KU-331-712

'I enthusiastically recommend this important book. It will stimulate much needed reaction and interaction among students of psychoanalysis, psychology, social theory, cultural studies and politics.' – *Contemporary Psychology*

'An interestingly comprehensive book on psychoanalysis and its bearing on social challenge and change.' – *Radical Philosophy*

'Anthony Elliott opts for a vigorously critical synoptic view, attempting to present both the strengths and weaknesses of classical psychoanalysis, ego psychology, object relations theory, Kleinian theory, Lacanian and post-Lacanian theory. In this book he strives to articulate the positive contribution of all branches, but he also searches deftly for the blind spots and problems of each psychoanalytic school.' – *Hysteric: Body, Medicine, Text*

'Anthony Elliott is quickly emerging as a one-person industry, intent in all of his writings to demonstrate both the relevance and the importance of psychoanalytic theory for critical social analysis ... *Psychoanalytic Theory* is more than an introduction in the conventional sense ... Elliott is boldly attempting to restore psychoanalysis relevant to a critical social theory but fundamentally respectful of human capacity for change and self-transformation.' – *Thesis Eleven*

'Elliott succeeds, in *Psychoanalytic Theory*, in showing that psychoanalytic theorists must explain not only how numerous cultural processes and social institutions structure the subject, but how the subject can meaningfully structure culture and social institutions ... Elliott is especially attentive to postmodern challenges of notions of the self and self-knowledge, as well as to the responsive critiques of postmodernism within psychoanalytic theory.' – *Journal for the Psychoanalysis of Culture and Society*

DONATIONS

1 0 JAN 2006

UCC LIBRARY

Also by Anthony Elliott

Psychoanalysis in Contexts (editor, with Stephen Frosh)
Subject to Ourselves
Freud 2000 (editor)
Social Theory and Psychoanalysis in Transition: Self and Society from Freud to Kristeva
The Mourning of John Lennon
The Blackwell Reader in Contemporary Social Theory (editor)
Psychoanalysis at its Limits (editor, with Charles Spezzano)
Concepts of the Self
Profiles in Contemporary Social Theory (editor, with Bryan S. Turner)
Key Contemporary Social Theorists (editor, with Larry Ray)
New Directions in Social Theory

HS 150·195 ELLI

Psychoanalytic Theory: An Introduction

Second Edition

Anthony Elliott

ι16616777

© Anthony Elliott 2002

All rights reserved. No reproduction, copy or transmission of
this publication may be made without written permission.

No paragraph of this publication may be reproduced, copied or
transmitted save with written permission or in accordance with
the provisions of the Copyright, Designs and Patents Act 1988,
or under the terms of any licence permitting limited copying issued
by the Copyright Licensing Agency, 90 Tottenham Court Road, London W1T 4LP.

Any person who does any unauthorised act in relation to this publication
may be liable to criminal prosecution and civil claims for damages.

The author has asserted his right to be identified as the author of this
work in accordance with the Copyright, Designs and Patents Act 1988.

First edition 1994
Published by Blackwell Publishers Ltd

Second edition 2002
Published by
PALGRAVE
Houndmills, Basingstoke, Hampshire RG21 6XS and
175 Fifth Avenue, New York, N. Y. 10010
Companies and representatives throughout the world

PALGRAVE is the new global academic imprint of
St. Martin's Press LLC Scholarly and Reference Division and
Palgrave Publishers Ltd (formerly Macmillan Press Ltd).

ISBN 0–333–91910–6 hardcover
ISBN 0–333–91912–2 paperback

This book is printed on paper suitable for recycling and
made from fully managed and sustained forest sources.

A catalogue record for this book is available from the British Library.

10   9   8   7   6   5   4   3   2   1
11 10 09 08 07 06 05 04 03 02

Printed and bound in Great Britain by
Creative Print and Design (Wales), Ebbw Vale

Nothing but a wish can set our mental apparatus at work.

Sigmund Freud, The Interpretation of Dreams

It is one and the same enterprise to understand Freudianism as a discourse about the subject and to discover that the subject is never the subject one thinks it is. The reflective reinterpretation of Freudianism cannot help but alter our notion of reflection: as the understanding of Freudianism is changed, so is the understanding of oneself.

Paul Ricoeur, Freud and Philosophy

The primary processes are present in the mental apparatus from the first, while it is only during the course of life that the secondary processes unfold, and come to inhibit and overlay the primary ones.

Sigmund Freud, The Interpretation of Dreams

The time-lag between consciousness and the unconscious is itself the stigma of the contradictory development of society. Everything that has got left behind is sedimented in the unconscious and has to foot the bill for progress and enlightenment.

Theodor Adorno, 'Sociology and Psychology'

For Keith and Jean Elliott

Contents

Preface

Many people have helped me in preparing this new edition. Special thanks must go to Stephen Frosh for suggesting the need for a revised edition, and for initially setting up a meeting with my editor to discuss the project. Frances Arnold has been a marvellous editor, generous with her time, and with helpful suggestions for the improvement of the text – I am grateful for her assistance with the project. Anthony Moran carried out research relating to biographical materials, as well as contributing to new sections on race and post-colonialism. His friendship and support have been vital. I should also like to thank the following people for their advice, criticism and help: Nick Stevenson, Steve Pile, Sean Homer, Nicola Geraghty, Jeffrey Prager, Alison Garrod, Jane Flax, Jessica Benjamin, Lynne Segal, Janet Sayers, Madelon Sprengnether and Kriss McKie.

ANTHONY ELLIOTT
Bristol

List of Tables

Introduction

Everyone, it seems, is familiar with the core cultural images of psychoanalysis. Declared variously as all-pervasive, strange, bizarre, as well as an impossible profession, psychoanalysis is inextricably intertwined with its ideas, methods and practitioners. We might, for example, conjure up the image of 'the couch', with the analyst dutifully taking notes as the patient speaks; or we might think of the founder and master of psychoanalysis, Sigmund Freud, working to unlock the mysteries of dreams and the mind, all while chain-smoking cigars; or we might reflect on psychoanalysis as having something special, perhaps precious even, to say about sex and sexuality, particularly the way in which desire influences personality; or we might think of the myths of psychoanalysis (the Oedipal complex, castration anxiety, primary repression), not to mention its surreal case studies – *Dora*, the *Rat Man*, or the *Wolf Man*; or we might conjure up that haunting image of Freud, old and frail, arriving in London, fleeing from the Nazis after the German annexation of Austria in 1938. We know these cultural images of psychoanalysis in one form or another. We know them either from reading Freud, or from books, films, cartoons and jokes. Everyone knows all this but still asks, what is psychoanalysis?

The cultural image I want to begin this book with is somewhat different: my nomination for framing psychoanalysis, and reflecting on the part it plays in contemporary culture, is the *political Freud*, or at least the Freud who asks what makes us political and what makes us value social relations? The terms of the question – positing a relationship between psychoanalysis and political, public affairs – direct us to a major difference from those prior cultural images of Freud and therapy that I have mentioned above. For the most part, Freud's legacy is generally understood to centre on the individual, and there remain many who believe that psychoanalysis is really only of concern to psychologists and others working in the field of mental health. But this is far from accurate. For if psychoanalysis deals with individual desire and private fantasy, it has also been the springboard for some of the richest cultural reflections on the impact of shared ideas and collective imagination. On this reckoning, psychoanalysis is interpersonal, creativity and mutual understanding, with sharp emphasis on sexuality as

1

outstripping the needs and limits of the body. The unconscious, as Freud tirelessly reminds his readers, truly transcends boundaries and influences the furthest reaches of our cultural and political lives.

'Psychoanalysis', wrote Freud in 1921, 'should never be used as a weapon in literary or political polemics.' Freud issued this warning in response to a book he was reading, *The Story of a Style* – a psychological dissection of the personality of American president Woodrow Wilson. Freud liked the book but was troubled by its gossipy tone. He concluded that you cannot psychoanalyse a patient who is not on the couch. Eight years later, however, Freud ignored his own edict and began working on a psychoanalytic study of a politician. That politician was – surprise, surprise – Woodrow Wilson. Freud's personality profile of Wilson concentrated on the leader's gift for self-deception, as well as his inexhaustible well of hidden hatred. Though Freud regarded his study of the American president as somewhat second-rate (indeed, he thought it embarrassing), his excursion into biography effectively opened the way for the application of psychoanalysis to politics.

Since Freud, the psychological interpretation of the inner fabric of public lives has taken on special significance. Today, a biography hardly seems worth reading if it only offers a chronicle of the exterior life. We want to know more. We want to know something about the key emotional events and psychic conflicts that make up the successes and failures of a life lived in the public eye. It is just this intriguing cross of the personal and the political in the frame of psychoanalytic ideas that biographers, sociologists, historians, political scientists and literary theorists have taken from Freud and begun to develop in productive, and sometimes novel, ways. Reading the inner lives of individuals, leaders or icons as symbols of who we are collectively – that is, connecting public lives to our deepest beliefs and values – invites us to reconsider the relationship between the outer and inner world, objectivity and subjectivity.

While Freud thought psychoanalysis potentially valuable for developing a better understanding of biography, his principal interests (beyond the consulting room) concerned big social changes and major political transitions – what he termed 'applied psychoanalysis'. From *Totem and Taboo* (1913–14) to *The Future of an Illusion* (1927) and *Civilisation and its Discontents* (1930), Freud sought to trace the complex, contradictory patternings of individual desire in relation to social forces, and especially the capacity for individual autonomy in the face of repressive social and political pressures. One of my principal concerns in this book is to situate psychoanalysis in political context. This means looking at the claims of psychoanalysis without losing sight of culture, society or politics. To stress the political context of psychoanalysis may appear to some, at first sight, somewhat odd. After all, many argue that psychoanalysis is anti-political, with therapy promoting privatism, a narcissistic turn inwards. This is not a view I share, and my subject throughout the book is the relationship between psychoanalytic theory and contemporary culture and politics. The political significance of psychoanalysis, I shall claim, is that it provides a kind of knowledge that can be used to assess the emotional strains and stresses of civilization, with particular attention to the humanity of a society. Psychoanalysis, as Freud argued, stimulates autonomy, honesty, trust and mutual understanding – or at least, this is the aim of psychoanalysis. It is no less the aim of a political psychoanalysis, one geared to the realization of autonomous social relations.

The force of Freud: situating psychoanalytic studies

'In psychoanalysis', wrote the German critical theorist Theodor Adorno, 'nothing is true except the exaggerations.' What Adorno meant by this remark, it seems, is that the more outrageous features of Freud's work – the fictions of psychoanalysis, if you will – actually contain key insights into contemporary social and political realities. From this angle, Freud's theory of, say, castration anxiety can be recast as an appropriate metaphor for the destructive and brutal nature of social relationships promoted in an age of multinational capitalism.

Notwithstanding numerous critical assaults on Freud in recent times, the exaggerations of psychoanalysis have continued to flourish. Mostly within the academic disciplines of sociology and social theory, comparative literature, cultural studies and feminism, psychoanalysis has been used to cross conventional intellectual boundaries, highlighting the masculinist bent of traditional separations of the rational and irrational, reason and emotion, science and art, culture and nature. Indeed, in the light of Freud's monumental discoveries about sexuality and the unconscious, the nature of critical practice in the human sciences has been radically transformed. Focusing on individual subjectivity, on the complex emotional experiences of people in relation to society and politics, on the quality of cultural relations, on gender divisions and our unequal sexual world, and on the fundamental assumptions of Western knowledge and science, psychoanalytic theorists have instigated a powerful restructuring of the major theoretical traditions in the social sciences and humanities. Despite the central place of psychoanalysis within the academy, however, the current perspectives and advances of the discipline are generally regarded as a terrain for specialist debate. Indeed there has been a genuine difficulty for students and the general reader searching for a critical introduction to psychoanalysis.

This book sets out to provide a reasonably comprehensive discussion of developments in psychoanalytic theory. The chapters that follow explore various traditions in psychoanalysis, setting them within the broader context of contemporary debates in the human sciences. Throughout, I have tried to examine psychoanalytic perspectives in a judicious manner, comparing and contrasting Freudian theory, American ego-psychology and self-psychology, British object relations theory, French Lacanian and post-Lacanian psychoanalysis, Kleinian theory, feminist and postmodern psychoanalysis. However, an introductory discussion such as this will necessarily involve certain simplifications, omissions and gaps. It would be too simplistic to attempt to represent the key conceptual problems of a discipline as complex as psychoanalysis. For this reason, I have opted for focusing on the work of particular theorists, highlighting certain themes and issues, similarities and differences, linking psychoanalysis throughout with developments in contemporary thought.

This is not a clinical study, but an expository and comparative introduction to the current state of psychoanalytic theory. I am not attempting to provide a history of all psychoanalytic ideas or an account of the institutional divergences between various psychoanalytic schools. Nor do I consider the complex issue of the scientific verification of psychoanalytic theories. A reader searching for such a discussion will have to look elsewhere. Rather, my aim is to provide an informative overview of the contemporary relevance of psychoanalysis to theory and social practice.

Despite numerous re-evaluations of his work, few would deny that Freud and psychoanalysis remain a pervasive influence on contemporary intellectual life. Yet according to some critics, especially in the United States, Freud is finished. When *Time* ran the question 'Is Freud dead?', the verdict was a resounding 'Yes'. Many argued that, as a psychoanalyst, Freud botched many of his clinical cases, and failed to prove the value of psychoanalytic treatment. Freud's talking cure has been declared obsolete by many, partly owing to advances in pharmacology. Drug treatment rather than therapy is now the preferred line of attack for mental distress. End of story – or so some would like to think. But in terms of understanding Freud's enduring political importance, we need to set Freudian psychoanalysis against a certain fashionable populism regarding issues about identity and the self, as well as drawing attention to the radical implications of the psychoanalytic account of fantasy and the unconscious.

Fifty years after his death, and despite the ongoing debate about the scientific status of psychoanalysis, we remain culturally fascinated by Freud. It is true that, following in the footsteps of the founder of psychoanalysis, there have been other psychoanalysts of whom the public has become aware – for example, Freud's own daughter, Anna; the child psychoanalyst, Melanie Klein; or Freud's French interpreter, Jacques Lacan. All of these figures are introduced and discussed in this book. Yet it is Freud who remains at the centre – as patriarchal father? – of psychoanalysis. Why should this be?

In examining the powerful fantasies that shape self-experience – anxieties about otherness, about envy and hatred, about need and desire – Freud demonstrated that a world of secrets, lies, doubts and fictions lurks within our individual and public lives. In introducing the notion of repression, Freud identified the submerged, hidden identities that imbued people's lives with a sense of fear, anxiety or shame. Most people have only the patchiest knowledge of the actual content of Freud's theories. Yet his ideas infiltrate and shape our daily lives and cultural interactions. Repression, projection, fantasy, repetition: these are terms that many people use to grapple with the more mysterious aspects of human relationships. My suspicion is that Freud's lasting cultural importance arises not only from the content of his theories, but equally from the symbolic importance we have come to attach to him culturally. Freud's legacy, in other words, is as much about the fantasy we have invested in him as it is about the truth value of his work. I suspect that many readers will find this viewpoint maddeningly postmodern. But perhaps it is worth pausing for a moment to consider this: whatever the fluctuating stock-market fortunes of psychoanalysis in the area of mental and public health, Freud's impact has perhaps never been as far-reaching as it currently is within the public sphere and intellectual debate. Psychoanalysis today is used by social and political theorists, literary and cultural critics, by feminists and postmodernists, such is its rich theoretical suggestiveness and powerful diagnosis of our current cultural malaise.

For example, if one turns to some of the most interesting cultural critiques of society and the whole shape of politics in recent years, ranging from the American historian Christopher Lash to the social theorist Cornelius Castoriadis, we find a strong engagement with Freud. This is also obviously true of various versions of feminism. So-called 'third way' feminists, such as Julia Kristeva and Luce Irigaray (both of whom are practising psychoanalysts), refer to Freud throughout their writings. Even the discourse that has caused much alarm and lament inside and outside of academic circles – that is, postmodernism – contains critical and descriptive terminology that reflects a Freudian debt. The French philosopher Jean-François Lyotard, widely considered the supreme analyst of postmodernism, remarked that his radical proclamation about the 'end of modernity' arose from concepts borrowed from Freud: 'remembering', 'repeating' and 'working through'.

There can be little doubt that the motivating force for this turn to Freud and psychoanalysis is primarily political. In a century that has seen totalitarianism, Hiroshima, Auschwitz and the prospect of a nuclear winter, intellectuals have demanded a language able to grapple with culture's unleashing of its unprecedented powers of destruction. Freud has provided that conceptual vocabulary. Far from being finished, I am confident that Freud will continue to have a huge influence on future generations of academics.

About this book

In preparing the second edition of *Psychoanalytic Theory: An Introduction*, I have sought to expand and to improve the text in a number of ways. In contrast to the first edition of this book, there are now detailed biographical portraits of the major psychoanalytic theorists – Freud, Klein, Winnicott and Lacan. In providing such biographical material, I have sought to connect aspects of the personal life and professional career – demonstrating the ways in which individual biography shapes particular theoretical concerns. I have also extended many of the chapters to encompass more recent trends in psychoanalytic studies. These include sections on the relationship between post-colonialism and psychoanalysis in Chapter 2, as well as new material on the psychodynamics of race in Chapter 3. I have added material to update the coverage of prominent figures working in the social sciences and humanities who draw from psychoanalytic theory. This is most evident in the reorganized chapter, 'Psychoanalytic Feminism', where I have added a new section on the writings of the American queer theorist, Judith Butler, and where I have extended the discussion of feminists including Nancy Chodorow, Jessica Benjamin, Julia Kristeva and Luce Irigaray. There is also an extended discussion now of Lacanian social theory, with new sections on the writings of the cultural theorist, Slavoj Zizek, and the neo-Lacanian, Jean Laplanche.

There are three central themes of this book. The first concerns the analysis of *human subjectivity*. At issue here is our understanding of the personal domain, self and self-identity. Psychoanalytic theory is of vital importance for understanding the emotional construction of selfhood. Whereas the social sciences have tended to see human agents as rational and autonomous, psychoanalysis recasts the relations between selfhood and desire, reason and passion. In psychoanalytic terms, the self is not a stable or unified entity. Rather, selfhood is constituted to its roots through desire, the self emerging as an outcrop of the unconscious. From this angle, we cannot really speak of the self outside of desire, fantasy, sexuality, and gender identification – indeed, issues of gender are fundamental to the psychoanalytic reconceptualization of identity. Existing versions of psychoanalytic theory conceptualize the impact of unconscious desire upon self-organization in distinctly different ways. For some theorists, the presupposition of an authentic sense of selfhood is crucial to psychoanalytic critique. For others, the self is seen as an imaginary fiction, a psychic strategy of accommodation aimed at masking the painful realities of desire itself. Many of the following chapters trace the consequences of these differing theoretical standpoints for conceptualizing the self, self-identity and subjectivity.

The second theme of the book is the *relation between self-organization and the contemporary social and political world*. Following directly from the first theme, psychoanalytic theorizing about selfhood carries important implications for analysing the wider context of social and political relations. That is to say, our understanding of the psychic conditions of self-organization can be used as a tool for generalizing about contemporary culture – interpersonal relations, the quality of social bonds, and political community. Particular attention is therefore given throughout the book to current debates on modernity and postmodernity. For in so far as psychoanalytic theory maps the internal world of the self, it is therefore well placed to assess the links between self-experience and the contemporary cultural and historical period.

The third theme of the book concerns *epistemological issues* – issues about psychoanalytic knowledge and its relation to individual and collective autonomy. As a model of social critique, psychoanalytic theory is concerned with uncovering asymmetric forms of power. This involves the study of the complex ways in which human beings question, alter or reinforce their affective relations with others and with the social world. Psychoanalytic critique gives explicit recognition to the possibility of disinvesting from certain ideological forms, and to the creative transformation of the self. Thus, many of the following chapters trace the manifold ways in which psychoanalytic critique enhances our understanding of, and therefore contributes to possibilities for, human emancipation.

The chapters that follow explore these core issues from differing psychoanalytic standpoints. Broadly speaking, they are all concerned with important advances in theoretical thinking about the self and the unconscious within contemporary culture. Thus the chapters trace a certain psychoanalytic narrative, the interconnections between self and society. However, I have tried to highlight the distinctive concerns and preoccupations of the theoretical traditions under consideration in each chapter. Therefore, chapters can be read in any order, and theoretical traditions can be studied according to the reader's interest. To facilitate this, every chapter is prefaced with an introductory overview as well as concise table summaries. In addition, the book concludes with an extended list for further reading in psychoanalytic theory.

The opening chapter provides a broad overview of the various conceptual traditions in psychoanalytic theory today, with the issue of the self to the fore. The concepts examined in this introductory chapter include the unconscious, repression, sexuality, fantasy, gender identity and power. In Chapter 2, I concentrate on how various psychoanalytic concepts have been used to analyse culture, society and self-identity, with repression as a central theme. This chapter examines developments in psychoanalytic–cultural criticism, from Freudian-Marxist integrations to debates over post-colonialism. In Chapter 3, I examine the psychoanalytic traditions of object relations, Kleinian theory and self-psychology. In this chapter, the connections between interpersonal relations and the internal world of the self are explored.

Chapter 4 examines French Lacanian psychoanalysis, post-Lacanian criticism and the theoretical current known as poststructuralism. Several key issues are assessed in this context: the reinterpretation of Freudian psychoanalysis in the light of structuralist and poststructuralist theories of meaning; the interweaving of language and the unconscious; and the structuring of desire within cultural relations. In Chapter 5, I consider developments in psychoanalytic feminism, tracing key conceptual differences between Anglo-American and Continental perspectives. The major themes in this chapter include the unconscious dimensions of patriarchy, sexual difference and the possibilities for transforming gender relations. Chapter 6 traces current debates about modernity and postmodernism, examining their social and cultural ramifications for identity. This chapter explores contemporary directions in psychoanalytic theorizing, ranging from French anti-psychoanalysis to postmodern theory. Finally, in the conclusion, I sketch out the prospects for a radical psychoanalytic criticism today, reframing the subversive potentials of the discipline within the plurality of perspectives and debates at the current time.

CHAPTER 1

The Making of the Self

Divergences in Psychoanalytic Theory

Psychoanalysis raises important issues about the personal and public contexts in which selfhood is constituted. In the hands of some theorists, psychoanalysis powerfully questions, indeed subverts, common-sense understandings of subjectivity itself. The key questions to be addressed in this chapter include the following. What is the self? How does a sense of selfhood emerge? What are the psychical mechanisms that link self-reflexivity and desire, reason and emotion? What are the interconnections between selfhood and culture, between personal meanings and the contemporary social world? In exploring these questions, the chapter ranges widely across core premises of Freudian psychoanalysis, ego-psychology, object relations theory, Kleinian theory, and Lacanian and post-Lacanian theory, connecting these standpoints with contemporary social theory and cultural criticism.

Imagining the self

What is meant by the notion of selfhood? At first sight, the answer seems obvious. A person's sense of self is usually understood to refer to their defining elements of personality and character. Implicit in this is the belief that there is something stable and durable about the self. I believe myself to be the same 'self' as I was yesterday; and, for purposeful social life to be possible at all, I must also believe that others have a fairly coherent sense of their own identity. Such presumptions about ourselves and others, unless a person is ill or disturbed, are at the root of our cultural life. The view that there is some such fundamental 'core' of selfhood has, of course, been central to the Enlightenment's basic understanding of humanity. The Cartesian understanding of the self as a fixed, indivisible and permanent whole ('I think, therefore I am') has underpinned dominant conceptions of consciousness and reason. Indeed, as Dennis Wrong comments, the human sciences have for the most part operated with a wildly 'over-socialized' conception of the self, a conception which sees the individual as essentially rational, unified and conflict-free.[1]

Psychoanalytic theory radically challenges such evaluations of selfhood. The self, which seems obvious at one level, is deconstructed by psychoanalysis as one region of subjectivity, a region that is merely the tip of the iceberg. The self, or 'ego' as it is termed in some versions of psychoanalytic theory, is shown to be a dimension of subjectivity which is internally fashioned through interpersonal relationships and intense emotional experiences, particularly experience in early infancy and childhood. Dismantling the notion of an essential unity to the self, psychoanalysis posits a *split* at the centre of the psyche between *consciousness of self* and that which is *unconscious*. Lurking behind all forms of self-organization – that is, our day-to-day fashioning of self-identity – there lies a 'hidden self', a dimension of subjectivity that is cut off from self-knowledge. Significantly, this hidden self, however we may choose to act or express ourselves, constantly disrupts and outstrips our intentions, through displacing and condensing our conscious experience and knowledge. Such splitting between practical consciousness and unconscious forms of experience is evident in the very act of self-reflection. I might, for example, reflect on the nature of my own identity, thinking about the attributes of my personality and my emotional investments in, or passionate attachments with, other people. However, a difficulty which inevitably arises is that this sense of self, on which I am reflecting, is actually located within myself as a human subject. On this line of reasoning, then, there will be aspects of what I desire, think and feel which arise outside and beyond the confines of my own organized sense of selfhood. It is precisely at this point, between the splitting of conscious intention and unconscious desire, that psychoanalytic theory inserts itself, seeking to uncover repressed or overdetermined aspects of self-organization.

We can get a better idea of the importance of this notion of a 'hidden self' by considering the subtle emotional knowledge that people display in daily life. In contrast to academic evaluations, our mundane accounts of ourselves, and of others, are often quick to highlight the emotional dimensions of human experience, particularly the nature of emotion and passion. Consider the following: What does it mean when someone during a dinner conversation makes the following remark about a close friend in the process of ending his marriage: 'Peter is just not himself at all at the moment – he's very mixed up, confused; he's got a lot of emotional stuff he's trying to work out.' To say in ordinary conversation that a person is 'not himself' is to indicate, implicitly, an awareness of the diversity and complexity of emotional life. This does not mean, of course, that such a comment appreciates the psychoanalytic distinction between self or ego and unconscious forms of experience. But such a comment does accord some place to conflicting emotions, the interplay of love and hatred, as well as the importance of a person's concrete emotional history in the development of their identity; the comment seems to recognize that the ending of a relationship, and especially an intimate sexual relationship, will bring into play complex, contradictory emotions involving considerable pain, turmoil and loss. Herein lies the significance of everyday talk: the implicit recognition that selfhood is shaped by broad emotional influences. At a theoretical level, these are the influences with which psychoanalysis is most directly concerned, tracing the fluid and multiple psychodynamics of emotional life on the construction of the self, and on human social relationships more generally.

Consider also the links between the psyche and the contemporary social world. In recent times, there has been considerable debate about global transformations affecting the late modern world in which we live, about the end of modernity itself, and about the possible transition to a postmodern social condition. In these debates, there has been a broad consensus that modern forms of life are increasingly marked by a kaleidoscopic variety of forces and events, by social contingency, uncertainty and ambivalence. The cultural and institutional processes of modernization which have launched the West upon a dazzling path of global expansion are said to have reached into the heart of selfhood and created new forms of personal identity. In postmodernism, particularly in its poststructuralist guise, contemporary cultural experience becomes permeated by fragmentation – an outcome of the dynamism and intensity of modern institutions. Significantly, one important consequence of this view is that human subjects, outflanked by a global network of communicational and computational processes, are now understood to inhabit a world in which meanings no longer have any lasting moral value. Social reality becomes a world of surfaces, images and fragments. (For further discussion, see Chapter 6: 'The Dislocating World of Postmodernism'.)

Psychoanalysis has made significant contributions to these theoretical debates on modern and postmodern identity, providing methods of analysis for understanding the connections between cultural trends and new patterns of self-organization. In these debates, as we shall see, psychoanalytic theory has been used to trace shifting psychic identifications as played out in the cultural sphere. To widen our sense of social and political reflectiveness, cultural critics have developed psychoanalytic concepts to trace processes of self-constitution in an era increasingly characterized by risk and uncertainty. For if contingency, ambivalence and instability of a threatening kind really do characterize the late modern age, then it is reasonable to assume that self-identity is also radically transformed. Indeed, according to the American cultural critic Christopher Lasch, our contemporary cultural condition promotes a 'minimal self', a self preoccupied with survival which has narcissistically turned back upon itself. This shrinking of the self, Lasch says, is directly connected to the waning of political life today and the lack of interest in the public sphere more generally. Alternative traditions of social thought are less inclined to link patterns of self-organization to contemporary culture in this way; instead, psychoanalytic theory is drawn upon as a way of understanding the constitution and reproduction of our social practice. Such accounts, as elaborated by theorists such as Erich Fromm, Cornelius Castoriadis and Anthony Giddens, have developed a more sociological appropriation of psychoanalysis for analysing social life. That psychoanalytic theory has inspired such diversity in the critical development of the human sciences will form one of the central concerns of this book.

Psychoanalytic portraits of the self

Current versions of psychoanalytic theory assess self-identity and the self in different ways. In order to explore their various meanings, let us at this stage list some definitions of the self and human subjectivity to be found in contemporary psychoanalytic theory and critique:

(a) the structural division of ego, id and superego;
(b) topological structure of consciousness, preconsciousness and the unconscious;
(c) defence mechanisms motivated by ego-organization;
(d) originary drives which are 'object-seeking';
(e) the conjuncture of 'true' and 'false' selves;
(f) the process of splitting, ranging from paranoid–schizoid positions to depressive positions;
(g) an imaginary structure of misrecognition and illusion;
(h) a process of linguistic closure in which repression is constituted.

There are several important points about this list which should be noted at the outset. First, no overall definition of the self can be extracted from these conceptual strands of psychoanalytic thought. If, for example, rationality and autonomy are central to the constitution of the subject, then clearly it fails to make sense also to speak of the self as a 'structure of misrecognition'. Accordingly, the gamut of meanings here is simply too broad in scope to nail down an all-inclusive definition of individual subjectivity. That this wealth of meaning is a positive gain for social critique, rather than something to be lamented, is a contention I will defend throughout the book. Secondly, all of these portraits of the self carry far-reaching implications for social, cultural and political criticism. In many of these approaches, the self is seen as fully anchored in social and historical contexts, with the development and enrichment of interpersonal relationships a political aim. Other definitions, however, view selfhood in more pessimistic terms – as an imaginary fiction, or as a repressive point of closure of human potential; to this extent, such perspectives carry rather different implications for thinking about social and political organization. Finally, it should be noted that these psychoanalytic portraits involve knowledge claims of different types. In some approaches, human beings are recognized as possessing the capacity for critical reflection and thus the ability for self-transfiguration. Other approaches, however, are more cautious about such humanist conceptions of autonomy, asserting that the best hope for social subversion arises from the mutations of desire itself. These differences form a conceptual backcloth for the critical examination of psychoanalytic theory contained in this book.

Let us now turn to consider some of the core concepts of psychoanalysis. To do this, it is necessary to examine the life and work of its founder, which necessitates returning to the origins of psychoanalysis.

The legacy of Freud

The talking cure: Freud's invention of psychoanalysis

Sigmund Freud, the great theorist of the enigmas of the human mind and founder of psychoanalysis, was born on 6 May 1856, in Freiberg, a part of the Austro-Hungarian Empire. His father, a Jewish wool-merchant, moved the family to Vienna in order to take advantage of business opportunities when Freud was only three years old. Freud was a studious child, who greatly enjoyed reading. Attending university at the age of 17, he studied biology, physiology and anatomy, while managing to find time to read widely in German, French and English literature. In 1881, he commenced a medical degree, and four years later this took him to Paris to work with the pioneering neurologist Jean Martin Charcot, who at that time was developing hypnotic techniques at his Salpêtrière Clinic.

Returning to Vienna, Freud established his private neurological practice, where he treated patients with hypnotic suggestion. He also lectured at Vienna University, though anti-Semitism prevented his appointment to a more senior and secure post. Pursuing his clinical interest in hysteria, Freud translated the works of Charcot, and began collaborating with a colleague, Josef Breuer, on a study of hysteria. *Studies on Hysteria* (1893–5), the book that emerged from the work of Freud and Breuer, examined symptoms ranging from hallucinations to the physical paralysis of arms and legs, and advanced a complex, and at times jumbled, theory of hysteria, one that underscored the central role of sexual memories in the formation of mental disturbance. The work laid a skeletal structure for the theoretical development of psychoanalysis, which emerged proper in 1900 with the publication of Freud's magisterial *The Interpretation of Dreams*.

The influence of sexual conflicts and their imaginative terrors on neurotic suffering is underlined most strongly in the celebrated case-study of 'Anna O.', which appears in *Studies on Hysteria*. She was the patient who coined the term 'talking cure', a term that Freud adopted in order to stress the radical power of language to relieve emotional torment. Freud became fascinated with Anna O., Breuer's patient, since she provided a near textbook example of hysteria: she suffered from hallucinations about snakes, skeletons and skulls, disturbances of speech and syntax (oftentimes mixing English, Italian and French), long periods of silence and depression, and the partial paralysis of her legs and arms. Freud viewed this patient's hysterical illness, particularly her depression and passivity, as resulting from a strong identification with, and devotion to, her father, a very wealthy Jewish businessman. Anna O. had led a sheltered life as a child, and was overprotected by her parents, especially her father – who fell ill when she was 21. In an act that expressed her own dependency on her father, Anna O. became depressed and ill at this time. As if caught between mania and depression, activity and passivity, her sense of identity shifted rapidly between two contrasting personalities; these schizoid states, Breuer and Freud observed, worsened considerably after the death of her father.

Up to this time, Freud had largely concentrated on the treatment of hysteria through hypnotism – as he had seen practised by Charcot in Paris. The treatment of Anna O., however, was radically different. Breuer is credited with the bold and impressive idea of encouraging his patient to talk freely about her feelings, a therapeutic innovation to which psychoanalysis owes a very great deal, though it would fall to Freud to pinpoint the exact connections between the talking cure and repressed desire. In working with Breuer, Freud came to concentrate on how the patient's telling of stories – the weaving of narratives of the self – produced a catharsis, a relief from disabling symptoms. Certainly, Anna O. seemed to find the talking cure, or what she also called 'chimney sweeping', liberating. The opportunity to reflect on the past, in the presence of a listening audience, permitted a reawakening of disowned memories as well as the reclaiming of intense, displaced emotion. This working through of past experiences, and exploration of painful memories, led in turn to the disappearance of symptoms – hence, the cathartic dimension of talking. In the case of one symptom, for example, Anna O. recounted to Breuer more than 100 episodes related to an experience of not hearing. During this exploration of memory, Anna O. was sometimes so deaf that Breuer could only communicate with her through writing. Significantly, when the disturbance was traced back to a memory involving her father, the symptom disappeared.

Happily, Anna O. was cured of all her symptoms – or, at least, this is what Breuer implied in *Studies*. Yet the truth of the matter was rather different. Anna O. continued to be afflicted with distressing symptoms for many years; though, in time, she did go on to enjoy a successful career in social work. It fell to Freud to take a more critical approach. Freud felt that Breuer's treatment had been ineffective, primarily because Breuer had failed to appreciate the emotional intricacies involved in this young woman's identification with her father, especially as this related to the adoption of sexual passivity. For Freud, Breuer had failed to grasp the power of psychology and fantasy that the case so graphically demonstrated, and the two men soon parted company thereafter. Yet one reason why the contradictions and ambivalences of the Anna O. case remained important to Freud is that he was very impressed by the emotional depth – the passion and energy – of her attachment to her symptoms, to her family, and especially to her doctor, Breuer. In reflecting on the case in this way, Freud did something highly unusual for a medical practitioner at the time: he was attempting to *learn* from his patient, to *listen* to her distress, her feelings and her desire for the future, to *think* about what occurs when very powerful emotions are mobilized in personal relationships (especially patient/doctor relations), and in particular to probe and question the origin, nature and meaning of those emotions in a broad psychological context.

Again, let us stay a little longer with the case of Anna O., since in considering the kinds of creative and destructive uses of imagination that Freud uncovered with the theory of psychoanalysis, it is important to remain close to the clinical material from which his formulations were drawn.

In *Studies on Hysteria*, Breuer noted that he omitted a large number of important details about Anna O. What the book left out of account, Freud subsequently revealed, were details relating to the sexual dimensions of Anna O.'s fantasies and identifications, particularly the nature of her erotic attachment to her doctor, Breuer. Indeed, reflecting on the case some 50 years later, Freud emphasized that the ambivalent passions that circulated between Anna O. and Breuer were consequential for an adequate clinical understanding of the case, even though at the time Breuer himself (and perhaps we should also add Freud) did not sufficiently appreciate the role of the erotic in Anna O.'s hysteria.[2] As Freud explained this missing erotic dynamic of the case, Anna O. had developed a passionate identification with Breuer, one that not only led to the formation of disabling delusions in her mind, but also implicated Breuer in the tangled frame of a complex sexual fantasy. On one critical occasion, Freud notes, Anna O. went into hysterical childbirth when Breuer was present, imagining that the doctor was the father of her child. The meanings Anna O. attached to her fantasied baby are complex (and are in much dispute in contemporary Freudian scholarship), though there can be little doubt that the acting out of this fantasy disturbed Breuer very deeply; he promptly broke off treatment, referring Anna O. to another colleague. It was as if Breuer was in flight from his patient's sexual attachment, and most significantly in flight from an engagement with female sexuality.

A fanciful tale spun by a young woman who, perhaps simply, had fallen in love with an older, authority figure – her doctor? Or, the story of a failed medical treatment, dressed up in the psychological language of pathology, hysteria and mental suffering? Perhaps we do not have to rush to judgement at this stage. For one of the striking elements of the case of Anna O. is the idea of a cluster of intense feelings which develop with regard to another person, a cluster of affects which, unknown to the individual, replays or repeats emotions experienced in relation to an important person in the individual's past – most usually, a parent. At this point, we plunge into what Freud calls 'transference', a concept that lies at the heart of psychoanalysis as a field of investigation, method of inquiry and psychothera-peutic practice. In *An Outline of Psycho-Analysis* (1940), Freud argues that, through the phenomenon of transference, the patient sees in the analyst 'the return, the reincarnation, of some important figure out of his childhood or past, and consequently transfers on to him feelings and reactions which undoubtedly applied to this prototype'.[3] The key notion in this definition is that of a return or reincarnation of the original relationship to a lost love (namely, the mother, father or both), and of the projecting of such unacknowledged positive and negative, affectionate and hostile, feelings towards the sympathetic listener, the analyst. Elsewhere, Freud speaks of the transference in terms of 'new editions' of displaced desires and 'facsimiles' of feared fantasies, noting that the clinical setting of psychoanalysis provides a privileged site for dismantling and reconstructing the web of impulses and fantasies that shape the unconscious complexes of individ-uals.

Against this theoretical backcloth, Anna O.'s fantasied baby raises some very interesting questions concerning the erotic transactions between patient and doctor, as well as complex matters pertaining to the ways in which past emotional experience comes to structure, indeed invade, an individual's relation to other people in the present. Recent Freud scholarship has proposed various, intriguing interpretations of the transference dynamics between Anna O. and Breuer. These range from Oedipal-styled scenarios, in which Breuer represents an emotional substitute for Anna O.'s father, to explanations that emphasize the astonishing ambiguity of erotic identifications at the level of the unconscious mind, with Breuer cast as hovering uneasily between the role of father figure and lover in the fertile imagination of Anna O. Still other interpretations underscore the connections between hysteria and femininity in the cultural imagination: active doctor and passive patient, male medical authority and female rebel. From this angle, Anna O. can be seen as a kind of proto-feminist, a rebel adept at seducing and duping her male doctors into embarrassing error, deceit, grand medical claims and scientific fictions.

The concept of transference can only be adequately grasped when defined in relation to Freud's other core ideas – the unconscious, repression, Oedipus and the like. We will turn to a broader examination of Freudian psychoanalysis shortly, but firstly I want to note that Freud's theory of transference undercuts the traditional distinction between inner and outer worlds, self and other, the individual and culture. The strong argument here, developed in various writings of Freud, is that the individual self holds a transferential relationship to other people, to social bonds and to the cultural realm more generally. In our emotional attachments to others, from intimate sexual relationships to the organizational structures of authority in public life, the phenomenon of transference is a fundamental dimension of human experience: we people our world, according to Freud, with emotions and fantasies drawn from the past, but projected on to current experience.

Fantasy and sexuality

In developing a general theory of psychical disorder (concentrating at first upon hysteria), Freud speculated that emotional suffering derived from sexual trauma, from an actual assault in childhood that in turn shaped neurosis in adult life. This was Freud's seduction theory of neurosis, the idea that psychical disorder is the product of sexual abuse or actual assault. The theory was arrived at on the basis of both Freud's medical research and through listening to the tales of his patients – many of whom spun highly eroticized accounts of incestuous experience with family members, especially fathers. In Freud's clinical work at the time, he sought to trace memories of sexual scenes back to an original trauma, to a defining event in childhood through which seductions and symptoms could be put into an orderly structure. The central problem for Freud at this point of his career, however, was that his patients refused to corroborate his painstaking detective work; his patients, though remembering scenes of sexual longing and disappointment in childhood, often had no recollection of actual seduction; or, if seduction had taken place, Freud's patients refused to accept the narrow interpretation that their neurosis could be traced back to a single traumatic moment.

Freud, accordingly, changed tack. He began listening more sympathetically to his patients' fantasies, noting the erotic charge and sexual anxiety that underpinned emotional symptoms; in time, he carefully arrived at the conclusion that memories and recollections of erotic experience might be interpreted in a different manner, as *signs* of the significance of desire, longing and passion. He came, in effect, to see that his patients' sexual fantasies were not so much subjective clues to be used, in the spirit of Sherlock Holmes, to reconstruct some original traumatic event, but rather were to be seen as part and parcel of the larger emotional issue of how the self is emotionally constructed and organized. Rejecting the idea that feeling states simply mirror external events, Freud opened a path for investigation into the complex ways that individuals structure themselves out of present and past relationships as mediated through intense desires, identifications and repressions.

In focusing on the power of fantasy in shaping personal and public life, Freud sought to grasp something of the glorious diversity in human personality, sexual behaviour and interpersonal relationships. His fundamental concern was with the import of fantasy, sexuality and imagination for analysing both the continuity and turbulence of human conduct. However, from the time that Freud first went public with his ideas on the unconscious and sexual repression, the scientific credibility and ideological bias of psychoanalysis have been sharply contested. On the specific issue of fantasy versus trauma for understanding the causes of emotional distress, there has been a marked rise in recent Freud-bashing, with some critics arguing that psychoanalysis was founded on a massive denial of the ubiquity of sexual abuse. This is, at any rate, the accusation made in Jeffrey Masson's best-seller *Assault on Truth: Freud's Suppression of the Seduction Theory* (1984). Charging Freud with turning a blind eye to the sexual abuse of women and children, Masson condemns Freud for dismissing actual trauma as mere fantasy, daydream, illusion. Here, once again, Freud's attempt to develop a map of fantasy life and its unpredictability is seriously misrepresented. Masson's critique of Freud is, in my view, greviously flawed – primarily for the reason that Freud did not dispute his patients' accounts of actual seduction and sexual abuse. What Freud did emphasize, however, and this is surely his crucial and lasting contribution to critical thought, is the complex, muddied way in which external events are suffused with fantasy and desire.

Above all else, Freud poses the question of the self in relation to human sexuality. He traces the genesis of desire to those early bodily experiences between the small infant and its primary caretaker – typically, the mother. At birth the human infant, says Freud, is wholly dependent on care from others for the satisfaction of its biologically fixed needs. The small child is incapable of surviving alone without the provision of care, warmth and nutrition from other people. It is thus, one might claim, the emotional interaction between child and significant others which is central to the constitution of selfhood. 'There is no such thing as a baby', says the psychoanalyst D. W. Winnicott, thus underscoring the origin of self in relation to others. According to Freud, the small infant first experiences its mother within a kind of imaginary space, completely apart from everyday structures of time and space. At this point, the infant makes no distinction between inside and outside, itself and the maternal body. Rather, the infant lives within a world of plenitude, satisfying its natural self-preservative needs. Yet self-preservation, says Freud, goes beyond the biological. Needs are, in fact, bound up with the attaining of libidinal enjoyment (or what Freud called the 'pleasure principle'), even if the latter actually separates out from the former. Freud's exemplary case is the small child sucking milk from its mother's breast. After the infant's biological need for nourishment is satisfied, there is the emergence of a certain pleasure in the act of sucking itself; and this, for Freud, is the core of human sexuality: 'The baby's obstinate persistence in sucking gives evidence at an early stage of a need for satisfaction which, though it originates from and is instigated by the taking of nourishment, nevertheless strives to obtain pleasure independently of nourishment and for that reason may and should be termed *sexual*.'[4] In Freud's account, sexuality is not some preordained, unitary biological force that springs into existence fully formed at birth. On the contrary, sexuality is *created*, not pre-packaged.

In *Three Essays on the Theory of Sexuality* (1905), Freud presents both a radical defence of sexual diversity and a plea for an enlarged or broader conception of the human potential for sensual pleasure. His focus was primarily on the variety and intensity of erotic passions in childhood, the notion of autonomous infantile sexuality and, in particular, the multiple forms of bodily pleasure as mediated in the child's fantasy life. According to Freud, sexuality is itself a 'perversion' – the infinite flexibility of the human sexual drive means that any part of the body, as well as any conceivable object, can provide erotic pleasure. He thought that all individuals are innately 'polymorphously perverse'; Freud's argument that there is an enormous fluidity of sexual desires shaping human experience came under attack from both the conservative medical establishment and from a disbelieving public. In the post-Freudian era, as we will see, Freud's theories on the origins of sexuality have retained their power to shock and disturb the reactionary insistence on a fixed dichotomy between 'masculine' and 'feminine' forms of sensual pleasure and sexuality; though it is also the case that some later versions of psychoanalytic theory turned away from the radical notion of polymorphous perversity in order to advance a normative account of gender relations fixed within the heterosexual nuclear family.

In *Three Essays*, Freud systematically reconstructs the key erotic phases and dominant emotional conflicts of early childhood. The oral stage, as Freud describes it, is the earliest phase of sexual life and is associated with the baby's sucking of milk. Oral pleasure becomes 'erotogenic', in Freud's terminology, because of the way the infant creates fantasy-infused images deriving from the comfort of the breast. As the infant develops, this linking together of pleasure, sexuality and the body opens out to other erotogenic zones. In the anal stage, the infant's pleasure derives from the 'letting go' or 'holding on' of faeces; such fantasy is primarily sadistic, as erotic pleasure derives from expulsion. The nature of the phallic stage is organized through the child's sexual energy (or libido) becoming centred on the genitals, and is associated with masturbation along with fantasies of control and self-sufficiency. What is happening with the unfolding of oral, anal and phallic forms of sexual pleasure, Freud suggests, is that the child creatively and imaginatively establishes an emotional relation to its own body, to other people and the wider world. It is from this enlarged understanding of human sexuality that Freud is able to read the turbulence of adult emotional life off from the primitive sexual desires and identifications of early childhood. Remarkably, social problems can now be recast with the assistance of psychoanalytic concepts – infantile sexuality, fantasy, identification and the like. Whatever the problem of reductionism (and this, as we will see, is considerable), the links between psychic fantasy and social constructions are palpable, evident in cultural symptoms from excessive drinking (orality) through dieting and over-exercising (anality) to sexism (phallic).

Freud believed that the imaginary plenitude of the child/mother dyad is broken apart through the intrusive impact of reality into the pleasure principle. For Freud, the 'reality principle' imposes severe restrictions on the pleasure-seeking drives of the unconscious. This opposition between pleasure and reality is fundamental to human life; it is the task of the precarious ego, or the self, to attempt to balance its unconscious demands for pleasure with the cultural constraints of external reality. The constitution of a reality-ego, rationality-testing and self-control are, Philip Rieff comments, the Freudian moral imperatives in the 'emergence of psychological man'.[5] Freud's insight – that the self is differentiated from unconscious pleasure through its contact with external reality – has been extensively developed in contemporary social, cultural and political thought. One central lineage, from the Frankfurt theorist Herbert Marcuse to the American Freudian-Marxist Joel Kovel, has been concerned with tracing how cultural forms disfigure unconscious pleasure in ways which produce 'surplus repression'. By contrast, other traditions of social thought, from poststructuralism to postmodernism, have sought to deconstruct the opposition of pleasure and reality back to the mutations of desire itself. Both traditions offer important insights into the connections between self and the social world. These will be examined more closely in the following chapters.

We need, however, to look further at this painful intrusion of the external world into the closed, imaginary world of the infant. In positing a fundamental opposition between the pleasure principle and the reality principle – or what is elsewhere termed the 'primary processes' of the unconscious and the 'secondary processes' of consciousness – Freud's thinking indicates its affinities with Enlightenment rationalism. The image of the self as purely pleasure-seeking, and only subsequently brought within the regularized control of society, certainly stretches back to classical liberal philosophy. Most significantly, the ideological implications of Freud's theory would seem almost entirely negative. For as many commentators have suggested, the victory of reality over pleasure in Freud's thought is at one with the elevation of rationality over the irrational, masculinity over the feminine, and reason over emotion. The extent to which these ideological blind spots are actually rooted in Freud's theory is a matter of ongoing debate. In my view, it can be plausibly argued that Freud's work is more complex and subtle than such characterizations suggest. This becomes clearer once we consider Freud's argument that there are two sides to the surrender of the pleasure principle to the reality principle. According to Freud, all individuals must negotiate the shift from unconscious pleasure to external reality. Where this is not achieved, schizophrenic tendencies and related pathologies are certain to result. Yet here comes the twist in Freud's argument. In negotiating the dictates of external reality, the ensuing surrender of pleasure is itself a kind of decoy. Freud says unconscious drives only defer immediate satisfaction in order to achieve a more durable type of pleasure. Pleasure is therefore not defeated; it merely takes new forms, via the unfolding of fantasy. It is this insight that will lead Freud, in 'On Narcissism' (1914), 'Mourning and Melancholia' (1917) and *The Ego and the Id* (1923), to the view that selfhood is inextricably intertwined with fantasy.

Our sense of selfhood, therefore, is not just magically assigned to us by the external world. Rather, identity has to be *made* or *created*. In this connection, Freud suggests that ego-formation occurs through the unconscious selecting or screening of objects by *identification*. Identification is a process in which the individual 'introjects' attributes of other people and transforms them through the unconscious imagination. This identification with another is made a part of the subject by *incorporation*: the taking in of objects, either wholly or partially, to form the basis of an ego. In relation to the imaginary dyad of child and mother, for example, Freud comments that the subject has 'created an object out of the mother'.[6] Identification and incorporation are thus twin boundary posts in the structuring of identity. For Freud, the identificatory process is engendered in and through painful feelings of loss. For it is the loss of a loved person which actually necessitates the introjection of that other into the structure of the ego itself. It is as if the hurt of losing somebody is so terrifying that the ego incorporates the lost love as an act of self-preservation. As Freud puts it, 'by taking flight into the ego, love escapes annihilation'. The links between loss and self-formation are made plain by Freud in *The Ego and the Id*:

> we succeeded in explaining the painful disorder of melancholia by supposing that [in overcoming this hurt] an object which was lost has been set up again inside the ego – that is, that an object-cathexis has been replaced by an identification. At that time, however, we did not appreciate the full significance of this process and did not know how common and how typical it is. Since then we have come to understand that this kind of substitution has a great share in determining the form taken by the ego and that it makes an essential contribution towards building up what is called its 'character'.[7]

It is clear from this statement that desire can take the self as an object in just the same manner as 'external' objects. This significantly complicates traditional understandings of the relation between the individual and society, inside and outside, private and public. For it underscores the point that, in the formation of the human subject, identity is created through picking out, and taking in, certain parts of other persons and objects through fantasy. From this angle, the rational ego of the Western philosophical tradition is shown to be constituted to its roots through unconscious mechanisms of fantasy, imagination and desire. Significantly, it follows from this that the relation between self-identity and modern social processes will be more complex and contradictory than is commonly assumed. For if structures of identity are formed in relation to others (and particularly our affective images of others), then so too will changes in social relationships affect the nature of the self. In this connection, the nature of social transformations this century are palpable. Modernity – with its global economic mechanisms, its restructuring of time and space, its capitalist commodification, its phantasmagoria of mass media – brings into existence new forms of personal identity and social relations. The impact of these social and cultural transmutations upon self and identity-formation are at present controversial. Some critics find new possibilities for self-actualization in the late modern age; whereas other commentators take a more pessimistic view of the expressive cultural possibilities for the self. These debates will be explored in later chapters.

The Oedipus complex, cultural regulation and symbolic order

We have seen that, for Freud, self-constitution arises as a consequence of loss. Selfhood is formed under the sign of the loss of the object, in an attempt to *become* like the lost love. Yet identificatory processes carry serious implications not only for self-organization but also for gender as well. The links between the pain of loss and gender consolidation are to be found in Freud's theory of the Oedipus complex – a theory which conceptualizes the psyche's entry into received social meanings. For Freud, the Oedipus complex is the nodal point of sexual development, the symbolic internalization of a lost, tabooed object of desire. Sexuality, deriving from the bisexual, polymorphous pleasures of infancy, is reordered within the cultural framework of instituted gender relations. In the case of the young boy (the model in which Freud first theorizes the Oedipus complex), the child develops sexual knowledge of the penis and fantasizes sexual union with the mother. This fantasy of sexual union is, however, subsequently to be broken from outside the child/mother dyad, by the father. Consequently, the boy comes to hate his father's superior control of the maternal body and, as passion reaches fever pitch, fantasizes his death. But recognizing that he cannot compete with the phallic authority of the father, and faced with the imagined threat of castration (the castration complex), the boy must renounce his primary erotic investment, repressing sexual desire for the mother permanently into the unconscious. Clearly, as far as culturally sanctioned heterosexuality goes, so far so good. However, there are difficulties in this psychoanalytic narrative of male sexual development. In his late writings, Freud notes that the child's inevitable bisexual tensions significantly complicate any forging of stable sexual identification, so that gender affinity is understood as always undermined by sexual ambivalence. This sexual ambivalence in intimately interwoven with either the mother or father, or both, as erotic objects.

The trajectory of the girl's passage through the Oedipus complex is a good deal more complex. Freud contends that in the case of female sexuality the Oedipus complex works in reverse fashion: instead of instigating the repression of Oedipal desire, the castration complex actually *produces* incestuous desire in the little girl. Several features of Freud's thought are relevant here. First, a masculine sexuality is the starting point of reference – 'the little girl is a little man' according to Freud. Second, sexual difference is founded upon 'the discovery' of the absence of the penis. As Freud puts this, 'She has seen it and knows that she is without it and wants to have it.'[8] This sets in train a series of sexual identifications. The discovery by the small girl that she lacks a penis with which to pursue her active sexual drives leads her to imagine that she has been castrated. As a consequence, she turns away in horror from her similarly castrated mother. In this connection, Freud believes that the girl's wish for a penis is sufficiently intense that it is subsequently transferred to a substitute, the desire to bear the father a child. It is this reversal from love of the mother to father that establishes gender affinity for the girl. Through penis envy, the girl renounces the more active elements of her sexuality and 'consolidates' feminine sexual passivity. In Freud's view, then, the development of heterosexuality in the girl is dependent upon an earlier sense of failed masculinity.

This description of sexuality as resting upon a male norm, with its consequent devaluation of the feminine, has been at the heart of the feminist debate with Freud. Freud's ideas have come under fire for their perpetuation of the misogynistic view that femininity is little more than a negation of 'normal' male sexuality. However, there are two quite divergent interpretations of Freud's ideas on female development in the current literature. The first ascribes to Freud the view that it is the *moment of actual perception* of sexual organs which is fundamental to the child's emotional investment in, and psychic structuring by, sexual difference. Yet the difficulty with this conceptual position, as many commentators have pointed out, is that it involves biological reductionism, and thus undercuts the critique of gender hierarchy. For if the 'inferiority' of the female sexual organ arises through such a 'sighting', then clearly the possibilities for restructuring gender relations also vanish. The second interpretation, by contrast, argues that in Freudian psychoanalysis the child's sexual knowledge is only given meaning within the *structure* of gendered, social relations. That is, sexual difference and gender identity are given meaning with reference to the patriarchal socio-sexual order. At this point, it is important to note that Freud's work deeply problematizes female sexuality. Unlike the boy's strong repression of incestuous desire, the girl's Oedipal stage is understood to be relatively unstable, forever shifting between maternal and paternal identifications, and thereby always incomplete. Freud's own work, however, fails adequately to trace either the girl's ambivalent affinity with the feminine gender role or how the Oedipus complex dissolves, if indeed it does.

A good deal has been written about the patriarchal bent of Freud's discourse. Certainly the notions of a primary masculine sexuality, penis envy and feminine sexual passivity suggest a widespread male bias in Freud's thought. The issues which arise, therefore, are these. Can psychoanalysis be defended as a progressive theoretical scheme for analysing sexist practices? Or is psychoanalysis simply the prisoner of the sexual and cultural assumptions which it seeks to investigate? The answer to these questions varies considerably in contemporary psychoanalysis and feminist theory. One line of argument is that Freud's theory is descriptive, not prescriptive. That is, psychoanalysis offers something like a 'thick description' of what actually takes place in current relations between the sexes. A major feminist defence of Freud along these lines is Juliet Mitchell's best-selling book *Psychoanalysis and Feminism*, which uses psychoanalysis to sketch a general critique of patriarchal culture. Similarly, Nancy Chodorow, Jessica Benjamin, Jane Flax and Madelon Sprengnether have suggestively used psychoanalytic theory to analyse asymmetric gender relations. An alternative tradition of thought, largely developed in Lacanian and post-Lacanian circles, has employed core concepts of psychoanalytic theory (the unconscious, displacement, identification and the like) to deconstruct the ideological fiction of 'stable gender-identity'. This line of enquiry has been central to the French radical feminism of Luce Ingaray and others. Similarly, the work of the French psychoanalyst Julia Kristeva has sought to undo repressive gender norms by reconceptualizing human subjectivity within a pre-Oedipal realm (known as the 'semiotic') as a means for rethinking identity. These different ideological perspectives in psychoanalytic feminism will be discussed in Chapter 5.

Freud himself was in no doubt that the Oedipus complex lies at the foundation of civilization; Oedipus ushers in the structure of sexual relations which prepares men and women for the repressions and sublimations required by culture. Significantly, Freud looks at how received social meanings are underwritten by the forces of unconscious desire, tracing inscriptions of power and domination within the primary erotic attachments of human subjects. Accordingly, Freud's work provides us with conceptual tools for understanding why individuals should come to have a positive psychic investment in social arrangements which are in fact oppressive and restrictive. (For further discussion, see Chapter 2: 'Modern Culture and Its Repressed'.) Yet there is a fundamental ambivalence at the heart of identity, says Freud. The internalization of cultural norms is at best a partial, contradictory affair, if only by virtue of the fact that such norms are shot through with the displacements and distortions of the unconscious itself. For example, the post-Oedipal child's connection to the mother as a separate, caring agent is always interwoven with a prior relation to the mother as an erotic object. Beyond the realm of social signification, as Slavoj Zizek points out, there is always a kind of leftover of unconscious desire which resists the basic dimension of ideology[9]; and it is this kernel of desire which serves as a support for forms of resistance (what Freud called 'reaction-formations') to the social and political order.

This point can be put in another way. There are strong ambiguities in Freud's account of culture and its encoding of unconscious desire. Indeed we could say that there is a modernist and postmodernist Freud on the powers and limits of cultural ideology. Freud, the modernist, views culture as incorporating our unconscious desires in that psychical act known as 'sublimation', the embedding of sexual enjoyment within the framework of social significations. This is the Freud who believes that psychoanalysis can confront the power of the unconscious in the governing of the soul. In this sense, Freud's enlightenment slogan 'Where id was, there ego shall be' refers to the possibility of making the unconscious conscious. The pain caused by paralysing unconscious feelings is to be undone through the rational mastery of self-reflection. Yet there is another Freud, perhaps more postmodern in political sensibility. This is the Freud who stresses that unconscious desire is intimately bound up with everything we do, who stresses that fantasy is a constitutive and creative feature of the human imagination, and who underscores the point that psychoanalysis is itself interminable. As Cornelius Castoriadis puts this: 'Freud's proposition can be completed by its inverse: "Where ego is, id must spring forth." Desire, drives ... have to be brought not only to consciousness but to expression and to existence.'[10] Significantly, both of these emphases in Freud's texts, modernist and postmodernist, are elaborated and reconceptualized in contemporary psychoanalytic theory.

Post-Freudian psychoanalysis: self and other

The portrait of the self now found in psychoanalysis has undergone dramatic change since the time of Freud. In this period, clinical and theoretical developments in psychoanalysis have significantly recast the notion of the self, as well as the broader connections between individual experience and society. Roughly speaking, attention has shifted from the intrapsychic world of the self to the interpersonal sphere, to relations between self and other. That is to say, post-Freudian theory focuses on the emotional relations *between* human subjects rather than the inner world of the individual self alone. From this *intersubjective* angle, the dynamics of personal and social conflict appear in a new light. The reproduction of the patriarchal and social order of modern societies is no longer understood as merely rooted in sexual repression and the denial of passion, as in the classical view of psychoanalysis. Rather, repressive social conditions are traced to various pathologies that underlie human relationships, primarily the complex way that interpersonal relationships can distort psychic life, selfhood and gender. Much of the impetus for this conceptual shift of focus has come from the failure of classical psychoanalysis to comprehend the sufferings of the modern clinical patient. In the post-Freudian period, the clinical picture of typical analysands has been, not one of individuals suffering from disturbances in sexual repression and self-control, but rather that of individuals experiencing a deep emotional poverty in relations with others, coupled with a more general estrangement from the self. Moreover, recent psychoanalytic accounts converge on the point that modern social conditions drive a wedge between self and others, generating in turn a waning in social ties and commitment to political and public life.

The study of the self *in relation* with others carries important implications for understanding psychic life. For many contemporary theorists, social relationships do more than just influence the development of subjectivity. Rather, the human subject's inner world is *constituted* through these relations. That is to say, the nature and meaning of a person's subjective and sexual experiences are actually formed in relationship with others. Such a recognition of the intersubjective foundation of the self has led psychoanalytic debate away from issues of Oedipal conflict and sexual repression to a concern with the earlier pre-Oedipal period, the imaginary dyad of child and mother, and emotional disturbances in ego-formation. More specifically, there has been a fundamental revision of Freud's atomistic and mechanistic language of unconscious drives. Instead, the psychological dynamics underlying selfhood depend upon mutually engaged subjects.

These changes within psychoanalysis are registered in the American post-Freudian tradition and the British school of object relations theory in very different ways. Both traditions of thought share the view that classical Freudian metapsychology is unable adequately to comprehend the nature of human motivation, problems of selfhood and contemporary difficulties in living. They also share a common emphasis upon interpersonal processes in theorizing problems of selfhood and relationship difficulties. Yet there are also fundamental differences between these psychoanalytic traditions. The American post-Freudian tradition divides into two schools of thought: (1) ego psychology and (2) the interpersonal (or culturalist) model of psychoanalysis. Ego psychology is generally concerned with the genesis, development and adaptive capacities of the ego. The key figures in this school of psychoanalytic thought include Anna Freud, Heinz Hartmann, Ernest Kris, R. M. Lowenstein, Erik H. Erikson and David Rapaport. The interpersonal tradition in psychoanalysis shares this focus on the rational capacities of selfhood, but also emphasizes the place of social and cultural conditions in its constitution. The key figures in this theoretical tradition include Erich Fromm,

Harry Stack Sullivan, Karen Horney and Clara Thompson. The British school of object relations theory, by contrast, focuses on the dynamics and structures of intersubjectivity itself, tracing the complex emotional links between the self and other people. The central figures in this school of psychoanalytic thought include W. R. D. Fairbairn, Harry Guntrip, Melanie Klein, D. W. Winnicott, John Bowlby and Michael Balint. In order to provide ourselves with a map of these post-Freudian theories, let us now trace the general outlines of these positions.

For Freud, the synthesizing capacity of the ego is continually outstripped by psychic reality (the unconscious) and external reality (society). As noted, the ego attempts to negotiate some sort of balance between inner desire and external necessity. As Freud puts this, the ego is like a 'man on horseback, who has to hold in check the superior strength of the horse'. In the reinterpretation of Freud developed in ego psychology, however, this steering capacity of the ego is shifted up a gear into a fully blown self-mastery. Ego psychologists emphasize the powers of the ego for masterful, rational action. We find an early theoretical outline of the ego as a powerful steering force in the psychic economy in Anna Freud's pioneering book, *The Ego and the Mechanisms of Defence* (1941). In this book, Anna Freud advances the view that human development unfolds through the emergence of bodily needs and capacities in a context of a sharpening awareness of significant-other people. The earliest interaction between infant and mother consists of an original oneness, known as primary narcissism. In successive phases, the infant separates out from mother, transforming him- or herself into an independent agent. This growing sense of the infant's independence, however, is seen as a *disengagement* from relationships. The ego's basic mechanisms of adjustment provide the psychic underpinning for a successive pattern of separations throughout the life cycle. In this connection, Anna Freud speaks of the ego as having a range of defences at its disposal against unconscious anxiety and dread. These defence mechanisms, such as an identification with the aggressor, are built up through human interaction and thus locate the ego within the wider frame of social relations. Accordingly, her work highlights the role of early interpersonal relations in the framing of our psychic world.

Anna Freud's work describes the mechanisms of ego growth and defence, but she fails to document much about the psychic structure which promotes such functioning. In the writings of Heinz Hartmann, however, the constitutional basis of the ego is given explicit attention. Hartmann describes his psychoanalytic enterprise as a 'general developmental psychology'.[11] As such, he is concerned with examining not only psychopathology, but everyday psychological functioning and associated processes of adaptation. Whereas for Anna Freud the ego arises as an outcrop of defensive mechanisms in the face of anxiety, Hartmann argues that the ego is both primary and autonomous. The kind of autonomy that Hartmann has in mind encompasses a remarkably broad range of ego functions, including thought, language, perception and memory. These ego capacities, Hartmann says, are essentially conflict free. By this he means that such functions can be smoothly performed in day-to-day social life in a way not anticipated by traditional Freudian theory, and which thus radically alters our assessment of the potentialities for self-control. Free from internal distortion or unconscious compulsion, the ego is released, in Hartmann's scheme, to pursue an autonomous existence in its relationship with the external environment. Since the ego for Hartmann is largely conflict free, it can enter into an adaptive role with social reality, incorporating the demands of the external world and making them a fundamental source of human motivation. This enlargement of the ego's power, specifically the self's immediate link with the social environment, means that Hartmann's psychoanalysis can underwrite the rationalization of selfhood and everyday life. From this angle, social relationships are less significant than is mastery of the inner world.

This focus on self-mastery and adaptation in ego psychology need not necessarily be taken as denying the importance of human relationships; it can be read as suggesting that autonomous selfhood is an essential precondition for equal interpersonal relations. By upgrading the powers of the ego in the face of its defensive struggles with external reality, Hartmann attempts to emphasize the capabilities of the individual self for insight and reason. His emphasis upon adaptation shows that the external world has a major impact upon the strivings of the individual subject. However, the notion of 'adaptation' is not without its difficulties. As Russell Jacoby has argued, such an emphasis leads psychoanalysis generally in the direction of social conformism, with every failure to 'adapt' a sign of psychopathology.[12] Questioning this conformist orientation, Jacoby argues that the dynamic unconscious surely implies that the self is not capable of such 'adaptation'. Perhaps just as significantly, Hartmann's work also results in a neglect of the *quality* of social relationships. Since the only criterion of assessment is that of adaptation, Hartmann has no viable way of confronting social critique. From this standpoint, human autonomy depends on a successful introjection of the values of society, no matter how insanely exploitative or emotionally destructive they may be. Moreover, the primacy attributed to separation in ego psychology would appear to go hand in hand with the American ethos of individualism, thus promoting a narcissistic expansion of the would-be autonomy of the self. This is a limitation which will be discussed in later chapters, especially when we turn to consider the work of Erik Erikson and Erich Fromm.

Whatever one makes of these ideological blind spots, ego psychology undoubtedly influenced psychoanalytic theory towards a deeper examination of interpersonal issues. This change in emphasis, from problems of drive regulation to those of relationship difficulties, is further expanded in object relations theory and related variants. Broadly speaking, object relations theorists view the self in emotional dialogue with others. For object relations theorists, the internal structuring of the psyche is seen as an outcome of interpersonal activity, reciprocity and emotional exchange. Relations with other people, and particularly the mother, become part of the psychical economy of the self. The emotional need for connection and recognition leads to a psychic incorporation of representations of otherness into the self; and it is precisely such representations of others which are essential to the formation of psychical structure. Significantly, the other side of the coin is that interpersonal distortions or pathologies will in turn be built into the structure of the self. In object relations theory, it is socially destructive relationships in the social world which pervert the self's capacities for relating to other people. Thus, cultural conditions underpin problems of self-organization.

The theoretical premises which inform object relational approaches involve a fundamental re-evaluation of issues concerning self-constitution and the nature of psychic structure. In contrast to classical Freudianism, object relations theorists hold that individuals want relationships with others for the intrinsic satisfaction of such connectedness, and not simply to reduce drive energy. In the words of Michael Balint, psychical life is itself characterized by a search for 'primary object love'. Relational needs are primary, and disturbances in self-constitution are seen as the result of a failure to obtain the love of significant others. In the view of W. R. D. Fairbairn, one of the pioneering analysts of the British object relations school, the self is object-seeking rather than pleasure-seeking. Pleasure is certainly still important, but in object relations theory unconscious enjoyment is itself regarded as a means of achieving emotional connection with others. From this angle, the privileging of unconscious drives as the underlying engine of human motivation and social interaction is too simple, since it obscures the complex processes through which the individual (ego) and social (objects) intersect. Rather, object relations theorists suggest that we should see the quality of interpersonal relations as structuring and transforming unconscious desire and passion. For the unconscious fantasy world of the self is only given specific content and emotional texture because it operates in the service of human relationships. What this means for Fairbairn, in the words of his acolyte Harry Guntrip, is that drives 'can only operate satisfactorily when they belong to a stable ego, and therefore cannot be the source of the ego's energy for object-relating. It seems more conceivable that the energy of the ego for object-relating is the primary energy.'[13]

The starting point for the analysis of ego structure in the work of Fairbairn and others is the maturational environment, specifically the quality of maternal care experienced by the small infant. In Fairbairn's view, the earliest months of life are characterized by a total merging between the infant and mother, a mode of relatedness termed 'primary identification'. In this state, ego and objects are harmoniously linked since no differentiation has yet occurred. For Fairbairn, it is this primordial unity at the centre of psychical life which provides the basis for genuine interactions between the self and other people, from which self-organization becomes more or less integrated. This emphasizes that problems in selfhood stem from these early relationships with primary caretakers – specifically, they have their roots in infantile experiences of maternal failure and emotional deprivation. Fairbairn argues that if parental availability and responsiveness are low, the emerging child will attempt to overcome the pain of frustration by ego-splitting and internal fantasy substitutes. Typically, this involves splitting the pre-Oedipal mother into good and bad objects. The inadequacy of actual interpersonal relations leads the infant to create internal fantasy objects as a substitute. Yet such compensatory fantasy limits the child's capacity for healthy development and interpersonal interaction. Such external frustrations – that is, the mother's failure to meet the infant's needs – are conceptualized as generative of splits and distortions in consciousness. Since object and ego only exist in connection with each other in this perspective, negative experiences in this early period will lead to distortions, as well as the formation of pathological defences, in the construction of the self.

From the foregoing considerations, it can be seen that the object relational perspective holds the promise for enriching our critical understanding of the interpersonal processes involved in the constitution of the self. By illuminating the subtle, yet profoundly important, interpersonal mechanisms of self-constitution, object relations theory suggestively reconfigures the relations between the self and social context. Significantly, the focus on the pre-Oedipal relationship between infant and mother in object relations theory provides a useful corrective to traditional Freudian theory, which tended to repress the role of the mother in self-development, instead making the father the centre-point of object-internalization and thus self-constitution. This focus upon the pre-Oedipal infant/mother relationship also directs our attention to important changes affecting social relations. For object relations theorists, the late modern age creates severe disturbances in object relating. Particularly for Fairbairn and Balint, the destructive nature of modernity impacts upon the nurturing mother–infant tie too early, thus preventing the establishment of a core sense of self and trust in human relationships. This can lead, in turn, to a lifelong search for primary love through substitute fantasy objects.

However, there are also serious difficulties with object relations theory, problems that will be addressed throughout this book. A fundamental principle of the object relational perspective is that ego and object are inseparable. The ego is bound up with objects from birth, and disturbances in object relating are, first and foremost, interpersonal problems. Yet Fairbairn's postulation of a unified, integral ego smacks of essentialism. It recalls the sort of ahistorical view of human nature that Freudian psychoanalysis explicitly challenges, privileging the consoling unity of personal identity over the fractures of unconscious desire. For if there really is a timeless core of personal unity, then the social, cultural and political possibilities for transforming the self are also acutely delimited. It is this tendency to project self-development as the unfolding of a human essence that leads many commentators to conclude that object relations theory is conservative in political orientation; this is a theme that will be examined in detail in Chapters 3 and 5. To be sure, there is an implicit assumption in object relational perspectives that the unconscious is an epiphenomenon – internal fantasy objects being merely derived from failures in real environmental relations. From this angle, fantasy is not so much generative or creative but rather a consolation for, or escape from, external frustration. Rather than viewing the unconscious as a constitutive source and productive wellspring for selfhood, as is the case with Freud, the object relational approaches of theorists such as Fairbairn, Guntrip and Balint find unconscious processes a distortion of human development. To this extent, there is a parallel with the German social theorist Jürgen Habermas, who takes the unconscious as a prime example of 'systematically distorted communication'.

Instead of bracketing unconscious processes in such a negative fashion, however, it might be more instructive to trace the processes through which imagination and desire interlace with those early object relations of the environmental surround. This line of approach is suggested by the work of the British paediatrician and psychoanalyst, D. W. Winnicott. Following Freud, Winnicott emphasizes that the newly born infant has to develop a sense of self from an original state of 'unintegration'. This struggle of the self for an individuated existence characteristically centres on the quality of object relation between child and mother. For Winnicott, the emergence of true and authentic selfhood is tied to a state of 'primary maternal preoccupation'. Through such preoccupation, the mother offers a special sort of presence, or devotion, which allows the child to experience itself as omnipotent and self-identical. The mother thus objectively provides support for connection with external reality, while at that moment the child is free to create a 'representational world'.

If all goes well during this process of maternal devotion, or what Winnicott calls 'good enough mothering', the small infant is able to develop a sense of independence in line with the exercise of her or his ego functions. In this connection, Winnicott suggests that it is vital for the mother not only to be responsive to her infant's needs, but also to establish a kind of non-intrusive presence, a presence which allows the child to freely create, imagine and desire. By offering non-demanding support, the mother leads the child to a positive experience of aloneness, thereby establishing a basis for 'going-on-being' in the world. Winnicott describes this as the child's move into 'transitional space', a concept which will be discussed in Chapter 3. At this point, let me simply note that Winnicott's portrait of the self underscores a key paradox at the centre of human development. The emergence of a stable core of selfhood, according to Winnicott, depends on establishing the kind of relationship that is at once liberating *and* supportive, creative *and* dependent, defined *and* formless. For it is within this interplay of integration and separation that Winnicott locates the roots of authentic selfhood, creativity and the process of symbolization, as well as social relations and culture. It is precisely from this angle that Winnicott draws his infamous distinction between the 'true self', a person capable of creative living, and the 'false self', a person unable to establish stable emotional relations with others. For Winnicott, the 'false self' is fashioned out of the loss of maternal sensitivity, as the small infant tries desperately to make some emotional connection with the mother by abandoning its own wishes and incorporating *her* demands, desires and feelings. It is as if the child, unable to adequately express inner needs and emotional longings, turns defensively against itself by internalizing the attitudes and reactions of others. Pathologies of selfhood thus screen authentic human strivings; and this, for Winnicott, is the essence of the 'false self' as it operates 'to hide the true Self, which it does by compliance with environmental demands'.[14]

In Winnicott's version of object relations theory, then, other persons play an essentially facilitating role in the construction of the self. It is only if the mother, and later significant others, are unable to provide a supportive, non-intrusive environment that a debilitating fragmentation of the self arises. What Winnicott's model of development can be said to overlook, however, is the intensity of unconscious passion and emotional fracturing, which for Melanie Klein functions in the form of fantasy. What is involved in the fantasy world of the individual, says Klein, is a kind of continual shuttling of inner and outer worlds, from which a sense of self emerges as an outcrop of unconscious 'internal objects'. The self for Klein is originally caught up in, and dispersed within, a world of 'part-objects' – for example, fantasies about the maternal breast. Adopting Freud's scandalous concept of the death drive, Klein puts aggression and destructiveness at the heart of psychic functioning. She contends that the tendency towards destruction is transferred or projected to the earliest 'part-objects', from which the mother (or more accurately, at this point, the breast) is, in turn, experienced as dangerous or persecuting. Such anxieties are in fact so terrifying, in Klein's view, that the infant must 'split' mother into good and bad objects, thereby displacing the pain of destructive unconscious fantasy. This splitting of the world into good and bad is what Klein terms the 'paranoid–schizoid' position. In order to get beyond these schizoid poles of paranoid displacing and projective idealizing, the infant has to integrate split representations (and the conflictive feelings that underlay them) and thereby accept that the mother is an independent and separate person. Klein argues that the main stumbling block in this respect is the child's fear that it has injured the loved object permanently, due to the infant's violent fantasies concerning the maternal body. To transcend this, it is necessary for the infant to 'make reparation' through the experience of guilt and ambivalence – a process Klein terms the 'depressive' position. The negotiation of depressive feelings in the

Kleinian framework carries a positive value, from which the creative and stable self emerges. Significantly, however, paranoid–schizoid mechanisms continually resurface in both personal and social life. It is this interplay between destructive expression and creative reparation, as we shall see when examining Klein's work in Chapter 3, that gives the Kleinian perspective a powerful critical edge for the analysis of self-identity and modern culture.

Before concluding this section, a few points should be made concerning the foregoing perspectives and their differing accounts of relations between self and society. In the object relations perspective, the emergence of selfhood is tied to the development of interpersonal relations. Because of this focus on the relational qualities of self, object relations theorists tend to see contemporary social experience as both opportunity and danger. There is a recognition of both the affirmative and destructive dimensions of modern life, as well as their impact upon the cultural sense of self. To the extent that contemporary culture restricts human relations, the object relations perspective argues that self-organization is stunted. Where this occurs, life becomes drained, society is experienced as dislocating, and superficial narcissistic relationships tend to predominate. By contrast, the Kleinian view of contemporary experience focuses less on relationships than affectively loaded internal objects. For Kleinian theorists, the interplay of paranoid anger and personal despair permeates all aspects of day-to-day social life. The key issue, therefore, centres on the extent to which modern culture provides opportunities for communal reparation and creative living. To the extent that cultural displacement swallows up personal strength, Kleinian theorists emphasize that self and world become disconnected, as paranoid anxieties prevail.

Postmodern identities: contemporary psychoanalytic strategies

So far we have examined a range of psychoanalytic portraits of the self. All of these portraits, notwithstanding conceptual differences, are premised upon the guiding ethos of autonomous selfhood. In classical psychoanalysis, autonomy is conceived as the self which is emancipated from distorting unconscious passions. In Freud's profoundly Enlightenment maxim: 'Where id was, there ego shall be.' In this account, what used to be unconscious shall be reclaimed for individual control and rationality. With the emergence of object relations theory, the psychoanalytic notion of autonomy undergoes significant transformation. The autonomous self can no longer emerge against the backdrop of a transformation of desire, but depends rather on the reconstruction of emotional links with other people. It is human relationships that matter, and the enhancement of the self's capacity for interpersonal relations may depend variously upon the rational mastery of inner drives (Hartmann), stable internal objects (Fairbairn), creative human relations (Winnicott), or reparation (Klein). Despite prescriptive variations, however, these standpoints offer a contribution to some future enlargement of the autonomy of the self. In psychoanalytic theories derived from semiotics and poststructuralism, however, there is a radical break with this search for self-coherence and autonomy. The distinguishing feature of poststructural psychoanalysis is the launching of a sustained critique on the very notion of 'self'. The problem of contemporary culture, it is argued, is not located in the failure of autonomy but rather in the idea that a stable, personal self is attainable at all. What this means, at least in its more thoroughgoing versions, is a complete deconstruction of the notion of subjectivity. In contemporary psychoanalytic perspectives, this deconstruction is characterized by unconscious contradiction and dislocation – which thus make the goal of stable personal identity problematical. One important implication of all this is that the modernist belief in the would-be autonomy of the self is rendered little more than an ideological fantasy.

The links between poststructural psychoanalysis and postmodernism are complex in character, and will form a central thread of discussion in later chapters. At this point, it can be said that postmodern theory refers to particular social transformations ushered into being in the twentieth century, and examines a social condition characteristic of advanced contemporary societies. Central to these social and institutional transformations is what Jean-François Lyotard has called the 'crisis of narratives'.[15] By this, Lyotard means that the lofty aims of the modernist epoch – rationality, emancipation, autonomy and revolution – are no longer sustainable. By contrast, the new postmodern attitude welcomes the institutionalization of contingency and ambivalence. Arguing against the grand ambitions of modernism, postmodern theorists suggest that we reject totalizing or unifying discourses and, instead, attempt to come to terms with the fractured and problematical nature of contemporary social experience. Significantly, it is at this point that the claims of poststructural psychoanalysis become most pertinent to postmodernism. For the emphasis on the illusory nature of the self and the polyvalency of unconscious desire in poststructural psychoanalysis fits neatly with the postmodern emphasis on surfaces, images and fragments. This decentring of the self is, in brief, at one with the postmodern account of contemporary social experience – an experience in which the flows of libidinal desire mesh with an attitude of 'anything goes'.

For postmodern theorists, the concept of self-identity is a fiction. Selfhood is an imaginary illusion, an illusion which serves to mask the painful reality that desire is itself insatiable. This deconstructive conceptual strategy is taken largely from the widely influential account of the human subject proposed by the French psychoanalyst Jacques Lacan. For Lacan, the narcissistic illusions of selfhood can be traced back to a very early stage in life, to a structuring event which Lacan calls the 'mirror stage'. This stage of human development comes about when the small infant, previously unintegrated and uncoordinated, finds its bodily image reflected in a mirror.[16] Whether the mirror stage is understood literally or metaphorically, the crucial point for Lacan is that the small infant is led to *misrecognize* and *misperceive* itself. According to Lacan, the mirror provides an illusory apprehension of self-unity that has not been objectively achieved. That is to say, the creation of an 'ideal self' – the self as it would like to be, self-sufficient and unified – is an imaginary construct, wish-fulfilment pure and simple. The implications of this narcissistic construction of the self are far-reaching. Lacan and his acolytes claim that, whether or not one is actually fascinated with one's own image, the distortions and traps of the imaginary order shape all interactions between the self and others. This ranges from family interaction, through school, early adulthood, to the work environment, and human social relationships more generally.

The Lacanian doctrine of the self as an imaginary illusion casts serious doubt on the question of autonomy as traditionally conceived. For if it is still possible to speak meaningfully of self-knowledge from this angle, then critical insight must shift to some other register than that of the narcissistic illusions of the ego. In Lacanian theory, as we shall see in Chapter 4, this possibility is linked to the entry of the individual subject into the symbolic order – that cultural plane of received social meanings, differentiation and individuation. The anchoring point of this transition from imaginary distortion to symbolic meaning is language. Taking a typically poststructuralist turn, Lacan contends that 'the unconscious is structured like a language'. What this means, essentially, is that social, linguistic processes and the inner depths of the psyche are intertwined. To be a member of society requires a minimum level of linguistic competence, in order to adopt the position of speaker or listener. This demands the acceptance of a *subject position* in terms of the social conditions of culture, sexual difference and ideology.

Lacan's linguistic reinterpretation of Freudian psychoanalysis has been taken up by social theorists, literary analysts and media and cultural critics. What has been especially influential in Lacan's writings is the argument that the imaginary and symbolic dimensions of psychical life are themselves ideological carriers of culture and history. Lacanian theory offers a powerful account of the organization of psychic life through the linguistic codes and symbolic structures of modern culture. The Lacanian emphasis on the decentring of the subject grasps the inherent difficulties of forging a core of personal selfhood in the late modern age. Caught between the narcissistic traps of the imaginary and the structural positioning of the socio-symbolic order, the portrait of the human subject in Lacanianism is in certain respects an apt characterization of how personal life is globally outstripped by social, political and economic mechanisms.

For Lacanian theorists, symbols order the psyche into socialized form, at once ripping the infant away from the world of imaginary plenitude and referring her or him to received social meanings. The symbolic field – that is, language – is the crucial means through which individuals are 'subjected' to the outer world. There is clearly a deterministic flavour to all this. The symbolic order structures the psychical reactions of people in the face of social and political institutions. In this connection, Lacanian theory might be said to suppress unconscious contradiction as well as the profoundly imaginary dimensions of human experience. Indeed, it is just this binding of unconscious desire to the social order that Gilles Deleuze and Félix Guattari in *Anti-Oedipus* find as lying at the root of the Lacanian ideological position.[17] According to Deleuze and Guattari, psychoanalytic theory (both traditional and Lacanian) is politically reactionary in character. The psychoanalytic privileging of Oedipal identity, or what Lacanians call the 'Law of the Father', is at one with the imposition of repressive discourses on the free flow of desire. To combat this, as we shall see in Chapter 6, Deleuze and Guattari emphasize the positive contours of unconscious desire, taking schizophrenia as a model for 'revolutionary action'. Deleuze and Guattari argue for a primary desire resistant to closure, a desire that can be ideologically marshalled to overcome the repressive constraints of modernity.

A similar, though less dramatic, critique of psychoanalysis is to be found in the writings of the French philosopher Jean-François Lyotard. Like Lacan, Lyotard sees all discourse as traced through the structuring force of the symbolic. However, Lyotard questions the supremacy that Lacan attributes to the symbolic order in fixing meaning. For Lyotard, the unconscious is less an organized system of language than it is a 'libidinal band' of pure traces, intensities and forms. It is precisely from this angle, as we shall see, that Lyotard analyses the production of culture.

It follows from all this that psychoanalytic discourse might itself be a repressive component of contemporary society. We might say that psychoanalysis is a prisoner of rigorous binary codes (conscious/unconscious, pleasure/reality, love/hate, primary/secondary), codes which are used to impose a rigid theoretical grid upon the complexity of human experience in its entirety. In the postmodernist perspective, psychoanalysis is often charged with violently homogenizing the complexities and differences of social experience in terms of concepts such as the unconscious, castration anxiety, Oedipus and the like. Thus, for the postmodern sociologist Jean Baudrillard, psychoanalysis functions as a 'mirror of desire', projecting its terms and concepts on to human subjects, and thereby constituting the unconscious and its effects.[18] Whether you find this sort of argument convincing or not depends, to a large extent, on how you evaluate the ontological conditions of desire and passion as well as the discourses we use to make sense of everyday life. It is, I shall argue in this book, an intellectual sleight of hand to imagine that discourse simply legislates into existence the concrete emotions, desires and aspirations of human beings. This is not to say that a reductive use of psychoanalytic categories does not limit our understanding of personal and social phenomena, nor is it to deny that people in modern societies often draw on psychoanalysis in framing and understanding their daily activities and decisions. But it is to make the point that psychoanalysis is not just a theoretical play of mirrors. Unless one is willing to embrace the idea that individuals are just magically born into the social network, or that desire is somehow always already true to itself, then one must concede that psychoanalysis provides valuable insights concerning the imaginary world of selfhood.

In contrast to the French anti-psychoanalytic claim that the intellectual fascination with Freudian theory is over, the enterprise of psychoanalytic critique is developing at a faster rate than ever before. Indeed, it has been via a thoroughgoing revision of the whole Lacanian framework that a number of theorists in recent years have sought to rethink the complex relations between self and society, as well as the possibilities for transformations of culture. This theoretical current is generally grouped under the banner of 'post-Lacanianism', though many of its leading figures tend to reject this label. There are numerous common themes that surface in post-Lacanian theory, and in subsequent chapters we shall review the influence of post-Lacanian motifs in contemporary theory. At this point, the following key themes of post-Lacanian theory are noted: the re-evaluation of the creative power of the imagination; the rejection of a monolithic symbolic Law; a profound questioning of the phallic, patriarchal order of modern societies, together with a stress on the immanent possibilities for alternative gender relations; and a peculiar concern with social and political interests as the product of contingency, lack and linguistic uncertainty. To date, post-Lacanian ideas have attracted strongest interest in feminist quarters. The writings of Julia Kristeva and Luce Irigaray, whose theories will be examined in Chapter 5, have provided feminism with a powerful reconfiguration of feminine sexuality and the female body, urging women to reject the prison-house of patriarchal language and overturn it for an alternative feminist vision of social relations. Significantly, though, post-Lacanian theory has also made important contributions to rethinking human subjectivity within a general theory of ideology. In this connection, the key emphasis is on social and cultural forms as imaginary traps which paper over the impossible nature of desire itself. In this sense, post-Lacanian criticism engages in a psychoanalysis of cultural objects, showing how people project desire into the social fabric of modern culture.

Summary

In this chapter, we have examined a range of psychoanalytic portraits of the self. In so doing, three fundamental themes have been developed: selfhood and its

Table 1.1   The making of the self

Psychoanalytic model	Self and sexual subjectivity	Key terms
Classical psychoanalysis	Structural division of the psychical economy; self as outcrop of unconscious fantasy	Id, ego, superego Oedipus and castration complexes
Ego psychology	Traced as the outcome of the separation–individuation scheme	Defence mechanisms Adaptation
Object relations theory	Seen as the internalization of early environmental surround	Internal object relations
Kleinian theory	Understood as the product of love and death drives, from which ego object relations undergo integration or disintegration	Splitting Paranoid–schizoid and depressive positions
Lacanian theory	Seen as an imaginary construct; structured by symbolic law of language	Imaginary, symbolic and real orders Law of the Father
Post-Lacanian theory	Interplay of libidinal forces and symbolic codes; at once subject to and subversive of the law	Pre-Oedipal imaginary

embedding in asymmetric relations of power; the links between personal meanings and the contemporary social world; and the relationship between psychoanalytic critique and individual and collective autonomy. These themes have been selected for their relevance to the central concerns of this book, and I shall seek to develop them in a substantive way in the chapters that follow.

In introducing these themes, an overview of different psychoanalytic traditions has been provided. Firstly, there was an outline of Freud's theory of the self as an outcrop of the unconscious. In classical psychoanalysis, the self, as well as our relations with others and with society, is fully shaped by unconscious desire. Following this a review of various object relational accounts of the self was sketched. In these theories, it was stressed that relationships themselves are taken as primary and fundamental to self-organization. In this respect, it was emphasized that both classical and object relations theories adopt certain modernist assumptions about self-identity, pathologies of self and social relations, and their possible transformation. Finally, there was an examination of contemporary psychoanalytic perspectives in the light of postmodernism, stressing the fragile links between unconscious desire and the self as an imaginary construct. It was argued that the self in postmodernism is seen as an alienating fiction, without psychic interiority of depth. Finally, some social and political implications of this general standpoint, as developed in Lacanian and post-Lacanian theory, were traced out.

We shall now turn to consider how these themes have influenced contemporary psychoanalysis and social-theoretical debates during the twentieth century. In the next chapter, I begin this examination by investigating various psychoanalytic interpretations of modern culture.

CHAPTER 2

Modern Culture and Its Repressed

From Freud to Lasch

Sexuality and repression: these are twin boundary posts in the psychoanalytic interpretation of modern culture. In the wake of Freud's discoveries concerning sexuality and the unconscious, a strong tradition of political radicalism has emerged which attempts to ground social theory in psychoanalysis. This brand of social psychoanalysis is concerned with the disruptive impact of unconscious desire as it affects whole societies. In applying psychoanalysis to the spheres of social, political and cultural life, the following key questions arise. How does the individual subject engage, at an emotional level, with general social relations? Do personal meanings merely 'reflect' social reality, or are they inseparably bound up with cultural life and thus capable of transforming the social world? How does the unconscious affect the complex connections between self and society? What of society itself? Does society play a facilitating role in emotional expression and psychic development, or does it serve to restrict and deform the self? In exploring these issues, this chapter ranges widely across a variety of conceptual standpoints. Broadly speaking, one central lineage, from Freud's cultural diagnosis to Herbert Marcuse's social theory, is preoccupied with the idea of sexual repression as the key to understanding the modern period. An alternative tradition of social thought, from the writings of Erich Fromm to Christopher Lasch, is concerned more with interpersonal issues of sexuality, love and emotional communication in modern societies.

Freud's social theory: survival, repression, ambivalence

Towards the end of his career Freud wrote: 'I recognized ever more clearly that the events of human history, the interactions between human nature, cultural development, and the precipitates of primeval experiences ... are only the reflection of the dynamic conflicts among the ego, id, and superego, which psychoanalysis studies in the individual – the same events repeated on a wider stage.'

This statement captures the essence of Freud's thought about culture. Analysis of culture and cultural forms, like the critique of personal subjectivity, requires the application of psychoanalytic knowledge. This involves tracing the institutionalization of the unconscious – the regulation of sexuality and desire – within social and cultural relations.

According to Freud, *ambivalence* lies at the heart of the relation between self and world. The ground of all human thought, feeling and action springs from a primordial ambivalence vital to the complexity of social life itself. To be precise, Freud says, such ambivalence precedes society. Consciousness and the unconscious, reason and desire, primary and secondary process, self-preservation and sexuality, love and hatred: these are permanent dualisms, contends Freud, of our psychic world. Because human sexuality is 'polymorphously perverse', because desire is filtered through fantasy, because the unconscious is always clamouring for expression: the torments of ambivalence are no mere accident that might be overcome in a different social world. In this respect, Freud's social theory engages with some of the most painful and distressing aspects of human experience. Modern culture, Freud says, is repressive. Society imposes severe psychic demands upon individuals, demands that produce intense personal misery. But it is precisely from this painful ambivalence or unconscious anguish that Freud also detects the roots of psychic resistance. Too much repression, Freud says, leads to intense hostility and rage. At this point, the pressure of unconscious desire can release the 'mental dams' of sexual repression in a far-reaching way.

Freud's earliest full-length consideration of the relations between self and society is his paper, ' "Civilized" Sexual Morality and Modern Nervous Illness' (1908). The theory of society embodied in this text is usually interpreted as a one-way impress of culture upon the individual. However, as is so often the case with Freud, this essay is at once a polemical engagement with traditional views about morality and cultural order, and a preliminary outline of the immense conceptual difficulties in linking the unconscious and social organization. Freud begins by considering the viewpoint that modernity – the transition from pre-modern to modern culture – has produced a general condition of neurosis, of 'exhausted nerves'. According to Freud, the competitive and materialistic quality of modern social life has given rise to much emotional suffering. Indeed, the overall tone of Freud's argument is that modern culture is lamentable. However, Freud does not wish to limit himself to only a sociocultural explanation of anxiety. For the crux of the matter lies elsewhere: in those points of unconscious pleasure through which sexuality interlaces with extrinsic moral imperatives. For Freud, the ambivalence of psychical life rebounds as cultural uncertainty. What this means, essentially, is that the emotional conflicts which Freud uncovers in humans are shifted up a gear into the antagonistic structures of social and cultural life. Conflict, generated in and through the psyche, produces anxiety which is turned against culture.

In the same manner that the ego seeks to establish order and control over the disruptive unconscious, it is essential for culture to incorporate the deeper emotional strivings of the subject, pressing the pleasure principle into the service of the reality principle. This is so, Freud contends, for the very reproduction of social and cultural life. The development of civilization, social bonds and the injunction to labour all depend upon self-control. However, it is precisely at this point – the disjunction between individual desire and social necessity – that Freud locates cultural pathology, the initial 'manifestations of nervous disturbance'. The fundamental problem, in short, is that culture robs the individual subject of unfettered instinctual enjoyment, and places gigantic restrictions upon sexuality. Listening to the miseries and anxieties of his bourgeois analysands each day, Freud discovered a deep connection between personal, inner desires and the repressive social forms which engender excessive self-control. The denial of feelings, the structuring of sexuality into narrow paths of monogamy and marital legitimacy, the rigid (male) insistence upon genital monosexuality: these are, Freud argues, the oppressive emotional repressions inflicted upon human subjects. Imposing order on the free flow of unconscious desire, Freud comments, is thus a key task of civilization. However, the balance between desire and order is constantly changing, and can easily become too much of a burden for individuals and collectivities. When the imposition of social control, order and structure results in repressive closure, cultural life is condemned to self-annihilation. Authentic communal bonds are reduced to little more than a façade. Hence, Freud places 'civilized' in quotation marks in this essay. As he concludes, 'when society pays for obedience to its far-reaching regulations by an increase in nervous illness, it cannot claim to have purchased a gain at the price of sacrifice; it cannot claim a gain at all'.[1]

Psychic ambivalence is therefore the route by which Freud sketches the psychoanalytic interpretation of culture. Desire and control, pleasure and reality, sexuality and self-preservation: these are the dualisms, in the early Freud, through which individuals come to face social regulation. Central to this structuring process of prohibition and repression is the Oedipus complex. The intervention of the father into the child/mother dyad is of key importance for grasping the institutionalization of extrinsic moral imperatives, primarily because the paternal role is symbolic and thus suggestive of social regulation. In seeking to demonstrate this, Freud traced the origins of collective moral prohibitions back in history, to an actual Oedipal event. The theorem of an original parricide, of an actual murder of the father figure, led Freud in *Totem and Taboo* (1914) to reconstruct a collective Oedipal moral imperative. Freud paints a picture of a 'primal horde', a collectivity of 'brothers' dominated by an all-powerful father who monopolizes women. In anger and frustration, the brothers eventually kill and eat the father. Due to ambivalence and guilt, however, the brothers come to feel remorse for the killing.

This unconscious anguish induces the brothers to identify with the dead father as a 'totem', and to invent moral anchoring restraints against the free expression of sexual desire. Like in the Oedipal fantasy itself, the terror of the father is now 'owned' on the inside and the regulation of society is instituted through the renunciation of desire, registered in the taboo against incest.

There is no need to rehearse here the grave limitations of Freud's account of social and cultural organization. In the light of subsequent anthropological knowledge this century, there are few advocates of this aspect of Freud's social account nowadays. Perhaps the most important point to note is that Freud's attempt to anchor the Oedipus complex in a foundational event displaces his crucial insights into the radically creative power of the human imagination. Seen from this angle, Freud's collective Oedipal myth ascribes to real events what are in fact products of fantasy, the life of the mind. Despite the limitations of Freud's account of the institutionalization of morality, however, there are still elements of considerable interest in this perspective. The problem of self and society, and their mutual imbrication, is fundamental in this respect. As Freud comments:

> The asocial nature of neurosis has its genetic origin in their most fundamental purpose, which is to take flight from an unsatisfying reality into a more pleasurable world of fantasy. The real world, which is avoided in this way by neurotics, is under the sway of human society and of the institutions collectively created by it. To turn away from reality is at the same time to withdraw from the community of man.[2]

This passage captures the essence of Freud's thinking about society and social institutions. First, Freud stresses that reality is not pre-given or natural. Reality, Freud says, is structured by 'human society', by the social and technical frameworks fashioned by human beings. Second, he underscores the point that individual subjectivity and society presuppose one another. To take flight from reality involves rejecting or foreclosing social bonds. For Freud, social forms thus constitute the self at the deepest roots of unconscious experience.

In his late writings, Freud comes to see human beings as living under the destructive force of a terrifying death drive – a primordial tendency within the psychic economy to return to non-being, to the inorganic. From this standpoint, psychic ambivalence is recast as the permanent co-presence of two drives: that of life and that of death, Eros and Thanatos. Freud developed the hypothesis of the death drive to account for a range of problems arising in clinical work. Issues relating to human aggressiveness, questions of sadism and masochism, the repetition of painful and traumatic experiences, the addictive character of neurotic suffering: these and other related phenomena could not be understood in terms of the pleasure principle of psychic functioning. Accordingly, Freud modified his earlier emphasis upon sexual pleasure and enjoyment. In *Beyond the Pleasure*

Principle (1920), Freud proclaims that 'the aim of all life is death'. After 1920, psychical life for Freud still has its origins in sexuality and libido, but the psyche is also shot through with aggressivity, sadism and hate. As Freud notes of this new dualism: 'only by the concurrent of mutually opposing action of the two primal drives – Eros and the death-drive – never by one or the other alone, can we explain the rich multiplicity of the phenomena of life'.[3]

In retrospect, Freud's positing of the life and death drives can be viewed as a preliminary cultural diagnosis, the essential underpinnings for his global model of repression. For Freud's theory of the death drive entails a radical reinterpretation of the repressive character of modern culture itself. Human misery and oppression are no longer understood as the outcome of sexual repression alone. Instead, Freud comes to equate culture with a fundamental constraint upon self-destructiveness. 'The main renunciation culture demands of the individual', writes Paul Ricoeur of Freud's metapsychology, 'is the renunciation not of desire as such but of aggressiveness.'[4] By incorporating this new dualism into his analysis of modern culture, Freud is able to rewrite the problem of self and society as a contest between love and hate. The Freud of *Civilization and Its Discontents* (1930) enfolds love and hate, Eros and Thanatos, in the following way:

> [C]ivilization is a process in the service of Eros, whose purpose is to combine single human individuals, and after that families, then races, peoples and nations, into one great unity. . . . These collections of men are libidinally bound to one another. Necessity alone, the advantages of work in common, will not hold them together. But man's natural aggressive instinct, the hostility of each against all and of all against each, opposes this programme of civilization. The aggressive instinct is the derivative and main representative of the death drive which we have found alongside of Eros and which shares world-dominion with it.[5]

The pathological compulsions of cultural life are rooted in a repressive structuring of love and hatred. To be sure, Freud remains faithful to his earlier view that the reproduction of society depends upon sexual repression. But in his late sociological vision this sexual repression becomes integrated into a deathly self-preservation, organized as a destructive assault on the human body, on others, and on nature.

The internalization of these repressive and deathly cultural norms is, according to Freud, carried out by the superego. Like the small infant in the Oedipal drama, human beings develop a relation to society through unconscious identifications with received social meanings and extrinsic moral imperatives. This is so, Freud argues, because human beings are born 'prematurely', and hence there is a dependence upon, and submission to, authority figures prior to the emergence of sexuality. What this means, in brief, is that human beings, at the level of desire, identify with political authority. From this angle, civilization is generally secure in enforcing a truce between desire and control. Sexual and aggressive passions are turned back upon individuals with a vengeance by social institutions, thereby introducing a sense of guilt, anxiety and unhappiness into the human condition. In this sense, the individual channels back 'unacceptable' desires into the psyche as the price paid for ordered social life. Yet in mixing the death drive with erotic impulses, civilization also outflanks these goals of security and social order. The integration of the life and death drives increasingly supplants cultural order, as unconscious desire swerves on to destructive paths of social expression. As Freud concludes: 'The fateful question for the human species seems to me to be whether and to what extent their cultural development will succeed in mastering the disturbance of their communal life by the drive of aggression and self-destruction.'[6]

Freud's signal contribution to social thought lies in the idea that culture is reproduced through a repressive structuring of the fantasy lives of individuals. However, Freud's social thought has been fiercely contested, both inside and outside psychoanalytic circles. It has been argued, for example, that modern societies are far more differentiated and conflictual in character than is recognized in the Freudian model of repression. Such critics argue that, since psychoanalysis sees cultural order as necessarily involving the overpowering of chaotic passion and desire, Freud's theories are, in effect, at one with the conservative-minded social thought of, say, Thomas Hobbes. This line of criticism involves a fundamental misunderstanding of Freudian psychoanalysis. I have already argued that it is mistaken to see Freud as equating culture with a one-way impress upon the individual. It is certainly the case that Freud finds modern culture repressive; often tyrannically so. But the fundamental tenet of his standpoint is that self and society interlock through ambivalence. There is a 'lack of fit', so to speak, between self and world; this disjunction arises from the existence of psychic dualisms (unconscious/conscious, sexual drives/self-preservation, life/death) that prevents the individual subject from becoming fully integrated into received social meanings. That this is the case, Freud says, is positive news. For it is ambivalence that drives the self forward, generating in turn the complexity of social life. Significantly, the Freudian image of conflict between unconscious forces and social reproduction helps to illuminate numerous aspects of contemporary social experience. Given the turbulence of modernity, Freud's social thought is in many ways an accurate reflection of the open, contingent and fragmented world in which we live. Political upheaval is a crisis of social relationships; repressed desires and passions threaten (and often invade) everyday life, disrupting the world as it is.

There is indeed a problem in Freud's theory, however, about how repression and culture are interwoven. For Freud, heightened repression is intrinsically associated with the complexity of modern culture. However, this thesis looks increasingly untenable in the light of various recent social transformations, especially changes in sexual mores and gender power. Put simply, the repression of sexual and aggressive drives no longer appears to be the key issue in a world which has broken with moral constraint almost everywhere. Whether we speak of the mass media's fascination with sex or the ideological turmoil of wars and revolutions the world over, modernity incorporates (and indeed bolsters) the erotic and aggressive passions of human subjects. Such trends suggest that culture is at once an essential medium for the expression and repression of unconscious drives. Society may place restrictions on various forms of emotional and sensual expression, but it also provides the means for self-representation through the constitution of cultural forms. In part, Freud's thought occludes this enabling dimension of the social network since he focuses primarily upon repressed passions of the self. This emphasis underscores the cultural repression of sensuality and sexuality, and related problems of self-control, but only at the expense of diverting attention from the complex patterning of social relations and their intersection with personal relationships. By contrast, in object relations psychoanalysis and related variants, as discussed in Chapter 1, the primary focus is away from the solitary language of sexual repression and towards the interpersonal dimension of desire. This psychoanalytical approach to the interpretation of culture will be critically examined in the following sections of this chapter.

Equally significant is the feminist criticism that Freud's account of social life and culture is unduly restrictive and gender biased. Here it is argued by critics that Freud is secretly held in thrall to the values of rationality and social authority that he seeks to disrupt. Though Freud is sceptical of Enlightenment reason, there is some truth to this charge. Civilization, in Freud's account, rests upon the repression of sexuality and aggression, itself the outcome of the Oedipus and castration complexes. In so far as Freud traces the psychic roots of Oedipal identity, it can be argued that his thought grasps the persistence of patriarchal domination. But there is also a defensive aspect here. By making Oedipus and the father central to his account of society and culture, Freud subordinates the role of the mother and pre-Oedipal experience as a whole. Paternal identification, for Freud, is the cornerstone of patriarchal culture, and the pre-Oedipal child/mother bond is cast aside as precultural. Society is equated with control, renunciation, organization and commerce. The pre-Oedipal maternal realm, by contrast, necessarily threatens subversion to male-dominated language and culture. This is a point that has become of considerable importance to some feminists, particularly those associated with object relations theory and also some post-Lacanians. For these theorists, Freud's social account is essentially a theoretical replication of patriarchal power. A discussion of these trends in psychoanalytic feminism is offered in Chapter 5. At this stage, a related but different point is made.

By viewing the Oedipus complex as preparatory to individuation and social reproduction, Freud's theory underlines the importance of male rationality and self-control in modern societies. Such a psychoanalytic model grasps how restrictive cultural norms are internalized, and thus reproduced, by human subjects. However, there are also limitations. By excluding the pre-Oedipal realm of sexuality, little is said in the Freudian scheme about love, empathy and emotional communication

Escaping society: Erich Fromm's humanistic psychoanalysis

We have seen that, for Freud, there is a fundamental ambivalence structuring relations between self and society. Inner repression, Freud argues, is the price paid for social co-operation. It is just this conception of social repression that is challenged in the writings of the post-Freudian cultural theorist Erich Fromm. An early member of the Marxist Frankfurt School, and later an émigré from Nazi Germany, Fromm argues – in a series of influential books – that psychoanalytic theory must be reformulated better to conceptualize the place of social and historical factors in self-constitution. For Fromm, the key error of Freud's work is that it abstracts from a specific socio-political situation – the sexual repression of Victorian culture – and projects interpersonal conflict into the solitary world of the individual subject. In contrast to Freud's approach, Fromm is out to show, not how we suffer repression in order to join society, but how society itself inscribes pathology at the heart of human relationships. Indeed, Fromm sees modern culture as offering false solutions to human needs. As he puts this, society is our 'escape from freedom'.

In his early writings associated with the Frankfurt School, Fromm attempts an integration of Freud's theory of the unconscious with Marxist social theory. According to Fromm, Freudian theory
order to grasp how social structures in
system, in Fromm's reinterpretation of I
subjects to fit the economic, cultural and
duces subjects adapted to the roles of ser
subjects as capitalists and workers; and
churns out subjects as consumers. Fromm
production of 'socially necessary characte
social individuals derives from the 'highl
instantiates a fundamental ordering of
values and processes into the deepest
Fromm, is individuals 'wanting to act as

For Fromm, as for Freud, the family plays a key role in the emergence of repression. The winning of parental love entails the repression and denial of inner selfhood and an adaptation to socially prescribed patterns of behaviour. As Fromm puts this: 'The family is the medium through which the society or the social class stamps its specific structure on the child, and hence on the adult. *The family is the psychological agency of society.*'[7] The nuclear family is an institution that implants objective antagonisms at the heart of individual subjectivity, sustains economic conditions as ideology, and infuses perceptions of the self as submissive, self-effacing and powerless. The central thread of Fromm's argument is that the destructive consequences of late capitalism are not only centred on economic mechanisms and institutions, but involve the anchoring of domination within the inner life and psychodynamic struggles of each individual.

If society, in Fromm's eyes, is a matter of sexual repression, libidinal renunciation and pathologies of self, then it is really not all that far from the general tenets of Freudian social thought. In arguing that social and political relations affect self-identity in different and changing ways, Fromm enriches Freud's account of repression. Fromm's later writings, however, change direction quite dramatically. Increasingly sceptical of Freud's dualistic theory of the psyche, he became convinced that the Freudian drive model of human motivation could not adequately grasp social relations. In particular, Fromm rejected Freud's notion of the death drive, arguing that the notion only served to legitimate the increasingly destructive and aggressive tendencies of the late modern age.

In his major work *The Sane Society* (1956), Fromm examines modern culture in terms of the pathologies it inflicts upon selfhood, considering the extent to which social structure deforms human relationships. In that book, he argues that Freud underemphasized social and cultural relations, and also the general impact of culture upon human needs. Selfhood, says Fromm, is best understood in terms of interpersonal processes. From this angle, psychical life is composed of emotional configurations derived from relations between self and others. For Fromm, self-organization, though influenced by unconscious drives and passion, is reflexively organized through 'awareness, reason and imagination'. Fromm's theory of selfhood can be stated in five theses:

Relatedness vs. narcissism. The human condition is rooted in an essential need
r relatedness – a thesis with which Fromm challenges Freud's supposedly
ial account of the individual. The need for relatedness is not instinctual but
om the separation with nature. Its flourishing depends upon creative
ions. Without such relations the self is impoverished, as in patho-
ism.

ativeness vs. destructiveness.* Against the backdrop of biological
ization of creativity unfolds in both positive and negative

forms. Creation and destruction, Fromm argues, 'are both answers to the same need for transcendence, and the will to destroy must rise when the will to create cannot be satisfied'.

3. *Rootedness-brotherliness vs. incest.* Creative social life, Fromm argues, depends upon an interplay of masculine and feminine values. Arguing against the 'patri-archistic–acquisitive' logic of Freud's Oedipus complex, Fromm contends that human potentiality depends upon the integration of feminine qualities (such as care and nurturing) into the masculine realm of reason and reflexivity. In this connection, Fromm says, feminine qualities are dangerous in modern culture since they threaten incorporation back into a 'state of nature'.

4. *Sense of identity-individuality vs. herd conformity.* The search for self-identity is intrinsic to the human condition, and modern societies play an essential role in structuring socio-economic possibilities for self-organization. The repressive transformation of this need, he argues, produces regressive ideologies such as fascism, racism and the like.

5. *The need for a frame of orientation and devotion-reason vs. irrationality.* The need for orientation and connection with the world is a precondition for human autonomy. Without this, symbolic forms become diffused, and the subject drained of ego-strength.[8]

The central feature of Fromm's theory is that helplessness, isolation and aloneness are key building blocks in relations between the self and others. In this respect, the patterns of relationship that a person makes can be either progressive or regressive. Progressive relations with other people involve a reflexive, rational understanding of the human condition. The pain of individual isolation must be confronted and accepted, in order for healthy intersubjective relations to develop. By contrast, a regressive involvement with other people is caused by denying individual separateness. In this mode of functioning, inner pain and emptiness are sidestepped by a neurotic immersion in infantile illusions. An endless menu of regressive fantasies is offered by mass consumer culture in this connection, fantasies which produce narcissistic pathology and related disturbances. The key feature in this neurotic unfolding of the self is that other people are used instrumentally in order to bolster self-identity, and thus to avoid inner emptiness and isolation. Here Fromm's standpoint converges on a crucial object relational distinction between self-development and self-distortion – as in Fairbairn's formulation of good and bad object relations, or Winnicott's account of the true self and the false self. However, Fromm proposes a more socially nuanced version of psychoanalytic theory by directly linking interpersonal relations and social context. The core of his argument is that problems of self, which link with social relationship pathologies, have their roots in already existing patterns of cultural domination. Because the spheres of economic, political and cultural life are shot through with the sadistic satisfactions of power and domination, regressive self-solutions are reproduced in the individual domain.

Given that contemporary social arrangements violently deform and warp self-constitution, is there anything that can be done to reverse this pathological state of affairs? Can human beings create, and sustain, any kind of meaningful liberation? Fromm believes that they can. Surprisingly, given the pessimistic tone of the foregoing analysis, Fromm contends that it is still possible to face painful realities of life in a mature and rational way. To do this, Fromm argues, it is vital for the self to *disengage* from the corrupting influences of mass culture in the media age. To live authentically means fashioning a creative and responsive selfhood, a self that can productively engage in intimacy and mutuality. Such a capacity, he contends, depends on coming to terms with individual separation and aloneness, usually experienced as isolation or emptiness in contemporary culture. A shorthand way of describing this is that Fromm is encouraging a more reflexive involvement with emotion and the self. But what then of social conflict? In this context, Fromm attempts to develop a moral dimension as an energizing vision for emancipation. The more that human subjects reclaim the possibility of authentic existence through introspection and self-reflection, the more a social order based on mutual respect and autonomous activity will develop.

Fromm's writings rank among the most important post-Freudian mappings of the relations between self and society. Indeed, his model has had a major influence upon the reception of psychoanalysis into social and cultural theory. There are, however, important problems with Fromm's humanistic psychoanalysis. It has been argued, for example, that his account of self-constitution and the social process leads to a form of sociological reductionism. What is meant by this charge is that Fromm reduces the complex, contradictory relations between self and society to a dull, mechanical reproduction of pre-existing social values. The subject is repressively constituted through certain agencies of socialization, which stamp the prescriptive values of society into the human soul and thereby deform the essential needs of the self. In this critique, Fromm presents an account of self-constitution that eliminates the profound role of the unconscious imagination, and leaves unexamined the diverse human possibilities for agency, creativity, critical reflection and transformation. He reduces Freud's notion of the unconscious to a deterministic conception of individual malleability. The limitations of such an approach are plain. The ambivalence that Freud locates between self and society – the tension between psychical and social reality – is obliterated. Although wanting to compensate for Freud's focus on unconscious drives, Fromm's cultural analysis proceeds too far in the other direction – sociologizing psychical reality out of existence. Ironically, then, it is the *post*-Freudian Erich Fromm that ultimately speaks up for a *pre*-Freudian conception of the 'total personality'.

A related criticism is that Fromm evaluates society against some 'human essence' of a non-cultural kind. It is as if Fromm, having diagnosed modern selfhood as thoroughly ideological, has to safeguard some resistant kernel of the human condition in order to articulate an emancipatory claim at all. Rationality, individualism, transcendence: these ideals may be absent from modern society, but they underlie all human experience and will potentially transform the social world. But in arguing that there is a transhistorical, universal 'human condition', Fromm seems blind to the fact that ideals such as rationality and self-mastery are often quite explicitly oppressive. Many contemporary world problems – global warming, the risk of massively destructive warfare, the exploitation and pollution of nature – are intimately bound up with the expansion of Western rationality and mastery. As one commentator puts it: 'Fromm revives all the time-honoured values of idealist ethics as if nobody had ever demonstrated their conformist and repressive features.'[9] Significantly, the ideals which Fromm stresses are also those of a male-dominated realm. Little is said about gender or the repression of female sexuality in Fromm's work. His humanistic psychoanalysis, and its under-writing of the 'essential needs of mankind', thus reproduces at a theoretical level masculinist fantasies of omnipotent self-control. Seen in this light, the inadequacy of Fromm's belief that authentic living is possible through social disengagement becomes evident: to turn inward in the hope of discovering authentic existence represents not a 'radical endeavour' but rather an illusory wish to overcome domination and suffering by escaping society.

Marcuse's Freudian revolution

For the Frankfurt School social theorist Herbert Marcuse, unconscious desire is at once subject to the social–historical process and also potentially transformative of that world. People suffer from too much repression in modern society, says Marcuse. Yet, by adapting Freud to radical ends, he argues that the liberation of repressed desire could produce social transformation of a far-reaching kind. Like Fromm, Marcuse sees psychological and political repression as interconnected. A critical reading of psychoanalysis is vital, Marcuse argues, for understanding how cultural domination penetrates the inner world of individual subjectivity, how monopoly capitalism and mass consumer culture shape personal desires, and for comprehending human passivity in the face of exploitative and destructive social processes. However, Marcuse does not accept that social forms repressively triumph over the individual subject completely. Critical of Fromm's humanistic psychoanalysis, Marcuse contends that the way forward is not through private disengagement, but through psychological and social transformation. From this perspective, Fromm's programme for 'authentic living' is fundamentally conservative since it implies accepting the world as it is. Whereas post-Freudians like Fromm graft society and culture on to psychoanalysis, Marcuse seeks to unfold psychoanalysis from the inside, in order to reveal its inherently critical edge. That is, Marcuse reads psychoanalysis as a critical theory of self-organization, one alert to the repression, domination and suffering of modernity.

In his seminal *Eros and Civilization* (1955), Marcuse traces how modern social processes deform the self and social relationships. According to Marcuse, it is necessary to recognize that the contradictions of capitalism pass into individual subjectivity itself. Capitalist processes of mechanization and automation – and the oppressive, dull labour which they spawn – inscribe themselves within the inner world of the individual subject through an intensification of repression. All social reproduction demands a certain level of repression, but in capitalist society the social organization of production institutes a crippling (though unnecessary) burden of renunciation. In this social–theoretical reading of Freud, the individual is, in fact, adapting to the interests of capitalist domination masquerading as the 'reality principle'.

Marcuse's cultural diagnosis proceeds from Freud's account of the conflict between pleasure and reality, sexuality and self-preservation. For Marcuse, as for Freud, conscious rationality depends upon the shift from the pleasure principle to the reality principle – a transformation that in fact safeguards the long-term interests of pleasure itself. According to Marcuse, however, the capitalist expansion of oppressive systems of technology and bureaucracy this century has led to a 'transubstantiation' of unconscious pleasure itself. What this means, essentially, is that pleasure has somehow become disconnected from the needs of the human body, being bent out of shape by the power interests of late capitalism. Indeed, this restructuring of the self has gone so far that the psychoanalytic division of the individual into id, ego and superego is today obsolescent. The psychical economy, says Marcuse, no longer has these sharp divisions. The Freudian image of man is *dead*. In this connection, Marcuse emphasizes the interweaving of the personal, technological and political spheres. Marcuse argues that, by a perverse kind of internal logic, unconscious desire is now subjected to – and manipulated by – techno-science and the globalized network of capitalist processes. The phantasmagoria of the mass media, the commodification of sexuality, and destructive warfare: these and other features of modern societies produce a general *disorientation* in self-identity.

From this angle, Marcuse's interpretation of Freud has certain themes in common with Lacanian and postmodern psychoanalysis. Like Lacanian and postmodern cultural criticism, Marcuse argues that the modern world is experienced as dislocating. The more that the stable psychological features of self-identity break down, the more people experience the world as fragmented, as a field of fleeting surface images. In contrast to these standpoints, however, Marcuse believes that an excavation of the repressed unconscious will herald personal and social emancipation. (Interestingly, some postmodern theories share this emphasis upon the truth of the unconscious, although their psychoanalytic base is deconstructive in orientation – as we will examine later in this book.) For Marcuse, repression and cultural domination are to be completely overturned by the disruptive force of unconscious desire and passion.

For Marcuse, the Freudian interplay of repressed desire and self-control is expressive of a wider social conflict. In conditions of modernity, the unconscious is denied true expression in the interests of capitalist domination. In Marcuse's view, however, Freud's emphasis on the contradiction between unconscious desire and cultural order was pulled in an ahistorical direction, making it the selfsame in all possible worlds. Seeking to recapture the historical dimension in psychoanalysis, Marcuse therefore distinguishes between two kinds of repression: 'basic repression' and 'surplus repression'. Basic repression refers to a minimum level of renunciation in desire or passion for facing social life and thus the tasks of culture. Marcuse uses this term to indicate that a certain amount of repression is necessary to produce a 'socialized subject', a subject capable of sustaining the business of social and sexual reproduction. Surplus repression, by contrast, refers to the intensification of self-restraint caused by asymmetrical relations of power. Marcuse describes the monogamic–patriarchal family, for example, as a realm where there is a surplus of repression. This repressive surplus operates through the 'performance principle', a culturally specific form of reality structured by the economic order of capitalism. According to Marcuse, the capitalist performance principle recasts repression as surplus in several key ways. The performance principle causes human beings to face one another as 'things' or 'objects', replaces general eroticism with genital sexuality, and fashions a disciplining of the human body (what Marcuse calls 'repressive desublimation') so as to prevent repressed desire from interfering with capitalist exchange values.

What of the possibilities for social change? Marcuse differs sharply from Freud as regards the nature of emancipation. Marcuse contends that the performance principle, ironically, generates the cultural conditions necessary for a radical transformation of society. What promises an end to surplus repression are the industrial–technological advancements of late capitalism itself. For Marcuse, the material affluence generated by Western capitalist industrialization and techno-science opens the way for an unravelling of sexual repression. The overcoming of cultural domination will release repressed unconscious forces, permitting the reconnection of sexual drives and fantasy to the social network. Such a reconciliation between culture and the unconscious will usher in a new, sensuous reality – a reality Marcuse calls 'libidinal rationality'. Libidinal rationality, though abstract as a concept, involves a radical reversal of surplus repression. Liberation from this surplus will facilitate a general eroticism, not only of the body, but of nature and cultural organization. Yet Marcuse's grounding of social theory in psychoanalysis stresses that emancipation requires more than just sexual freedom. It demands an integration of sexuality and love into transformed social, institutional life.

How are we to understand this notion of libidinal rationality? Is it just some emancipatory dream of the Frankfurt School theorist Herbert Marcuse, or does it unearth certain psychical tendencies that point towards an alternative social condition? As a resexualizing of social life, libidinal rationality can be interpreted as an encouragement of emotional communication and intimacy. Fantasy occupies a special place in this context, Marcuse says, since desire contains a repressed truth value. As he puts this: 'Imagination envisions the reconciliation of the individual with the whole, of desire with realization, of happiness with reason. While this harmony has been removed into utopia by the established reality principle, fantasy insists that it must and can become real, that behind the illusion lies knowledge.'[10] Fantasy is itself a longing for reconciliation – between pleasure and rationality, desire and reality. For Marcuse, this recovery of unconscious desire will facilitate the resexualization of the human body, thus creating harmonious social relations. Against the repressive structuring of 'sex' under the performance principle, the release of fantasy will eroticize all aspects of society, allowing for a spontaneous and playful relation to life.

Marcuse's influence over debates on sexuality has been immense in recent decades. What he has contributed in particular is the idea that sexuality, rather than a 'private space' internal to the self, is a thoroughly psychosocial phenomenon which is transformative of the social world. It was this strong emphasis on sexuality as revolutionary that shot Marcuse to international celebrity, as a prophet of the student and sexual liberation movements in the late 1960s. Due to this, Marcuse's work has sometimes been represented as elevating the personal over and above the political. However, Marcuse himself did not equate sexual liberation with a non-repressive society. The transformation of culture, he argued, 'involves not simply a release but a *transformation* of libido'. The transfiguration of sexuality presumes the flowering of emotional communication in social institutions. In this context, the conflict between life and death will diminish as Eros infuses social activity and culture.

Notwithstanding the socio-political importance of these ideas, many psychoanalytic commentators would now agree that Marcuse's work is unsatisfactory in several respects. To begin with, Marcuse's account of the individual and repression is wanting. He tells us that repression is socially imposed, with no aspect of psychical life escaping the total penetration of cultural domination. However, this view sits badly with psychoanalysis and, indeed, Marcuse's own social theory. Repression, as we have seen, involves a dynamic conflict between the unconscious and conscious self-organization. In the making of the self, the unconscious is expressed in particular, idiosyncratic ways that reflect the impact of specific sexual and familial experiences. But the crucial point, as Freud and others affirm, is that *internal psychical conflict* underlies self-organization and social relationships. Yet Marcuse ignores these psychodynamic aspects of unconscious experience, focusing instead on the power of society to shape and control the individual. The result is a socially top-heavy conception of repression which destroys the existence of psychical conflict and turmoil, individual agency, critical self-reflection and the capacity to act differently. Marcuse's focus is thus radically individualist: the complexity of self-identity and emotional life is evaluated simply in terms of how far society represses unconscious desire. Many object relational and related psychoanalytic theories, by contrast, make the quality of relatedness, of interpersonal bonds and community, and self-continuity central to evaluating the nature of repression in the modern epoch. The emphasis here is away from drive energies and potentials and towards interpersonal issues of social life – an approach that will be examined in the next section of this chapter.

Secondly, as a consequence of this totalistic image of repression, Marcuse is forced to round the individual back upon itself in order to find an escape route from the contemporary performance principle. The way forward is through the unconscious – which, ultimately, is beyond the scope of social domination, and thus prefigurative of an alternative society. However, despite the explicit aim to develop a new political vision, Marcuse has little to say about new forms of social relationship or improved cultural association. Rather, his vision of collective autonomy focuses on the overcoming of sexual repression. But such a vision of liberation is highly questionable. A mechanistic conception of unconscious desires, and not people, is the perceived agent of social transformation. Human agency is reduced to domination, while the repressed unconscious is linked to emancipation. But if the individual subject is obsolescent and repression complete, who exactly might possibly transform the truth of the unconscious? Who exactly would be capable of sustaining a liberation known as 'libidinal rationality'? Marcuse's focus upon unconscious potentialities, although valuable in some respects, actually mirrors an individualist culture which constantly forecloses issues about cultural bonds and political community. Here comparison with Fromm is instructive. If Fromm is in danger of losing the unconscious by sociologizing the ego, Marcuse risks a reductive account of social and political life – society being refracted through drive energies alone. Significantly, Marcuse's argument in favour of the liberation of repressed drives also smacks of essentialism. It recalls a *pre*-Freudian view of human passion as somehow natural and timeless, outside and beyond the reach of the social structure. The view that the repressed unconscious, or fantasy itself, will only gain expression in the non-repressive society fails to see that fantasy structures are already bound up with institutional life. Such a view fails to recognize that the 'truth of the unconscious' is already interconnected with embattled human relationships, violent gender tensions and ideological conflict.[11]

Finally, Marcuse's work raises serious difficulties for the interpretation of modern culture. His downplaying of human agency, and idealization of repressed drives as the basis of human liberation, do not allow students of psychoanalytic social theory to see how creative self-organization intersects with social processes, what goes into the making of interpersonal relations or politics, or of how individual subjects reflect critically on, and disinvest from, destructive ideological forms. Writing in the social context of the American cold-war period, as a refugee from Nazi Germany, it is perhaps not surprising that Marcuse holds a gloomy view of late capitalist consumer culture. Yet, however much this cultural diagnosis captured the dulling conformity of individuality at this historical time, it is plainly inadequate as a measure of the internally differentiated social formations that exist in the contemporary epoch. The emancipatory struggles of peace, feminist and ecological groups, among others, clearly suggest the bankruptcy of Marcuse's thesis concerning the total penetration of the psyche by social forms. To find an account of creative self-organization, and its links with interpersonal relations and the social process, it is necessary to look elsewhere.

Psychoanalysis and post-colonialism

One of the more interesting and important areas of public and academic debate in which psychoanalysis has made a strong impact in recent times is post-colonial theory. Post-colonial theory has had an ambivalent relationship with psychoanalysis, on the one hand ignoring it or even deriding it for its supposed collusion with colonial oppression, and on the other making interesting critical use of psychoanalytic concepts for the analysis of colonial domination as well as processes of post-colonial decolonization. In this context, psychoanalysis has afforded post-colonial theorists an opportunity to extend their work beyond a concern with socio-economic forces to the psychic trauma, tension and anxiety produced in encounters between imperial cultures and cultures of resistance.

The politically radical psychoanalytic critic Frantz Fanon is widely regarded as a founding figure of post-colonial studies. Prior to his untimely death at an early age, Fanon wrote such seminal works as *Black Skin, White Masks* (1952) and *The Wretched of the Earth* (1961). In the former, his most famous work, Fanon explicitly takes up psychoanalysis to explore the colonial terrain. Fanon's psychoanalytic influences were eclectic; he drew, for example, from the Freudian theorist Alfred Adler and also the French psychoanalyst Jacques Lacan. But in addition to psychoanalysis, Fanon's work also reflects the imprint of various philosophical influences, most particularly Hegel and Jean-Paul Sartre.

Psychoanalysis had been drawn upon, either explicitly or implicitly, by various authors for the study of colonialism prior to Fanon. Of particular interest for our purposes, given that Fanon directly confronts aspects of his work, is Octave Mannoni's *Prospero and Caliban* (1964). In this pioneering psychoanalytic attempt to understand racism, Mannoni argued that 'natives' suffered from an inferiority complex in relation to their colonizers; the sense of 'inferiority', says Mannoni, explained certain aspects of relationships of dependence and resentment evident in colonial societies. Now Fanon's critique of Mannoni's inferiority thesis is interesting, partly because he does not simply dismiss *Prospero and Caliban* as replicating the racist discourse of the surrounding culture – though it is surely the case that Mannoni failed to theorize his own conceptual vantage point in the wider scheme of race. Fanon accepts some aspects of Mannoni's argument concerning the native's inferiority complex. Unlike Mannoni, however, Fanon does not see such dispositions of inferiority as an inherent weakness in the structure of native societies, a weakness only brought to the surface in confrontation with a superior colonizing culture. Rather, he sees sentiments of inferiority as emerging from the terrible physical and emotional oppression under which the colonized suffer. Fanon argues that Mannoni's psychology of colonialism failed to grasp the debilitating psychic consequences of imperial oppression.

A double process, says Fanon, is involved in the creation of the 'inferiority complex' of the native: the first economic, the second psychodynamic (which involves the internalization, anchored in fantasy, of projected images of inferiority). Interestingly, Fanon also suggests that feelings of inferiority have flowed the other way – from colonized to colonizer. In this connection, he points to feelings of sexual inadequacy among white people, specifically as whites confront an erotically charged, sexually potent black phantasm of their own imagining. Fanon suggests that the 'Other' (blacks) became a repository of vice and desire for the white. White people relentlessly scrutinized, endlessly (consciously and unconsciously) referred to, pitted themselves against, felt repulsed by and attracted to, the imago of blackness and the black body. What this amounts to saying, in effect, is that whites have played out on the bodies of blacks, through the destructive use of imagination, their own racial fantasies. 'The civilized white man', writes Fanon, 'retains an irrational longing for past eras of sexual license, of orgiastic scenes, of unpunished rapes, of unrepressed incest. In one way these fantasies respond to Freud's life instinct. Projecting his own desires onto the Negro, the white man behaves "as if" the Negro really had them....'[12] In keeping with Freud's insights into the psyche and identity, sexuality looms large in Fanon's account of racialized identities, discourse and feeling.

The post-colonial theorist Homi Bhabha has written of Fanon that 'his psychoanalytic framework illuminates the madness of racism, the pleasure of pain, the agonistic fantasy of political power'.[13] Fanon presents the reader not only with a critique of the white Western psychological imperative to disown multiple forms of human sexuality and sensuality, and to displace it on to people of colour as other; rather his work also uncovers the complex ways in which such an imperative informs the place of the dispossed and marginalized. Fanon, writes Bhabha, 'speaks most effectively from the uncertain interstices of historical change: from the area of ambivalence between race and sexuality; out of an unresolved contradiction between culture and class; from deep within the struggle of psychic representation and social reality'. Fanon's argument that blacks often strive to be white in order to escape an imposed inferiority structure is relevant here. Fanon sees such annihilating forms of black identification arising in and through the taking on of belief systems and cultural values of the white Western world; even the eroticized body came to be experienced as animal like, and thus as something to flee from towards 'humanity'. 'In the white world', wrote Fanon, 'the man of color encounters difficulties in the development of his bodily schema.'[14] Blacks, according to Fanon, have for too long wanted to completely efface their identities in the presence of white people. Yet white people have been equally neurotic, a 'phobic' in his or her apprehension of the black body; the black body has been imbued with extraordinary, hallucinatory power and is resistant, at a very primal level, to reasoned argument. Forms of regression involved here are also sexual: 'Is there not a concurrent regression to and fixation at pregenital levels of sexual development? Self-castration? (The Negro is taken as a terrifying penis.) Passivity justifying itself by the recognition of the superiority of the black man in terms of sexual capacity?'

What comes through strongly in Fanon's work is a remarkable degree of self-questioning. Reflecting on his own sense of identity, as a black man, he comments: 'There is no help for it: I am a white man. For unconsciously I distrust what is black in me, that is, the whole of my being.'[15] The failure of psychoanalysis to theorize its own biases and prejudices in the study of racism greatly perturbed Fanon, though he thought Freudian theory could be better deployed to contest and combat racism. He wanted to move beyond the traditional psychoanalytic emphasis on the family as the breeding ground of neuroses to see their mainsprings in racist culture. Fanon's work can also be seen as anticipating postmodern concerns with the breakdown of identity and the fragmentation of selves. However, the destructiveness of racism did not prevent him from trying to maintain a utopian longing for transformations in race relations, the creation of a new social space where whites and blacks would truly recognize each other in their authentic humanity.

I have already mentioned the work of Bhabha, and it is worth briefly looking at how he has built upon and extended Fanon's critique of colonialism, since Bhabha has become one of the most influential theoreticians of diasporic culture and multiculturalism writing today. Like Fanon, Bhabha draws extensively from psychoanalysis – in particular Lacan, but also the post-Lacanian perspective advanced by Kristeva. He is also heavily influenced by the poststructuralist writings of Michel Foucault and Jacques Derrida. In *The Location of Culture* (1994), Bhabha recontextualizes Lacan's account of specular identity-formation to rethink the relation between colonizer and colonized. He agrees with Fanon that the visual lures of racialized, interpersonal relations means that racism as an institutionalized phenomenon is always in process, shifting, transformational. But he devotes rather more attention to exploring the ambivalence of psychic identifications affecting colonial relations. In particular, Bhabha argues that colonial identities are always fabricated upon a marginalized, excluded Other. For Bhabha, such psychic exclusion never fully succeeds. The repressed unconscious returns to derail the colonial language of power, and this for Bhabha is nowhere more evident than in colonial strategies of 'hybridization' and 'mimicry'. The attempt to imitate, copy or blend racialized identities must necessarily come unstuck, says Bhabha, because colonized subjects are in fact different from those that advance the strategies of colonial power. Against this backdrop, Bhabha situates racial stereotyping in colonial discourse in relation to the psychoanalytic notion of repetition. Repetition of racial insults indicates that the relation between colonizer and colonized is highly ambivalent, such that meanings (slurs, denigrations, etc.) are continually in danger of coming unstuck, from which actors work to make and remake relations of domination and submission.

Bhabha, a product of Elphinstone College, Bombay and Oxford University, has sometimes been rebuked by his critics for preaching the rights of native peoples, migrational groups and marginal cultures from the lofty heights of European poststructuralism. Whatever one makes of this charge of elitism and elitist language, there can be little doubt, in my view, that Bhabha has powerfully engaged psychoanalysis with the rapidly changing social and demographic movements unleashed by the forces of globalization. Moreover, following in the footsteps of Fanon, Bhabha has fashioned a very particular politically informed psychoanalytic critique of post-colonialism, one that deploys concepts of hybridity, liminality and mimicry to challenge neo-colonial forms of political power over the colonized Third World and to deconstruct imaginary constructions of national and cultural identity. He forcefully argues against the colonial tendency to essentialize Third World cultures as homogeneous, the bearers of historically continuous traditions; rather, he suggests relations between First World metropolitan and Third World cultures are constantly changing and evolving, involving creative hybrid interactions of various cultural identities. The theme of equal respect for cultures has emerged in his more recent writings, though it is not clear at this stage how Bhabha intends the more politically pessimistic threads of Lacanian and post-Lacanian theory that he uses elsewhere in his work to fit with this emphasis on rights in the context of multiculturalism and hybridization.

The post-colonial critic Ashis Nandy has also drawn upon psychoanalysis to explore the complexity of identity in the post-colonial world. Nandy refers to the way that 'colonialism colonizes the minds in addition to bodies' so that it 'releases forces within the colonized societies to alter their cultural priorities once and for all'. This is post-colonialism shifted up a gear into a fully blown critique of Western modernity, transformed from a 'geographical and temporal entity to a psychological category'. 'The west is now everywhere', writes Nandy, 'within the west and outside; in structures and in minds.'[16] Like Fanon before him, Nandy emphasizes the way that colonialism psychologically deforms and disfigures, not only the colonized, but the colonizer. But Nandy also focuses upon the role of new forms of British masculinity, especially in the late nineteenth and early twentieth centuries, in the development of colonial practices and texts, through which the colonized other was feminized. Nandy argues that the critique of colonialism has often neglected the damage done to the humanity of the colonizer, who often seemed to come out of such critiques unscathed. He argues that British colonizers, for example, through their emphasis on a reified masculinity, did damage to their own selves and cultures. The victory within Britain over feminized softness de-emphasized reflection, cognition and speculation as feminine, and thus as irrelevant to the public sphere. British imperialism sanctified ruthless social Darwinism, created a false sense of cultural homogeneity, itself a lever on cultural dynamism and the capacity to institute social change by covering over social differences and conflict, and provided mechanisms for the siphoning off of resistance to the colonies. Imperialism, as E. M. Forster put it, became a cosmology that contributed to the 'undeveloped heart of the British'. This involved a rigid separation of cognition from affect, an emphasis on being hard and powerful. 'Colonialism', writes Nandy, 'encouraged the colonizers to impute to themselves magical feelings of omnipotence and permanence. These feelings became a part of the British selfhood in Britain too.'[17]

Narcissism: sign of the times?

In earlier sections of this chapter, I examined the complex links between selfhood and culture in various versions of psychoanalytic critique. In the drive model of psychoanalytic theory, we have seen that unconscious ambivalence underlies the structuring of sexual and aggressive drives within culture at large. Libidinal and destructive unconscious forms are fused to make possible the reproduction of society. In relational psychoanalysis, by contrast, social context and relationships are not something just tacked on to the self, but are actually constitutive of personal identity. Here it is social relations themselves that constitute the fabric of self-identity and daily life. But what happens to self-identity when social relationships themselves go awry? What happens when cultural experience becomes permeated by a thoroughly global capitalist system, and when social relationships are in the process of fragmentation and dispersal?

One major response to these questions in contemporary theory is the debate over narcissism. The ever-increasing randomness and contingency of modern social life are said to have led to a shrinkage of the public world, thus promoting a defensive, yet painfully empty, search for self-gratification. The key image is one of 'dead' social experience – culture becomes thoroughly structured by media images, centred upon consumption and surface appearances. The self in this context becomes permeated by a deep sense of cultural emptiness, fractured by the repetitive life-rhythms of monopoly capitalism. In fact, for many authors the modern world has become so emotionally drained that human autonomy and creative social relationships are rendered redundant. Modern culture is simply unable to provide the emotional conditions necessary for autonomous social relationships – the self being left distorted, deformed and brittle.

In this final section of the chapter, we will look at some painful emotional costs of modernity by examining this narcissistic void at the heart of the self. In particular, we will concentrate on the links between narcissism and contemporary cultural forms. To do this, the influential writings of Joel Kovel and Christopher Lasch will be examined.

Kovel: narcissism, de-sociation and late capitalism

In an essay entitled 'Narcissism and the family' (1980), the American psychoanalytic Marxist Joel Kovel explores the connections between narcissism and advanced capitalist societies. Narcissism, Kovel says, is a fixing of desire in the self which underpins basic psychic functioning and self-esteem. In this potentially healthy mode, narcissism regulates all self and other relations – supplying the vital libidinal components for self-regard, ideals, values and so on. In exaggerated form, however, narcissism becomes a character disorder, a disorder which produces a general estrangement from the self and from other people. To understand narcissism as a character disorder, Kovel returns to Freud's distinction between primary and secondary narcissism. Primary narcissism is constituted in the imaginary child/mother dyad, prior to the infant's distinction between self and other. In this fusion of desire with part-objects (specifically, the breast) the infant jubilantly feels itself to be self-identical, living in a magical world of omnipotence and fulfilment. Secondary narcissism refers to the break-up, yet continuation in new form, of this raw and primitive state of narcissistic self-unity. Secondary narcissism thus occurs with the first emotional separation of the infant from mother – a time in which the infant learns of mother as a separate person and thus forms a prefigurative sense of social reality. This gradual learning or finding of reality, however, is a painful experience since it is connected to a primary loss: the loss of that blissful imaginary state of self-unity. Yet, in so far as the infant forges a broader connection with mother and world, there is a kind of reflux of primary narcissism; but it is a reflux which is now securely centred within a human relationship and thus tempered by social factors. Secondary narcissism thus substitutes for infantile omnipotence; what makes the infant a socialized individual is this internalization of the other, an internalization that brings the child into the wider context of social and cultural relations.

Narcissistic disorders, Kovel says, have their origin in this transition from primary to secondary narcissism. The key problem here is that the child remains stuck within raw and destructive early omnipotence, thus preventing the development of healthy boundaries between the self and the external world. In modern social conditions, the internalization of the early parental relationship fails to provide a widening of social and cultural objects – deemed so vital for the emergence of individuality. Instead, the child remains a prisoner of primary omnipotence, the result being a narcissistically troubled relation to the self and to others. In fact, the narcissistic character can at best relate to other people only as suppliers of general approval and admiration. Lacking emotional connection with others, the narcissist inhabits an unintegrated world, a world in which persons and objects are split off, either powerfully idealized or arrogantly denigrated. However, there is another side to all this. Kovel, drawing on the post-Kleinian research of Otto Kernberg, argues that narcissistic states of grandiosity in fact hide deeper feelings of worthlessness and inadequacy. The narcissist's continual search for approval, and absorption in superficial pursuits, is in reality a defence against a painfully weak and fragile sense of self. The underside of the grandiosity of the narcissist is thus a ravenous rage, a rage which threatens to devour and destroy the self. This narcissistic rage, in Kleinian terms, is bound up with early paranoid–schizoid processes – such personalities simply cannot tolerate depressive feelings in which other persons are experienced as ambivalent. Instead, the narcissistic personality undergoes a process that Kovel terms 'de-sociation'. De-sociation, in Kovel's description, refers to the relation between all-consuming narcissistic rage and the social network. Cut off from realistic social engagement, and in the face of intensive feelings of powerlessness and inadequacy, the narcissistic self can cope with reality only through sadistic attempts at manipulation, control and self-aggrandizement.

Advanced capitalism, with its colonization of social relationships under the sign of the commodity form itself, plays a key role in furthering narcissistic rage. Indeed monopoly capitalism, according to Kovel, replaces earlier Enlightenment processes of subjective differentiation with a 'non-human other' – the commodity. Late capitalism creates a thoroughgoing commodification of the personal sphere, thus engendering an age of consumerism which tears wider social relationships apart. Kovel's central point here is that the loss of social texture generated by capitalism becomes deeply inscribed within self-organization. This can be seen, says Kovel, in the increasing tendency to treat human beings just like commodities in modern Western culture – and this is nowhere more clearly evident than in family life today. Suffering under the emotional impoverishment of modern culture, the developing child is said to encounter parents who themselves are on the brink of unthinkable rage and despair. In late capitalism, parents relate to their children primarily as 'investments'; an investment which might bring a future yield of narcissistic satisfaction. This distorted parent/child link thus reproduces narcissistic pathology, generating inauthenticity and rage within the wider social environment. According to Kovel:

> the bourgeois age is, among other things, that age of a family centred upon children. It is therefore the era in which childhood emerges for the first time in history as a distinct category of existence. Pathological narcissism is then fundamentally the outcome when the family, so to speak, is not merely centred on children but collapses upon them as well, crushing them beneath its weight. It is therefore a specific disorder for that phase of capitalist development in which such a collapse occurs. Pathological narcissism is a pox of late capitalism.[18]

Lasch: narcissism and survival

The American historian Christopher Lasch in two of his best-known books, *The Culture of Narcissism* (1979) and *The Minimal Self* (1984), utilizes psychoanalytic theory to explore the relation between narcissism and contemporary culture. Whereas Kovel sees pathological narcissism as an outcrop of capitalist relations, Lasch relates the phenomenon to the flux and unpredictability of modernity itself. Capitalist production and, perhaps more significantly, consumption, certainly play a key role in Lasch's analyses of the self in the modern world. As Lasch says, we live in a world in which mass production and mass consumption drive a wedge between creative self–other relationships; restructuring the self as a 'consumer' who measures everything in terms of market attractiveness and the approval of others. However, narcissistic self-distortions, in Lasch's writings, are shown to depend, not only on capitalism, but on fundamental social transformations which have arisen this century. Lasch thus links narcissism as a modern experience with globalization, mass communications, the end of history, the decline of tradition and so on. Here contemporary identity-formation is shown to be increasingly thin and precarious, as the self is outstripped by the dislocations and terrors of modernity. Against this background, selfhood and meaning begin to evaporate. For Lasch, the personal sphere starts to shrink in the face of an incomprehensible social environment – so much so that most people shut out this threatening external world, turning inward towards personal preoccupations in the interests of 'survival'.

Lasch, like Kovel, suggests that a deep sense of hatred underpins narcissistic self-organization. Locked into psychic splitting, narcissism brings into play an over-idealization of the object as a defence against infantile rage. This rage focuses on a complete inability to accept reality itself – with grandiose fantasies of omnipotence being used in the hope of returning to a state of imaginary self-unity. However, such states of narcissistic self-regulation are only bound to disappoint, and processes of idealization are quickly overshadowed by devaluation. In this way, Lasch says, feelings of infantile grandiosity alternate with feelings of complete emptiness and abject inferiority in the narcissistic personality. Linking this narcissistic orientation to contemporary culture, Lasch argues that the modern self is: 'facile at managing the impressions he gives to others, ravenous for admiration but contemptuous of those he manipulates into providing it; unappeasably hungry for emotional experiences with which to fill an inner void; terrified of ageing and death'.[19] The general point is that an interplay of grandiosity and emptiness, idealization and rage, intersects with social processes. In the modern world, the subject is narcissistically dependent on others in the forging of self-identity. Yet, far from helping to provide a sense of meaningful identity, other persons remain cut off from the narcissistic self.

Lasch believes that it is social conditions which generate narcissistic pathologies; they do not arise out of any internal necessity. The unpredictability and dynamism of modern social life make us narcissistically dependent on others in the making of our own identities. The problem, however, is that human beings are increasingly estranged and disconnected from each other since social life is itself fractured. Here Lasch concentrates on the breakdown of historical continuity in the public realm, and the subsequent emergence of mass-produced commodity images in the present age. He observes that the modern world is no longer one of durable objects. Instead, the high technology of mass communications inaugurates a world of fleeting images. These images take on a kind of hallucinatory character, spilling into everyday activities and the personal sphere. For Lasch, this dream world of media images not only restructures self-identity but also blurs the boundaries between the self and its surroundings. The self is today forged in a fantastic space of mirrors, divided between inner and outer boundaries. Yet this mirror-centredness of the self is deeply problematic. For just as the social world enters a phase of unprecedented flux and unpredictability, so too the self becomes structured by a deep sense of emptiness and despair.

Thus modernity for Lasch – with its commodified forms, its liquidation of intimate relationship, its globalization, its destruction of local historical meanings

– makes the achievement of selfhood extremely precarious. Yet the self does not simply internalize these more terrorizing elements of the modern world. For Lasch, the interplay between the self and the social world is much more subtle than one of external intrusion into the personal sphere. Instead, the contemporary stunting of human relations involves the perversion of that intermediate realm between the inner world and the outer world, namely transitional space. Connecting this analysis to Winnicott's theory of transitional objects, Lasch observes that modernity downgrades cultural and aesthetic domains. Today, culture is patterned after the cold and detached images of economic calculation promoted through mass communications and consumption. As Lasch puts this:

> Instead of providing a 'potential space between the individual and the environment' – Winnicott's description of the world of transitional objects – [culture] overwhelms the individual. Lacking any 'transitional' character, the commodity world stands as something completely separate from the self; yet it takes on the appearance of a mirror of the self, a dazzling array of images in which we can see anything we wish to see. Instead of bridging the gap between the self and its surroundings, it obliterates the difference between them. Far from providing a creative bridge between self and world, then, our contemporary one-dimensional culture at once mirrors and intensifies an alienated subjective world, a world of inner emptiness.[20]

The contemporary narcissistic zoning of the self, designed to avoid the meaninglessness and emptiness of modern experience, connects directly to what Lasch terms our 'culture of survivalism'. In this argument, survival signifies both a loss of selfhood, but also a desperate attempt at self-management in a brutal and chaotic world. Lacking a framework of meaning for a fulfilling human life, individuals are forced to live one day at a time, in order to survive the conflicting processes that characterize modern life. Emotional disconnection from others, apathy, lack of concern about the future – these are the key features of Lasch's surviving 'minimal self'; a self turned defensively inward upon personal preoccupations in a world felt to be out of control.

Lasch, and also Kovel, provide detailed assessments of the prevalence of narcissism in modern societies. The analyses set out by them highlight the extent to which modern social processes promote unconscious feelings of despair and emptiness. Yet there are dangers to such characterizations of the modern period. Lasch and Kovel frequently demarcate narcissistic pathologies as the central dynamic of modernity. Such a standpoint, however, violently homogenizes the complex, contradictory cultural patterns of identity-formation in the contemporary epoch. One consequence of this is a loss of critical perspective on the imaginary contours of self-formation as well as the dynamism and diversity of modernity. In this respect, I contend, it is better to read Lasch and Kovel as offering a description of narcissistic disorders, as a warping of the self which modern social life in some part promotes. However, in this perspective the forming of the self is not necessarily deformed by narcissism. For, as Marcuse has reminded us, narcissism is also an essential condition for a creative and autonomous engagement with the self, others and the outside world.

Concluding remarks

The cultural–psychoanalytic criticism examined in this chapter represents one of the richest traditions to have emerged from Freud's own theories. Sexuality and unconscious desire, as we have seen, are central to the reproduction of societies. In the drive-centred theories of Freud, and Marcuse after him, sexuality is pressed into the service of cultural reproduction, but it also retains a relative autonomy in respect of the social process. From this angle, emancipation presumes the undoing of sexual repression in conjunction with a transformation in social and political institutions. In cultural and interpersonal psychoanalysis, by contrast, it is social relations themselves which distort and pervert the relational capacities of the self.

Table 2.1   Modern culture and its repressed

Theorist	Analysis of modern culture	Key terms
Freud	Self-society structured through ambivalence; culture reproduced through unconscious repression	Ambivalence Primary/secondary process Life and death drives
Fromm	Modern societies deform human needs and relationships	Human needs Authentic living
Marcuse	Modern societies reproduced through surplus repression	Surplus repression Performance principle Libidinal rationality
Fanon/Bhabha	Colonialism and decolonization analysed as cross-cutting forms of ambivalence and cultures of resistance	Post-colonialism Hybridity
Kovel	Narcissistic pathology outcrop of capitalism	De-sociation
Lasch	Narcissism connected to general social conditions of modernity	Survival Minimal self

In the work of Fromm, Fanon and Lasch, it is pathologies in social relationships which are constitutive of dislocations in self-organization, which in turn feed narcissistic and related conditions.

A few concluding observations might be useful at this point. The drive model of psychoanalysis underscores in a remarkably clear manner how personal desire is intricately interwoven with modern social processes. Yet, as I have suggested, an undue emphasis on libidinal enjoyment is unlikely to be of much help in tracing contemporary transformations in social relationships. In this respect, the various relational models of psychoanalysis examined offer alternative leads on the dynamics of repression and cultural life. We can learn from relational psycho-analysis that oppression and domination are deeply structured by a complex interpersonal pattern of emotional relations. This is not to say, however, that the analysis of unconscious passions and conflicts should be sidestepped in cultural analysis. On the contrary, we need to know more about the interlinking of drive configurations and the social context. The psychoanalytic tradition of social enquiry, I think, must confront structural processes of intersection between unconscious desire, interpersonal relations and modernity. For the trans-formation of modern institutions, involving developments such as globalization and techno-science, is increasingly important in the constitution of selfhood and in social relations.

CHAPTER 3

Object Relations, Kleinian Theory, Self-Psychology

From Erikson to Kohut

In the previous chapter we examined the relationship between social and political organization in modern societies and the psychological repression of the individual subject. In this chapter, the focus is reversed. Rather than looking at social organization as such, we shall concentrate on the various ways in which culture shapes emotional life and personal identity, endeavouring to examine the emotional processes by which repression and pathology are generated in everyday life. Such a shift in focus necessarily entails a concern with self-organization, as well as interpersonal relationships. Seen from this angle, psychoanalytic theory is used to yield information about deeply layered human emotions and desires by which social activity and structures can be judged. In what follows, I shall review some of the major social–theoretical contributions that investigate these links between patterns of selfhood and contemporary social experience. Beginning with an examination of object relations theory, I shall link this version of psychoanalysis to issues of self and society in the late modern age. Following this, Kleinian psychoanalysis is critically examined, with particular attention given to the concepts of paranoid and depressive anxiety. Finally, there is an examination of contemporary American self-psychology.

Object relations theory: self, trust and transitional space

Object relations theory offers a powerful account of the interconnections between selfhood, gender, autonomy and social relations. In classical Freudian theory, culture is largely evaluated in terms of the possibilities it offers for sexual gratification and the release of repressed erotic energy. In object relations theory, by contrast, it is the form of relational processes that counts most in the assessment of the quality of cultural life. For object relational theorists, it is only through our intimate relationship with primary caretakers, and especially the mother, that a sense of difference between self and others is at all possible. Human relatedness is the backdrop against which a sense of selfhood is formed, and thus relational processes are at the heart of individual experience and self-definition. In mapping the relational processes that underpin the development or inhibition of the self, object relations theory has much to contribute to the formulation of desired social and political outcomes. That is to say, certain aspects of the object relations perspective can be used to assess how cultural activity and social institutions facilitate autonomous social relations.

The relation between self and other, for object relations theorists, is a dynamic one – a complex series of interactions and expressions that unfold through time. The key tenet in this perspective is that human beings are 'object seeking'. Whereas Freud's robust individualism constructs self-organization in terms of sexual drives and unconscious desire, object relations theory sees a fundamental linkage between self-formation and the environmental and emotional provisions provided by significant other persons. Of course, unconscious enjoyment is inseparably bound up within this context of human interaction. But what object relations theorists stress is that sexual pleasure is never merely an internal affair, the regulation of drive tension alone. Rather the gratifications and frustrations that we first experience in life are fundamentally structured by the dynamics of human interaction. The small infant experiences 'being with' the mother in the opening out of a *shared reality*. It is within this space of coexistence between the child and its providers that a sense of selfhood, as well as faith in others, gradually begins to emerge. The origins of this emergence of self, as portrayed by American object relational theorists, are rooted in feelings of trust. Striving to construct a core of meaningful selfhood, the small infant learns to trust in the reliability and responsiveness of the mother and hence, by extension, the external world. A sense of trust in the consistency of parental figures is deemed vital for psychological development. It is also fundamental in this perspective for the creation of meaningful social relationships.

Erik Erikson, who deeply influenced the development of American object relations theory, and whose views I have been paraphrasing, provides a detailed account of the links between trust and social reproduction in *Childhood and Society* (1963). What Erikson calls 'basic trust' is a fundamental condition for the individual's binding of unconscious anxiety, and especially for the achievement of separation and autonomy in the network of social relations. Basic trust, Erikson argues, is forged against the backdrop of presence and absence of the mother. In order to establish a sense of self-continuity, the small infant must learn to cope with its mother's periodical absences, and develop trust that she will return. To make such a commitment to trust, however, is emotionally very taxing. The infant has to adapt to the mother's absence against a background of pervasive unconscious anxiety. The capacity for basic trust, Erikson says:

forms the basis in the child for a sense of identity which will later combine a sense of being 'all right', of being oneself, and of becoming what other people trust one will become.... But, even under the most favourable circumstances, this stage seems to introduce psychic life (and becomes prototypical for) a sense of inner division and universal nostalgia for a paradise forfeited. It is against this powerful combination of a sense of having been deprived, of having been divided, and of having been abandoned that basic trust must maintain itself throughout life.[1]

In discussing the formation of trust, Erikson stresses that self-organization is fundamentally tied to the adaptation or incorporation of cultural norms. I am not free, according to this view, to become merely anything I want. In order to create an 'ego-identity', I have to rely on trust networks, which involves incorporating what other people expect of me into my own sense of self. It is this focus on questions of 'identity' that leads Erikson away from the usual psychoanalytic terrain of infancy to a broader focus on adolescence and adulthood. The human agent, for Erikson, has a basic need for identity. What this implies is that, in order to achieve separation and autonomy, human beings must enter into a kind of self-interrogation about their own needs and desires, as well as cultural meanings more generally. Provided basic trust is established in infancy, the individual will be relatively free in constructing a world for him- or herself. To Erikson, people pass through a series of transitions, or 'identity crises', which can only be resolved through synthesizing cultural contingencies into new patterns of self, trust and meaning. Ideological world views are thus inseparable from mechanisms of self-adjustment.

But what, exactly, are the connections between the creation of ego-identity and society? How is self-organization structured by modern social conditions? Erikson takes up these issues in *Identity, Youth and Crisis* (1968). What Erikson makes clear here is that the social world is in continual interaction with revisions of ego-identity. To Erikson, society is essentially beneficial for self-definition; society provides the ideological matrix of meanings for new definitions of identity. The child who visits the dentist, for example, subsequently takes to cutting up paper and sharpening pencils, redirecting aggression through an 'identification with the aggressor'. Or the student who learns of socialist ideas may now have an appropriate 'object' to displace, and thus in a sense recover, his or her repressed ideal self. Though perhaps bordering on psychoanalytic reductionism, Erikson elaborates a complex account of identity-formation, and of how identity connects to society – his work includes such notions as 'negative identity' (a fascination with certain self–other prohibitions), 'ego diffusion' (a reckless experiment with inner selves), and 'totalism' (wild mood swings between personal hope and despair). Such constructions of the ego are linked to a broader social dimension, in Erikson's view, since identity is an active synthesis of inner and outer worlds. 'Identity', Erikson writes, 'is a process "located" in the core of the individual and yet also in the core of his communal culture, a process which establishes, in fact, the identity of those two identities.'[2] Erikson then, in contrast to both Freud and Marcuse, stresses the 'identity' of self and society. Or, to put the matter slightly differently, Erikson's liberal humanism leads him to rewrite psychoanalysis, appropriately enough, so that all belief-systems are incorporated within the cultural system. In other words, there is a kind of fit between creative and expansive identity on the one side, and patterns of cultural development on the other. 'For in all parts of the world', Erikson writes in modern-day liberal vein, 'the struggle now is for the anticipatory development of more inclusive identities.'[3]

Erikson's theory, as the reader might have gathered, contains some serious conceptual difficulties and ideological blind spots. His concept of 'identity' is premised on the belief that there is a fundamental essence of selfhood, an essence from which human subjects strive for greater cultural inclusion. Such a definition of self-identity, however, overly domesticates psychoanalysis, reducing it to little more than bland talk about personal concerns and anxieties. Indeed, Nathan Leites has suggested that this reductionism actually accounts for the popularity of Erikson's ideas in the United States; Erikson's popular rendition of psychoanalysis allows people the use of a certain psychological terminology to talk about 'self', yet somehow manages to close things down just at the point where interesting issues arise.[4] As regards psychoanalytic theory, Erikson's work is problematic because he brackets the split and fractured nature of repressed desire, replacing such unconscious dislocation with a focus on 'ego-adaptation'. That the individual subject is internally divided – repressing painful feelings, denying parts of the self through projection and splitting, investing distorting self-images through unconscious fantasy – is thus sidestepped in this perspective. This has serious consequences for Erikson's analysis of social life. His stress on identity as adaptive and unified leads to an uncritical linkage of self and society. Such an assumption allows him to postulate that contemporary social conditions provide an all-inclusive framework for affirmative identity, an ideological vision which is at one with much contemporary multinational advertising, such as the projected world unity of 'The United Colours of Benetton'. Here Erikson's positive gloss on society, while trying to account for personal development, change and autonomy, becomes a way of underwriting the cultural values of late capitalism. By contrast, Freud's social thought registers more faithfully than Erikson's, it seems to me, the pathologies and repressions of everyday life. In Freud's work, as we have seen, self and society are mutually interlocking, but their relation is not one of mere equivalence. The unconscious, Freud tirelessly repeats, cannot become fully incorporated into the social realm. That this is the case is positive news, politically speaking, since – contrary to Erikson's pronouncements – modern societies are not 'affirmatively inclusive'. Rather, society functions through asymmetrical relations of power and force, relations that repress, exclude and marginalize social identities. It is against this background, I think, that the social and political relevance of the Freudian 'split' subject, a self that is dislocated but also a self that can creatively resist social domination, should be located.

Not all object relations theorists see the self in such ideologically blinkered terms as Erikson. The work of D. W. Winnicott stresses that, even though selfhood is constituted through interaction, there are many things that can restrict or inhibit self-organization. Winnicott, as noted in Chapter 1, provides important insights into the connections between selfhood, creativity, symbolization and culture. Whereas Erikson understands the self as entering into social interaction through adaptation, the relation between self and other is for Winnicott one of (possible) mutual understanding and recognition. That is to say, there is a *transitional realm* where minds can come together, enjoying authentic interaction while maintaining a separate and autonomous subjective space. Yet as Winnicott shows, this postulation of intersubjectivity does not involve an overestimation of the harmony between self and other, nor the quality of social relationships. For Winnicott, interpersonal processes foster many forms of self-pathology, or what he calls 'the false self'. Significantly, Winnicott's theory also implicitly raises the issue of how social life and institutional arrangements enhance or distort human relationships.

In Chapter 1, Winnicott's emphasis on the crucial importance of responsive mothering to self-development was sketched. In what follows, I want to examine in more detail some of Winnicott's provocative ideas, and to do this it will be helpful to briefly look at his own personal history and professional development. It is interesting that Winnicott was born into a family of, in his own words, 'multiple mothers' – given his conceptual emphasis on, and therapeutic preoccupation with, the mother–infant relationship. It is perhaps also relevant that Winnicott had an emotionally distant, and frequently absent, father. Born to a Methodist family in 1896, he was the youngest child and only son; in addition to his mother and two maternal older sisters, he was also looked after by a governess and a nanny. Winnicott's own mother remains a shadowy, vague figure. It seems that she suffered from depression when Winnicott was a child; he, in turn, felt it his job to make her smile. It is said that Winnicott's mother was unable to hold him, or soothe him, as an infant; and, again, it is interesting to note, against this biographical background, that holding was a central image for Winnicott in his description of mothers.[5]

In his own style of writing and lecturing, Winnicott personified the adapting mother he celebrated in his work on child development. He would adapt his language to his audience, pitching theoretical concepts to suit his readers or audience. This was also strongly true of his own professional work with children and other adult patients. Margaret Little, a former patient (and later herself a psychoanalyst), described how Winnicott, in response to an outbreak of intense anxiety, spent a session holding both of her hands as she cowered under a blanket. Others spoke of his deep intuition. It is said that he would oftentimes gauge the relationship between a mother and her infant by simply observing the way that the infant handled a spatula which he gave it in the presence of its mother.[6] Many referred to his capacity to tolerate paradox and doubt, key themes of his work.

In his highly influential essay 'The Mirror-role of Mother and Family in Child Development' (1967), Winnicott traces the processes of interaction between baby and mother which lead to the emergence of a sense of self. The starting point of his analysis is the primary unity of the baby/mother dyad; at this point, says Winnicott, the small infant makes no distinction between inside and outside, itself and mother. Winnicott suggests that it is within this context that the mother objectively provides emotional resources for the infant to create and develop an inner world. In this account, the mother functions as a 'mirror', reflecting back to the infant its own experiences and gestures. What is significant about this mirroring is that it provides the infant with a shared experience of human passion. The infant learns about need and love, as well as fear and anxiety, through the reflecting face of the mother. There are certain parallels here between Winnicott and Jacques Lacan's theory of mirroring, as we shall see in Chapter 4. Lacan views mirroring as necessarily leading to a false self (since the mirror is no more than mere image); whereas Winnicott understands mirroring as an essential basis for creative, ongoing human relationships. The mother, as mirror, shows the infant that she understands emotional states of jubilation and distress, and that she accepts these feelings. This acceptance, in turn, permits the incipient self to begin symbolization of inner feelings and to make emotional connections with other people.

If all goes well at this stage, Winnicott says, the mother's mirroring permits the infant a 'moment of illusion'; an emotional experience in which the infant feels that she or he alone has created the loving object (i.e. the breast) which the mother objectively presents. The mother's emotional sensitivity to the child – what Winnicott calls 'primary maternal preoccupation' – allows an illusion of omnipotence. This narcissistic illusion, according to Winnicott, is vital for the emergence and development of the self. For it is through experiences of good enough mothering that the child develops a sense of contact with the real world. As Winnicott puts this: 'The mother's adaptation to the infant's needs, when good enough, gives the infant the illusion that there is an external reality that corresponds to the infant's own capacity to create.' The importance of this can be seen in what occurs when emotional sensitivity is not established between mother and child. If the mother fails to mirror, and rejects the needs of the infant, pathology will result through the 'annihilation of the infant's self'.[7] In this situation, the infant is left emotionally unable to make contact with other people. Lacking a sense of trust, human interaction is itself perceived as terrifying. Winnicott suggests that such an individual

...empt to deal with such anxiety through withdrawal into a 'false self', a self that compulsively anticipates the reactions of others. This false self is at once a defence against the failure of the maternal object as well as an attempt by the infant to establish some form of object relationship, however frail or brittle. Accordingly, the small infant strives desperately to make human contact, but the absence of feelings of inner trustworthiness are inevitably projected on to an outside world, a world which, in turn, is perceived as uncaring and harsh.

A sense of mutual understanding and shared feeling is thus vital for the emergence of a stable sense of self. All this depends, as noted, upon good enough mothering and the child's creation of a rich, internal fantasy world. It should be clear, though, that the infant at this stage is not yet capable of entering, let alone sustaining, fully fledged social relationships. Caught in an imaginary realm of illusory omnipotence, the small infant is unable to recognize that she or he does not create and control the world. How then does the child make the transition from a world of inner, illusory objects to the world of outer reality? For Winnicott, the child forges a connection with the outside world through actively discovering the characteristics of other persons. Unlike Freud, who posits a brute enforcement of the reality principle at the time of the Oedipus complex, Winnicott does not view the object-world as repressively imposed upon the individual. Rather, the child emotionally searches for certain boundaries between inner and outer experience. This orientation towards aspects of outer reality is forged, in Winnicott's terminology, through 'transitional objects'. The establishment of a transitional or 'not-me' object (such as a blanket or toy) is a bridging between the inner world of fantasy and the outer world of objects and persons. The child at once creates and discovers such objects. Yet such transitional objects are neither subjectively nor objectively located; instead they exist in a liminal realm between these two worlds. For Winnicott, the child 'creates an object but the object would not have been created as such if it had not already been there'.[8] Transitional space is thus a paradoxical realm in which the infant feels he or she creates and controls the object, yet also perceives that this object belongs in the world of other people.

The capacity to use and play with transitional objects is fundamental to the child's construction of symbols. Winnicott calls this the opening out of 'potential space', a space which links fantasy and reality, self and other. Potential space, Winnicott argues, is essential for creative involvement with interpersonal relations and cultural life. From this angle, culture is not something that indivudals just suddenly encounter at some stage. It is, rather, creatively made and remade through a transitional realm of learning, tradition, ideas and invention. It is within this space between subjects, the bridging of inner and outer worlds, that culture and social life arise.

It may be useful to review the key elements of Winnicott's view of self-organization at this point. The emergence of self depends upon a *primary maternal preoccupation* with the needs and gestures of the infant. By functioning as a 'mirror' to the child, the mother plays a central role in the development or inhibition of the self. This emerging sense of self links to a stabilized world of objects and persons through *transitional space*, the bridging of inner and outer reality. Transitional space is essential to both individual creativity and cultural experience. Winnicott thus characterizes psychical development in terms of a *true-self/false-self distinction*. In the case of the 'true self', development has led to the creative and spontaneous expression of human needs and feelings. In the case of the 'false self', there is an annihilation of personal integrity and subsequent emotional vulnerability in the face of social relations. Yet, significantly, Winnicott argues that personal continuity is a precarious and fragile phenomenon. There is always tension and anxiety in relating inner and outer realities – which is experienced in and through the symbolic world of transitional space.

Winnicott's focus on mothering, and specifically the mother/child dyad, draws attention to the importance of early pre-Oedipal relations in the formation of the self. Whereas classical Freudian theory sees selfhood as constituted through the Oedipus complex, and thus ties individuation to the intervention of the father, Winnicott's theory stresses the centrality of the mother/child relation to ongoing self-organization and social context. This emphasis upon mothering in human development has had important implications for critical enquiry. It has been especially influential in feminist theory, where object relational theorists have contributed to a re-evaluation of the social context of parenting and gender asymmetries. There have also been severe criticisms, however, levelled against this aspect of the object relational perspective. For some commentators, Winnicott's theory romantically idealizes motherhood, and thus eliminates the complexity of maternal desire itself. In this respect, it has been suggested that the whole concept of 'good enough mothering' is politically regressive; a myth used *against* women as both fantasy and blame.[9] Another difficulty is that Winnicott's theory refers to, but ultimately fails to theorize, the role of general social relations in the constitution of the self. That is to say, Winnicott's work lacks a critical account of social structure as shaping the self and interpersonal relations. In this connection, a number of questions can be raised. How is the mother/infant relation mediated by contemporary social conditions? In what ways have recent social, cultural, political and technological transformations affected self and self-identity? And how might the increasingly informationalized and globalized framework of modern social processes affect the transitional realm in which culture is embedded?

One of the most promising uses of object relations theory to address these issues is to be found in the writings of the British sociologist Anthony Giddens. Giddens approaches the question of the self/society interface on a fairly grand scale, tracing mechanisms of self-formation to global institutional transformations associated with modernity. To do this, Giddens develops in *The Consequences of Modernity*

(1990) the concept of trust, by which he refers to the necessary confidence in the continuity of self and in the constancy of the surrounding social world. Drawing on the object relational theories of Winnicott and Erikson, Giddens argues that the forging of personal trust is a central element in the structuring of self-identity as well as the essential basis for a creative involvement with the broader institutional contexts of modernity. Trust, in Giddens's view, is a basic psychic mechanism for handling the demands and dangers of everyday social life; trust is crucial for establishing what Giddens terms 'ontological security'. It is because an individual learns a sense of trust in other people that feelings of inner trustworthiness come to predominate over anxiety. Trust established between self and others is fundamental to creative, ongoing human relations; trust enables individuals to achieve a practical engagement with the open-ended nature of modernity.

Giddens analyses trust against the backdrop of a highly original account of modernity. The dynamism of what he calls 'high modernity' – with its globalizing tendencies, its mediation of human experience by mass communication, its ceaseless technological innovation – reaches into the very heart of self-organization. Arguing against the much-repeated claim that society has entered a postmodern age, Giddens contends that what we are currently witnessing is modernity coming to terms with itself. Modernity, says Giddens, has become radicalized. To experience these institutional transformations is to experience what Giddens aptly terms the 'juggernaut of modernity', a realm of mixed possibilities. Modernity for Giddens, although racked with contingency and uncertainty, empowers men and women in the search for individual and collective autonomy. To live in modern society, he argues, involves living with ambivalence. It means facing new global opportunities and dangers. Trust is of key importance in this context. Mechanisms of trust provide an anchoring point, not only for personal relations, but for an engagement with the abstract, institutional systems of modernity. Significantly, trust is a means of coping with certain 'high-consequence risks' of the late modern age, such as the risks of nuclear war, ecological catastrophe, global economic recessions and the like. Yet since modernity is essentially a risk culture, the self can never be entirely secure. Rather self and society intersect, according to Giddens's portrayal, through generalized states of trust and risk, security and danger.

But how is individual trust embedded in certain forms of social and technical framework? How do individuals face the disturbing and unsettling risks of late modernity? And how can such traumatic 'high-consequence risks' be experienced without a dislocation and dispersal of the self? In *Modernity and Self-Identity* (1991), Giddens concentrates upon the implications of these issues in terms of the transformation of the personal sphere. He argues that the forging of trust between an infant and its caretakers is pivotal for a subsequent handling of the potential risks of day-to-day social life. Drawing upon Winnicott, Giddens relates the creation of a transitional realm between infant and others to a broader interpersonal organization of time and space. Transitional objects for bridging the space between the infant and others are seen as a basis for 'going-on-being' in the world; the cultivation of a sense of self that, in turn, protects the infant from unbearable anxiety. What matters most in this forging of self, according to Giddens, is 'what goes without saying' – that is, the establishment of routines and habits. It is through an early involvement with parental routines and habits, says Giddens, that anxiety is contained. A sense of self, trust and object relationships is therefore forged through a transitional realm of *routinization*. Thus, Giddens concludes that the child receives 'a sort of *emotional inoculation* against existential anxieties – a protection against future threats and dangers which allows the individual to sustain hope and courage in the face of whatever debilitating circumstances she or he might later confront'.[10] In this reading of psychoanalysis, trust and transitional space operate as screening devices against unconscious anxiety; they provide what Giddens calls a 'protective cocoon' for the self in its dealings with the social world.

The bracketing of anxiety by trust is thus essential to the formation of self-identity. Where this is achieved, the individual can approach social life through calculations of risk and opportunity. Where trust is not achieved, self-pathologies such as disturbed narcissism are likely to result. Giddens contends that the relation between trust and routine, which is vital to early psychological development, is also of paramount importance for maintaining and revising 'narratives' of self-identity. What this means, essentially, is that trust intersects with routine individual activity as an emotional basis for a stabilized world of objects and persons. Trust in this context is invested in day-to-day routines as a way of creating a 'normal' and 'uneventful' world, from which an individual can pursue his or her own projects and activities. Significantly, the investment of trust in routines also functions to bracket fear and unconscious anxiety. As Giddens develops this point:

> Awareness of high-consequence risks is probably for most people a source of unspecific anxieties. Basic trust is again a determining element in whether or not an individual is actively and recurrently plagued with such anxieties. No one can show that it is not 'rational' to worry constantly over the possibility of ecological catastrophe, nuclear war or the ravaging of humanity by as yet unanticipated scourges. Yet people who do spend every day worrying about such possibilities are not regarded as 'normal'. If most successfully bracket out such possibilities and get on with their day-to-day activities, this is no doubt partly because they assess the actual element of risk involved as very small. But it is also because the risks in question are given over to fate.[11]

In a nutshell, then, trust brackets risk.

It is clear enough from what I have said so far that Giddens draws on object relations theory to decipher how modern selves negotiate the troubled waters of modernity. For Giddens, the postulation of a relatively stable, reflexively grounded self is a precondition for any lasting and meaningful engagement with contemporary culture. That is to say, a coherent sense of personal identity is essential for navigating the dizzying risks and opportunities of the late modern age. This position puts Giddens in opposition to the theoretical currents of poststructuralism and postmodernism, which instead theorize a 'decentred subject', thoroughly fragmented in and through language. Yet Giddens's stress upon identity does not imply that the self is immune from dislocation and dispersal. The ambivalence of modernity, itself the upshot of global economic upheavals, reaches to the very heart of self-experience. In this connection, the creation of new identity patterns within such fluctuating social boundaries can lead to emotional disquiet. As Giddens puts this, 'the narrative of self-identity is inherently fragile'.[12] However, it is true to say that Giddens's stance on self-definition is essentially affirmative. He argues that modern social processes integrate as much as they fragment. Society provides opportunities for personal appropriation as well as generating feelings of powerlessness. In this context, Giddens offers the example of a person on the telephone speaking with someone on the other side of the world. This, to be sure, is an electronically mediated experience. However, as Giddens points out, the person's interaction with this 'distant other' may be more emotionally intense than his or her relationships with other people sitting in the same room.

What are the gains and losses of Giddens's appropriation of psychoanalysis for understanding self-identity? To begin with, the constructive side of Giddens's work is that he alerts us to the necessary emotional capacities that are required to engage practically in modern social life. Reconceptualizing the object relational view within a comprehensive social theory of modernity, Giddens is able to demonstrate that anxiety, trust and transitional space are fundamental psychical mechanisms which lie at the root of social interaction. Significantly, this shows that individual development and relational processes are not closed off in an asocial world (the imaginary dyad of child and mother), but are intimately bound up with general social relations. The learning of self and other in a transitional realm involves a good deal more than merely adjusting to social reality; it is actually constitutive of an emotional acceptance of the socio-symbolic world of other persons and objects.

While accounting for the social context of self-organization, however, there are difficulties with Giddens's work. For one thing, Giddens's whole vocabulary of self-organization – 'bracketing anxiety', 'emotional inoculation', and 'protective cocoon' – has a very different intent from that proposed in object relations theory.

For Giddens, individuals must be capable of trust, relatedness and routine in order to go about day-to-day social life. Once these emotional capacities are secured, the individual is deemed to have met the basic requirements for generating self-coherence and consistency. Yet psychoanalytic theory, including Winnicott's version of object relations theory, radically questions whether the self can ever be 'normalized' in this way. Winnicott stresses, on the contrary, the fractured and divided nature of self-experience – a product of unconscious sexuality itself. In Winnicott's theory, as previously noted, the self is never free from the task of relating inner and outer worlds; significantly, the self is always subject to dissolution through unconscious fragmentation and dread. Yet Giddens offers no account of this. Instead, the realm of the unconscious is generally 'bracketed' by social routines. What this standpoint fails to acknowledge, therefore, is that social routines may be constituted to their roots by unacknowledged desires; social routines may involve pathological, obsessional or narcissistic components. A person may 'live' a consistent self-identity, for example, following the routine of staring at his or her reflection 60 times a day in a mirror. Clearly, an obsessional routine such as this has direct links with the narcissistic overvaluation of appearances. Yet it is unclear whether we could critically interrogate the psychical contours of such self-pathology from Giddens's model. A central problem, then, is that Giddens's theory pays too little attention to the ways in which social systems of modernity disfigure and warp the unconscious constitution of the self. So too, Giddens fails to examine how unconscious desire intersects with social symptoms which distort the transitional realm of cultural experience.

Melanie Klein: paranoid and depressive anxiety

In much of his late work, from *Civilization and Its Discontents* (1930) to *Analysis Terminable and Interminable* (1937), Freud concentrated on the nature of human destructiveness. In exploring the ways in which personal and cultural life is threaded with despair, depression and destructiveness, Freud emphasized the dynamic force of the death drive, a universal aggressive force. From hostile jokes and family rivalries to military violence and war, Freud saw the tendency towards aggression, towards death and destruction, everywhere. Many psychoanalysts, commentators and critics have long been sceptical of Freud's notion of the death drive; this aspect of Freud's corpus is oftentimes dismissed as an expression of the master's pessimism as he encountered old age and suffered from various illnesses. Yet the idea that individuals are regularly caught in the grip of envious destructiveness, paranoid aggressiveness and hateful passions remains central to the psychoanalytic vision of society and culture.

Perhaps more than any leading figure in post-Freudian psychoanalysis, it is Melanie Klein who extends and challenges Freud's thinking about the potential for human destructiveness. In radicalizing object relations theory, Klein understands individuals in a way that makes aggression, destruction, grief, envy and mourning central to the achievement of mature and creative living. Klein worked for many years as a child psychoanalyst, and her pioneering studies about the fantasy lives of children placed in question orthodox Freudian theory. In her book, *The Psychoanalysis of Children* (1942), for example, she argued that psychic conflict and anxiety begin long prior to the Oedipus complex, as suggested by Freud. In subsequent papers and books, including *Contributions to Psychoanalysis* (1948) and *Envy and Gratitiude* (1947), Klein traced the complex interplay of love and hate, anxiety and guilt, in shaping the internal world of the self. Her clinical observations of children's fantasy life led her to stress that the infant, in the earliest months of life, experiences intense, and sometimes violent, feelings towards the mother. The infant, says Klein, experiences fantasies of attacking and destroying the maternal body, and in turn suffers paranoid anxieties that it too will be destroyed. In Klein's picture of psychological development, the infant's emotional world is filled with paranoid anxiety (what she terms the 'paranoid–schizoid position'), in which other persons become invested with persecutory powers, and only gradually shifts to depressive anxiety (what Klein calls 'the depressive position'), which involves acknowledging and owning feelings of loss, guilt and ambivalence.

It is fruitful to briefly consider some details about Klein's life – for just as Freud's work is substantially based on his own self-analysis, so too Klein drew from personal experience in developing her theoretical concepts. Klein's childhood, it would seem, was every bit as tumultuous as that suggested by her notion of the paranoid–schizoid position. She was born in Vienna in 1882, into a Jewish family and was the youngest of four children. Her family life, according to biographer Phyllis Grosskurth, was 'riddled with guilt, envy and occasionally explosive rages, and infused with strong sexual overtones'.[13] The key reason for this, says Grosskurth, is that she suffered from an overwhelming sense of being unwanted and unloved: she was told by her mother that her birth had been 'unexpected'. Perhaps not surprisingly, she was envious of her siblings – so much, in fact, that envy remained a constant preoccupation throughout her life, both as expressed in her intimate relationships and her theoretical concerns. In various influential papers, she questioned the meaning of envy, particularly its relationship to creation and destruction. Klein's theoretical interest in destruction – specifically the intertwining of desire, depression and the death drive – had its roots in painful childhood experience. Her sister, Sidonie, died of tuberculosis when Klein was only four years of age. This was the first in a long line of private tragedies. More traumatically, since she greatly idealized him, her brother,

Emanuel, committed suicide in 1902. Klein was devastated and experienced great sorrow and suffering.

While trying to come to terms with the devastating grief over her brother's death, Klein married and raised a family. Her marriage was not a particularly happy one, and after the death of her mother, Klein suffered a mental breakdown. Beginning to feel that loss, grief and mourning might play an essential role in emotional development and maturity, she in time developed various insights into the role that grief had played in her own life. What set her thinking along these lines was the work of Freud, for it was by chance in 1914 that Klein stumbled upon Freud's essay 'On Dreams'. The ideas that Freud explored in this essay – the unconscious, sexual repression, emotional conflict and its tragic inevitability – struck a powerful chord with Klein's personal life. She in turn became fascinated with psychoanalysis, and in time became involved with the Budapest Psychoanalytic Society, whose members included the influential psychoanalysts Karl Abraham and Sandor Ferenczi. Klein underwent a training analysis with Ferenczi, and he encouraged her (as he did with other women) to undertake psychotherapeutic work with children. The psychoanalysis of children was highly controversial at this time, and many questioned whether children could possibly obtain any therapeutic benefit from psychoanalysis. Klein, however, was not one to shy away from dealing with the most difficult areas of sexual and violent feelings towards parents. Through her clinical work with small infants, Klein came to the view that children want to hurt or damage their mothers, or at least this is so in fantasy at any rate. Indeed, unconscious fantasy is at the heart of every experience of love and hate that infants feel towards mothers; unconscious fantasy, according to Klein, structures and colours the infant's whole perception of the world. In exploring the shadowy and subterranean fantasy world of earliest infancy, Klein dramatically extended Freud's account of the way in which children's anxieties structure, shape or interfere with the development of their emotional world. Klein's work, in time, attracted considerable interest within the international psychoanalytic community, and she was invited to give lectures at the British Psycho-Analytic Society by Ernest Jones in 1925. She settled permanently in Britain in 1926 and became the first European psychoanalyst to become a member of the British Psycho-Analytic Society. She died in Britain on 22 September 1960.

In her earliest work, Klein was very much interested in the importance of anxiety in the emotional world of babies and small children. She found anxiety over destructive wishes flow from the earliest relation with the mother, and that babies routinely *project* anxiety outwards, attacking in fantasy the mother or parts of her body. If you think of the way that a screaming baby will often arch his or her back, hitting out at anything and throwing themselves about in an angry fashion, then this is perhaps what Klein was getting at when she said that hate and destructiveness are expelled by the small infant into the outside world. Many refused to accept Klein's suggestion that babies might want to hurt or inflict harm upon their mothers. But it is important to note that Klein is not speaking about actual physical damage, but rather about fantasies of attack on the mother. Klein regarded such fantasies as indicative of normal emotional development. If anxiety about the mother's body can be tolerated, this becomes a central driving force in the development of emotional growth and symbol formation in the child's psychic structure, according to Klein. However, if anxiety becomes too acute, because of excessive projection of extremely painful emotion, emotional development can be constrained.

We can get a better idea of the way in which children's anxieties interfere with emotional development by briefly examining Klein's essay, 'The Importance of Symbol-Formation in the Development of the Ego' (1930). In this paper, Klein provides a fascinating clinical account of a four-year-old boy, Dick, whom she described as psychotic, but who would probably be diagnosed today as autistic. The paper is historically interesting as it is the first published report of a psychotic child. Klein's theoretical arguments in this paper generated intense interest as she sought to demonstrate that psychoanalysis could, in fact, make emotional contact with a child cut off from speech. Her central theme was that Dick was overly anxious, indeed terrified, of his own hatred and aggressiveness; as a result, she said, his emotional development and capacity for symbol-formation had come to a standstill. Klein linked Dick's severe emotional difficulties in relating with people principally to his relationship with his mother, to whom he was often indifferent and showed no signs of affection. As Klein could not use language to make contact with Dick, she used a number of different toys – including trains and cars – in order to gain access to Dick's emotions and anxieties. Although Dick was slow to respond to Klein's psychoanalytic play technique, he did have an interest in trains and railway stations, in particular the opening and shutting of carriage doors. This interest, Klein suggests, had to do with anxiety over penetration of the mother's body, in particular the sexual relationship between his father and mother. In playing with the trains, Dick was demonstrating a rudimentary form of symbol-formation, and it is worth quoting from Klein at some length here:

> The first time Dick came to me ... he manifested no sort of affect when his nurse handed him over to me. When I showed him the toys I had put ready, he looked at them without the faintest interest. I took a big train and put it beside a smaller one and called them 'Daddy-train' and 'Dick-train'. Whereupon he picked up the train I called 'Dick-train' and made it roll to the window and said 'Station'. I explained: 'the station is Mummy; Dick is going into Mummy'. He left the train, ran into the space between the outer and inner doors of the room, shut himself in saying 'dark' and ran out again directly. He went through this performance several times. I explained to him: 'it is dark inside Mummy. Dick is inside dark Mummy'. Mean-

time he picked up the train again but soon ran back into the space between the doors.... Received it simultaneously with the appearance of anxiety there had emerged a sense of dependence ... and that at the same time he had begun to be interested in the words I used to soothe him and, contrary to his usual behaviour, had repeated them and remembered them.

In her clinical work with Dick, Klein sought to demonstrate that his defences against his own destructive wishes acted as an impediment to his own emotional development. As Klein puts this, 'Dick's further development had come to grief because he could bring into fantasy his sadistic relationship to the mother's body.' It is worth noting here that Klein departs considerably from Freud, primarily because she traces Oedipal anxiety back to the earliest months of life. The core of her analysis seeks to demonstrate that the toleration of anxiety depends on the use of language and the elaboration of fantasy and symbolization in the attempt to resolve and manage anxious situations. A child who is too anxious of his own destructive impulses is unable to emotionally deal with the self and others.

Let us now look a little more closely at Klein's idea of the paranoid–schizoid position. According to Klein, the small infant begins life under the sign of the death drive. Destructiveness, hatred and envy are all emanations of the death drive, and it is through a desperate attempt to deflect anxiety that the infant, according to Klein, projects primitive fantasies into the outer world, specifically towards the mother or parts of her body. Deflecting anxiety in this manner is soothing for the infant, as aggression is no longer experienced on the inside and bad feelings are projected and installed outwards. This anxiety-reducing strategy is, however, of short-lived value. Getting rid of destructive feelings actually makes the small infant even more anxious. This is because the child fears that the object on which it has displaced its rage (that is, the mother) will retaliate and attack it. As it is the mother's body which is now felt to be bad, or more accurately parts of the mother's body invested with the death drive, the mother's presence becomes in turn an object of fear. What Klein is getting at here, in so many words, is that the infant's fear now rounds back upon itself, giving rise to intense feelings of persecution and dread. Klein argues that the child consequently fears aspects of the maternal body, entertaining fantasies that the breast will devour it, cut it into bits, destroy it and scoop out its insides. There is, if you like, a kind of 'eye for an eye' mentality at this psychological stage. If I sadistically attack you, then I can only expect retaliation in return.

The infant's attempt to rid itself of bad feelings, in rounding back upon itself, produces fears of complete disintegration. So precarious is the infantile ego in the earliest stages of life, says Klein, that destructive feelings often cannot be tolerated. In order to break from this destructive cycle, the child is led to *split* the object into good and bad. By splitting, Klein means that fantasized aspects of the 'good mother' need to be kept quite distinct and separated from the 'bad mother'. In the earliest days of life, the infant constructs an image of the mother as an ideal, 'good' object; through projection, the infantile ego fills the maternal object with narcissistic, loving feelings, and experience itself as magically self-identical. Due to the impact of the death drive, coupled with actual experiences of maternal deprivation or frustration, such good feelings are in danger of being swamped by destructive feelings, or more accurately, the bad aspects of the beloved object. The result, according to Klein, is a state of paranoid anxiety. In this state, a 'bad' breast predominates, and the child's world is coloured by persecution fantasies. The infant is beset by fears of annihilation; good experiences are wiped out and the ego depleted. The crucial task for the infantile ego in this 'paranoid–schizoid position' is to keep at bay the persecutory powers of the death drive, and keep the bad breast on the outside through taking into the self more positive aspects of the beloved 'good' breast. 'The leading anxiety of the paranoid–schizoid position', writes the Kleinian commentator Hanna Segal, 'is that the persecutory object or objects will get inside the ego and overwhelm and annihilate both the ideal object and the self.' At this early stage of development, the infant splits its world: into the loved and loving breast and the hateful and hating breast. Anxiety in this position is generated from a muddling of these fantasized states, and the key task is to continually distinguish and keep apart good and bad.

Klein argues that splitting is a self-protective manoeuvre; it is through the splitting of the object that the fragile and precarious ego strives to keep idealized and persecutory objects as far apart as possible. This phase of paranoid splitting is characterized by the defence mechanisms of *projection* and *introjection*. In projection, the infant projects both positive and negative feelings outwards; in introjection, the infant takes into itself what it imaginatively perceives of others and the outside world. Klein essentially follows Freud here. However, she extends some of Freud's arguments by examining the ways in which projection and introjection operate in and through *unconscious fantasy*. For Klein, the psyche is a constant flux of fantasies that structure relations between self and others. The implications of this for psychoanalysis are significant. Whereas Freud understood projection as involving a channelling of unconscious drives towards objects, Klein instead suggests that projection involves the imaginative insertion of *actual parts of the self* into others and the external world. To capture this more interactional view, Klein speaks of 'projective identification', getting rid of parts of the self into others, and 'introjective identification', taking attributes of others into the self. In projective identification, for example, bad parts of the self may be attributed to others so that destructive feelings can be safely expressed. Alternatively, good parts of the self may be projected on to others in order to keep these feelings safe from bad and destructive fantasies inside. But in all of these schizoid mechanisms described by Klein – splitting, idealization, denigration, and projective and introjective identification – the key psychical task remains the same: to limit the pernicious anxiety generated by the death drive.

Klein's account of paranoid anxiety develops and deepens Freud's insight into aggression and destruction. Culture, Freud said, constructs individual subjects seething with unconscious rage, a specific elaboration of the death drive that is continually on the brink of complete self-destruction. This drive to destructiveness is mobilized and reordered into social order through repression. Klein's work allows us to see that it is not only a repression of rage – or its potential return – which is at issue. When aggression is projected outwards, and deflected on to others through projective identification, it rounds back upon itself in a persecutory manner. The typical defence against persecutory anxiety, Klein contends, is schizoid splitting. This view has considerable explanatory power with regard to social and institutional life. From this angle, the paranoid–schizoid position might be seen as institutionalized within whole sectors of modern culture. Various spheres of social, political and cultural life can be viewed as structured by a kind of perverse splitting, between the narcissistic, idealized 'good' and the denigrated, hated 'bad'. The imaginative life of the pre-school infant, for example, is bent into a two-dimensional fantasy world by television, as numerous images of good heroes and bad villains, strong men and submissive women, fairytale loves and protracted violences, are disseminated. Such images reinforce a fabric of desires, fantasies and feelings in the small child which become recurrent psychological themes in adult life. One can see how such splitting, when institutionalized, can lead to acute ambivalence in sexual relationships, as the desire for the perfect other generates a profound sense of frustration within interpersonal relations. Or one can see how mechanisms of splitting, idealization and denigration take hold of entire nations – fuelling terrors of actual and imagined security threats, or even the prospect of nuclear self-destruction. Indeed, one of the most striking aspects of the risk of massively destructive warfare in the contemporary age has been the response of general public apathy, a kind of psychic *denial* that comes to the fore under states of extreme splitting.[14]

Before proceeding too far with cultural diagnosis at this stage, however, it is necessary to stay with Klein's clinical picture of psychological development. For while schizoid mechanisms certainly underpin individual and social pathologies, Klein also emphasizes that splitting can play a facilitating role in emotional life. Klein stresses that paranoid–schizoid mechanisms are a normal defence against early, primitive anxieties. For example, the splitting into good and bad allows the primitive ego to emerge from a primary condition of psychic fragmentation. Splitting also lies at the basis, says Klein, of our capacity for judgement and discrimination; without splitting, individuals could not adequately distinguish between core experiences of love and hatred. When constitutional hatred is excessively strong, Klein argues, splitting is likely to occur in exaggerated form and thus distort human capabilities. This means that splitting into good and bad becomes excessive, with objects being either narcissistically idealized or destructively denigrated. In this condition, the infant feels that persons and objects are intensely persecuting, which in turn generates further splitting and overwhelming anxiety. Such excessive persecutory anxiety leads to perpetual dread and feelings of unreality, and sometimes into psychosis and schizophrenia. Klein emphasizes, however, that in normal psychic development good objects and feelings predominate over bad ones. In this connection, Klein's argument is that the paranoid–schizoid position, although underpinning all subsequent schizoid functioning, facilitates emotional development. Provided there is a predominance of good experience over bad experience, the ego gradually *gains* in strength, as the threat of the bad object diminishes. This means that persecutory and idealized objects are no longer ruthlessly split.

From this tendency towards integration, the small infant is led in the second half of its first year to perceive other people as whole objects. This involves an emotional shift from part or split object relationships to object relations proper. That is to say, the infant no longer relates exclusively to part-objects of the mother's body (such as her breasts, eyes, skin surface, hands and so on) but rather forges a connection to the mother as a *person*. The infant thus revises its previous split perceptions of mother, and comes to see that there is only one mother, a mother with good *and* bad human qualities. The recognition that mother is a whole person, an independent person with separate relationships, is pivotal to the child's emerging sense of selfhood. Significantly, this new phase also results in a decrease in persecutory anxiety, as the child comes to learn that the same mother is a source of good and bad feelings, and not a separate 'bad mother'. In the same way that a picture of the mother as a whole person is developed, so too the child will come to emotionally understand that it loves and hates the mother. That is to say, the child gets a kind of return dosage of the emotional pain and anger displaced on to 'bad objects'. The child comes to realize, at an unconscious emotional level, that such fantasized attacks are actually directed at the beloved mother. This leads to intense feelings of guilt and sorrow, and is termed by Klein the 'depressive position'. Whereas anxiety in the paranoid–schizoid position involves a fear of self-annihilation from outside objects, anxiety in the depressive position involves fears about the fate of others, the result of destructive fantasies generated by the child's own hatred. Having transcended schizoid splitting of the mother, it is as if the child realizes that others are no longer simply a receptacle for destructive fantasies. Instead, the child's connection to others becomes intensely social in form; and the emerging ego will respond to any damage inflicted upon others through feelings of guilt and depressive anxiety.

Let me briefly summarize the foregoing arguments. Klein posits a primary mode of psychic functioning in which child and mother interconnect through an unconscious communication of violent, destructive fantasies about part-objects and split objects. In this paranoid–schizoid position, the splitting of mother into good and bad facilitates the containment of the child's destructive drives and allows for a creative development of projective and introjective processes – deemed vital by Klein for successful self-organization. If constitutional hatred is excessive, the lure of paranoid–schizoid processes will be deformed and self-pathologies will result. If all goes reasonably well, however, good experiences predominate over bad experiences and the child is led to withdraw projections of destructive urges and to construct the object-world in more realistic terms. In this depressive position, the child develops the capacity to form emotionally durable relationships and to experience the other person as a separate, and ambivalent, object. Feelings of guilt, loss and reparation are crucial to this mode of psychic organization, and are connected to the interplay of destruction and reintegration which underpins mature self-organization.

Applications of Klein

Responses to Klein's work in social, political and cultural theory have taken a number of directions. Klein's doctrine initially made its deepest impact in England, at the Tavistock Institute of Human Relations, where her concepts were employed to trace unconscious mental processes in social relations. The Kleinian analysis of social institutions in the UK was developed especially in the work of Isabel Menzies Lyth and Elliott Jaques, whose research traced institutional defences against emotional pain and other related social aspects of splitting. Klein's ideas have also been significant in European and American academic contexts, and have been used for rethinking the nature of our social practice more generally: for example, in the philosophical writings of Richard Wollheim, the feminist analyses of Dorothy Dinnerstein, the work of the French social theorist Julia Kristeva, the art critic Anton Ehrenzweig, and psychoanalyst Hannah Segal's underlining of the unconscious dynamics of warfare and the nuclear arms race. Kleinianism, in these differing conceptual contexts, is invoked to examine the interconnections between pain, destructiveness and loss in human social relationships.

Perhaps more than any other area of psychoanalytically influenced social science, it is the paranoid nature of racism which has been most powerfully illuminated by academics drawing from Klein's ideas. A good example of this can be found in Rae Sherwood's *The Psychodynamics of Race* (1980). Sherwood's book emerged from a research project she conducted involving extensive in-depth interviews with families from different ethnic backgrounds (including black immigrant families). From these interviews, she developed long narrative accounts, and particularly rich psychoanalytic interpretations, of the experience of race and racism in Britain during the 1970s. Influenced not only by Klein, Sherwood drew from classical Freudian metapsychology, object relations theory and Erik Erikson's study of the stages of identity development.

What Sherwood developed from her reading of Klein's work, as the title of her book suggests, was an appreciation of the *psychodynamics* of race – how the self becomes caught up in racist thinking, particularly the ways that 'unresolved identity conflicts' become linked to the 'misuse of racial groups'.[15] Examining Klein's account of the various psychic means for managing, containing and displacing anxiety, Sherwood argues that, like individuals, groups function as repositories for holding and delimiting anxiety. Groups can be used either to explore, or to get rid of, aspects of the self that are emotionally too difficult to tolerate or reflect upon. 'The most important function served by groups', writes Sherwood, 'is largely an unconscious one. Throughout development, but especially when under stress, we all at times use social groups as repositories for our projections, providing a way out for the individual from experiencing inner conflicts that he would otherwise consider too disturbing or painful to face.'[16] Such projections comprise not only bad but good or idealized parts of the self – the latter may be held safely outside for periods of time if inner conflicts threaten to overwhelm or destroy them. The selection of physically and socially distant groups, like racial others, becomes useful in this context, as it helps maintain the necessary emotional distance required in order to get rid of parts of the self.

It is against this theoretical backcloth that Sherwood develops the provocative notion of vicious and benign racial spirals. Sherwood uses the concept of 'spiral' to capture the sense of increase and decrease in intensity of racist ideology and associations. It is clear that Sherwood is talking about a relationship, largely unconsciously driven, between racial groups when she speaks of spirals. Groups interact with each other unconsciously, pitting their identities against each other, and playing out against, and in relationship with each other, their unresolved identity conflicts. The flow of projections back and forth between groups is based upon, and in turn intensifies, projective processes. As Sherwood writes:

> The target racial groups which are used as repositories for the projections of the primary racial groups are provoked into protecting themselves from these impingements upon, and infringements of, their identity processes. This, in turn, modifies and affects their unresolved identity conflicts and so leads them in turn to use defence mechanisms also and thus to resort to the misuse of racial groups. This impinges back upon the primary groups, and begins to promote a further twist to the spiral. This is the essence of the spiral, interlocking processes linking unresolved identity conflicts with racial misuse.[17]

Sherwood argues that this process can be benign and even constructive, if projections are transitory and help to place before one's eyes aspects that can then be reintegrated into the self. But in certain situations projective processes become more constant, and racial groups become permanent receptacles of paranoid projections. This can lead to violence and vicious racist spirals. The racialized other becomes a 'locked safe': identity conflicts cannot be resolved, and defensive energy keeps the process going (p. 498). Sherwood is particularly interested in how unresolved conflicts remain and constitute 'vulnerable areas' of the self; these are areas which might be touched off, resonated or stimulated by contact with racial others. She emphasizes that this process is largely unconscious. Racist, paranoid thinking can be touched off by quite seemingly trivial things about a person's behaviour or activity: there may, for example, be something about the racially denigated other that might reverberate with an unwanted part of the self; through stereotypical thinking, a whole group can in turn be characterized as exhibiting that feature almost as their exclusive, and dominant, cultural characteristic (p. 499). Of special importance in this context are the activators and constraints that relate to racial misuse. For example, governments and social agencies can give subtle messages of approval to the continuation of racist practices.

Sherwood's work represents, as I say, an interesting application of some of Klein's ideas to the study of racism. Significantly, there have also been engaging attempts to connect Klein's thought to social and cultural theory more generally. A useful way of charting the relevance of Kleinian psychoanalysis to social analysis in more detail is by briefly examining the work of the British social scientist, Michael Rustin, and the American political theorist, C. Fred Alford. Both authors want to show the wider cultural meanings of psychoanalysis, and in particular to demonstrate the importance of the Kleinian tradition for the analysis of social and political relations. Alford, for example, argues that Kleinian psychoanalysis should not be used merely to fill the gaps in social and political theory; rather, it should be integrated with social theory on the grounds of its exceptionally rich psychological understanding of individuals and group processes. He suggests that social theorists have not made adequate use of Klein because they have too readily seen her work in reductive terms, as pertaining only to the private sphere or internal world. By contrast, Alford contends not that Klein's categories are already social and relational, but that they have fundamental political and philosophical relevance, even though Klein herself only provided scattered remarks about the implications of psychoanalysis for thinking about social relations. Similarly along these lines, Rustin asserts that Kleinian psychoanalysis is of fundamental importance not just for social science, but radical political action and a progressive public sphere more generally.

A prime instance of Rustin's application of Kleinian thought to politics can be found in his analysis of racism, in his book *The Good Society and the Inner World* (1991). For Rustin, as for Sherwood, racial antagonisms, as destructive forms of cultural oppression, are not only institutionalized within the social world but are deeply inscribed at the heart of self-experience. Rustin uses psychoanalysis to argue that racist ideology goes beyond the institutional structures of modern culture; racism penetrates deeply into unconscious modes of desire and feeling. The relevance of Kleinian thought to understanding the phenomenon of racism, Rustin argues, derives from its account of the emotional, unconscious structures in which hatred, envy and paranoia are expressed in human relationships. Klein's account of paranoid–schizoid and depressive anxiety offers a significant purchase on how destructive, negative feelings intertwine with socially valorized racial attributions. The key psychic mechanism fuelling racism, says Rustin, is splitting. From this angle, racism is a displaced expression of persecutory anxiety. The racist splits the world into rigid categories of good and bad, white and black, the in-group and the out-group. Unwanted feelings are projected on to others, who are then seen in objectified form. Yet racial domination involves more than just projections of fantasy. According to Rustin, the ideological attribution of hatred through projective identification is an *interactive process*, in which the victims of antagonism regularly absorb the fear, anxiety and guilt of the persecuting group. There is a self-reinforcing logic here: the emotional damage caused by projections of persecutory anxiety and hatred are such that victims more neatly fit the delusional worlds of their oppressors, thus serving to bind unconscious fantasy and to intensify the fear of racial retaliation. It does not take much imagination to see that whole societies may find themselves acting out emotions which in part derive from such racial categorizations. Think, for example, of the problems, mysteries and implications of race relations in South Africa, in which hatred, anxiety and aggression are formed around such fantasy scenarios.

Emotional pain is thus a central theme in Rustin's work. There is a continual spilling of hatred and destructiveness in the social and political world. Yet however distorted unconscious passion may be, Rustin argues we should not give up in our collective attempts to foster more caring, empathic social relations. For the most important feature of social life is the essential relatedness between human beings; it is through the fostering of this emotional relatedness that Rustin believes we might realize alternative social futures. In this connection, Rustin contends that the Kleinian framework provides a *moral energizing vision* for the radical trans-formation of society. For Rustin, Klein's exploration of unconscious pain, guilt and anxiety, as lying at the root of our moral concern for other people, provides an ethical norm for the assessment of political life and cultural organization. Whereas Freudian theory sees culture as repressive of individual desire, and thus focuses on the emancipation of the self from sexual repression, Klein's emphasis on emo-tional relatedness highlights the *primacy of social relationships*. Kleinian thought stresses that individuals are first and foremost social beings, capable of intense moral relatedness. As Rustin puts this:

Innate concern for the well-being of the other, at a very deep level, appears in [the Kleinian standpoint] to arise from the earliest lack of differentiation between self and other, and from the process whereby this differentiation comes about. Pleasure and pain are only slowly located in space and time, and in relation to whole persons. This intense experience of pain, as given and received, and this deep involvement with the caring person as the perceived source of all well-and ill-being, gives rise to the capacity to experience the pains and pleasures of the other with an intensity comparable to the pains and pleasures of the self.[18]

The Kleinian account of human experience – of unconscious intersubjective transactions of love and hate, anger and envy, pain and anxiety – thus brings *social relatedness* to the fore.

Rustin presses this account of human development into a social theory with utopian intent. Society, and the task of improving social conditions, can be assessed in terms of concrete emotional experiences: of the signal importance of love and care for others; of the quality and intensity of emotional relationships; of institutional support for creative human development; and of membership from birth to a social community. This constitutes what Rustin calls a 'critical human-ization' of the personal sphere. The reconstruction of contemporary society demands attention not only to institutional processes but also to the quality of emotional, interpersonal structures in which people interact. The principal link between emotional and institutional processes for Rustin is the family. The family provides a relational context, according to Rustin, that is usually absent in society at large. The critical point here is that familial life, notwithstanding various problems, can be located as a carrier for altruistic and caring values. As the emotional site of compassion and understanding, the family might potentially be harnessed to rebuilding cultural life under an ethic of mutual help and develop-ment. At issue here, Rustin says, are new definitions of self-identity, gender and interpersonal relations.

Like Rustin, Alford directly connects Klein's psychoanalysis to broad issues in social theory. In *Melanie Klein and Critical Social Theory* (1989), Alford develops a critique of current social arrangements by combining Klein's account of the paranoid–schizoid and depressive positions with critical sociology. More specific-ally, he makes an intriguing case for the refashioning of the major concerns of the Frankfurt School – primarily the writings of Max Horkheimer, Theodor Adorno, Herbert Marcuse and Jürgen Habermas – in terms of Kleinian psychoanalysis. We have already looked at the psychoanalytic cultural critique developed by Marcuse in Chapter 2, where Freud's account of sexual repression is linked to a detailed social analysis of political domination. The social theorists associated with the Frankfurt School that Alford discusses are, like Marcuse, primarily indebted to Freud for the manner in which they probe the depth emotional consequences of capitalist social relations. However, this singular reliance on Freud within the Frankfurt School for theorizing personal identity and the self is for Alford highly limiting. To adequately grasp the emotional contours of individual lives and group dynamics, Alford notes, Freud should be supplemented with Klein. 'Klein and the Frankfurt School', writes Alford, 'speak the same language, even if they did not speak it to each other.'[19]

For Alford, what the Frankfurt School termed 'instrumental reason' – a socially dominant form of reasoning governed by technical rules – can more fruitfully be interpreted, from a Kleinian perspective, as an expression of primitive anxiety and greed. The alternative form of reason – what Habermas called 'communicative reason' – can best be understood as 'reparative reason', drawing on the processes and affects characteristic of Klein's depressive position. Reparative rationality does not deny aggression, but refashions it, puts it to constructive use, and operates with a 'loose and flexible symbolic structure'.[20] According to Alford, Kleinian theory is centrally concerned with the passions. As Alford writes of Kleinian doctrine, 'greed, hatred, aggression, the guilt that these ugly passions evoke, and the attempt to make reparation for the damage they cause ... [are] the same themes that recur in the Frankfurt School's attempt to reformulate humanity's relationship to nature, as well as the concept of reason on which this relationship is based'.[21]

Alford, then, has his own version of Frankfurt School social theory, one that tracks divergent paths between paranoid projection and depressive anxiety in the management of social affairs and public life. Only if the Frankfurt School project of theorizing society in apocalyptic or utopian political terms is reinterpreted in the light of Kleinian categories will culture become more emotionally reflective and literate. But how can individuals engage with popular culture in more meaningful ways if society is already held in thrall to schizoid processes and a paranoid, individualizing consumer logic? Alford thinks the Frankfurt School overly pessimistic in this respect, and suggests that critical theory should concentrate more than it has on analysing the emotional underpinnings of group dynamics and institutional processes. In this connection, he notes that Freud saw groups primarily as modelled on the authoritarian relations of the family, whereas the Kleinian view is that the group is used by individuals as a defence against primitive anxiety. Probing the mysteries of why love, affection and concern are so rarely found within the group, Alford rejects the idea – sometimes implicit in classical psychoanalysis – of a group mind. Group relations are, he says, suffused with private passion: he writes, 'we purchase harmony in our private relations by investing our aggression in the group'.[22]

A related and perhaps more sophisticated use of Kleinian concepts can be found in Alford's study of violence, *What Evil Means to Us* (1996). In this book, Alford draws from interviews conducted with American prisoners who had engaged in very violent and destructive acts. Alford asked his subjects in these interviews to talk about what evil meant to them, what is involved in inflicting violence upon others, and what one is trying to resolve or get away from. Alford returns to the Kleinian model of paranoid–schizoid and depressive positions and considers the way that action is structured through these; but he complements these concepts this time with post-Kleinian psychoanalyst Thomas Ogden's notion of the autistic–contiguous position, which he argues precedes the paranoid–schizoid position as a more primitive way of experiencing the world. Ogden, in *The Primitive Edge of Experience* (1989), defines the autistic–contiguous position as follows:

> The autistic–contiguous position is understood as a sensory-dominated, presymbolic area of experience in which the most primitive form of meaning is generated on the basis of the organization of sensory impressions, particularly at the skin surface. A unique form of anxiety arises in this psychological realm: terror over the prospect that the boundedness of one's sensory surface might be dissolved, with a resultant feeling of falling, leaking, dropping, into an endless and shapeless space (p. 4).

Evildoers attempt to escape pain and suffering; the doing of evil is especially associated with the fear of losing sensory boundaries. Rather than suffer such loss, such terror is turned outwards, against the other. Through invading and destroying the boundaries of other selves, the doer of evil imagines him- or herself to have escaped their worst anxiety. That is the simple idea that Alford works with, but he evokes it powerfully through the many accounts of evil he retells, through narrative and analysis, reflections on philosophical arguments concerning, and literature dealing with, the myriad forms of evil. The result is Kleinianism as political theory.

Critique of Klein and Kleinian theory

What are the contributions and limitations of Kleinian theory and cultural analysis? To begin with, Kleinian theory significantly enhances our understanding of the relation between self and society. As we have seen, the individual subject in Kleinian thought is not only internally divided, split between consciousness and the unconscious, but also caught up in fantasies of identification with surrounding objects and people. In this view, the relation between self and society is extremely dynamic and fluid; aspects of self are deeply lodged in external objects and also continually reintegrated into emotional life. The concepts of projective and introjective identification offer a significant purchase on this mixing together of reality and fantasy in contemporary culture. For it is certainly arguable that a good deal of the imagery of modern culture – the superficial gloss of flashy commodities, seductive advertising images, and the like – are shot through with powerful paranoid feelings and idealizations. In this connection, media responses to a range of social issues – terrorism, racism, sexual crimes, poverty – are powerfully driven by unconscious fantasies, and lapse into dichotomous evaluations of the good and the bad. The consequences of such excessive projections and denials, as already suggested, are that victims of aggression become infused with persecutory feelings, which in turn leads to a perception of such persons and groups as even more menacing and threatening. Such a spiralling of projection and splitting can lead to delusional social feelings of persecution. At this point, society as a whole starts to trade in stereotyped emotional responses.

The Kleinian view of destructiveness and hate is also of paramount importance, especially in the face of ameliorist psychoanalytical theories (such as ego-psychology) which put an optimistic gloss on the potential harmony of self and society. Klein's theory, by contrast, addresses the existence of human pain, depression and despair. The implications of this for critical social analysis are considerable. That envy, hate and destruction are prime components of modern culture is obvious from the amount of violence generated in social relationships, as well as from the fascination with violence throughout the population as a whole. The Gulf War in 1991, for example, was a powerful indication of just how far contemporary political violence interconnects with inner hate, as was shown by our perverse interest in high-technology military destructiveness, encapsulated in the television presentation of the war. Viewed sociologically, the unlimited destruction of the Gulf War went beyond any mere unleashing of the Freudian death drive. Rather, the war was a product of a complex interplay between military and political forces on the one side, and destructive paranoid fantasy states on the other. The contemporary world system, it can be argued in Kleinian terms, maintains itself less through an attempt to repress or control destructive drives *in toto* than through mixing destruction and reintegration, fragmentation and reunification. In this view, social meanings and cultural identities are forged and integrated only to be destroyed, and in turn are thereby open to renewal. It is this interplay, between hate and love, and pain and joy, that takes us to the heart of the Kleinian position. An awareness of pain, despair and anger is fundamental if we are to confront successfully the implications of violence to the self and to others. For provided reparation can be made for prior damage and pain, then creative possibilities exist at both the personal and social levels.

Kleinian theory thus offers a complex account of interpersonal interaction. But if Kleinianism breaks with the individualistic focus of Freudian theory, substituting human relationships for the psychic energy of the solitary subject, it does so only by working outwards from the internal world alone. That is to say, Klein's privileging of the internal realm of fantasy leads to a crucial neglect of the role of social and cultural factors in the structuring of human relationships. Instead of examining how modern social conditions enter into the construction of the self,

Kleinians locate fantasy producing fundamental contradictions and deformations of human interaction – even though such processes are said to be installed in the outside world through projection and thus 'institutionalized' to some degree. But, as Cornelius Castoriadis points out, the Kleinian view that social life is distorted by fantasy leaves entirely open the question of *what* is being 'distorted' here.[23] How does fantasy inherently distort the social world in the act of constructing it? What about the role of social institutions, politics and gender relations in deformations of the self? How might political conditions affect and determine the systematic distortion of formations of fantasy which underpin social life? What seems to happen to the concept of fantasy in Kleinian theory is that, while it is correctly seen as the crucial psychic underpinning of all social activity, it is not recognized as inseparably bound up with the material conditions of its making. Instead, fantasy as the basis of intersubjective distortion is closed off from the social world and rounded back upon the human subject itself. As Stephen Frosh puts this: 'Kleinians seem to be responding to the terrors of modernity by theorising them as necessary elements in human nature; it is then up to the individual, mediated and supported by the containment which a caring environment can provide, to make reparation for them – to produce creative and integrative acts and artefacts which symbolise the possibility of recovery from loss.'[24] The critical point here is that, without attention to the social context in which fantasy is experienced and reflected upon, it is extremely difficult to imagine how radical politics might reverse the emotional damage produced by current social processes. Of course, it is important to recognize that some elements of social relations might be too deeply sedimented to be changed in present conditions. However, as with Freud, the starting point for such an analysis should give due recognition to the mutual imbrication of desire and law, fantasy and culture, in the social network.

Self-psychology: self-objects and meaning

Object relational and Kleinian thinking examines psychical life in terms of relationship difficulties. In contemporary American self-psychology, there is a similar concern with the experience of social relationships. In this theoretical current, however, more emphasis is placed upon the manner in which relationships affect the organization and coherence of self. The vision of the subject's inner, psychic world in self-psychology is one of a complex interplay between self-creation and social connection, individuality and affiliation. Heinz Kohut, the major theorist of self-psychology, develops a powerful account of the expansiveness of the self as refracted through interpersonal processes. For Kohut, absorption in other people is the central means through which the self is established, boundaries defined, purposefulness articulated. Kohut says that narcissism is vital to the emergent self, especially in the infant's early relationship with others. Narcissistic idealization and grandiosity, if supported by significant others, is a basic prop to a sense of self-esteem and therefore psychological well-being. However, if the child's narcissism is not underwritten by empathetic relations, self-identity can become severely warped, and disturbed narcissistic tendencies are likely to result.

For Kohut, the child is born with a need for emotional relatedness. In the same manner that humans require air for their physical survival, there is for Kohut a psychological need for relatedness and connection. This need is usually met through emotional contact with the child's own parents, who provide emotional security for the gradual development of the self. That is to say, Kohut views the child as naturally embroiled in adult experience of the world; this form of experience is 'lent' to the child, to use a kind of shorthand, in its creative involvement with others. Kohut calls this primary interchange of self and other 'selfobjects'. Selfobjects, though in actuality drawn from the outside world, pass into the child's own psychic structure, providing the essential building blocks for emotional experience and self-constitution. There are certain parallels here with Winnicott's notion of transitional space. Lacking any defined boundaries, selfobjects permit the bridging of inner world and external reality, a transitional realm from which the infant can take into itself parts of the object in order to secure identity. Significantly, this imaginary immersion in selfobjects also provides for a reflexive involvement with the self. As Kohut puts this: 'The child's rudimentary psyche participates in the selfobject's highly developed psychic organization; the child experiences the feeling states of the selfobject – they are transmitted to the child via touch and tone of voice and perhaps by still other means – as if they were his own.'[25]

Psychical life contains two types of selfobject: mirroring selfobjects and idealizing selfobjects. The mirroring selfobject arises through the child's sense of grandiosity and omnipotence. If we imagine the small child expressing basic narcissistic needs in relation to an admiring, mirroring other, we can grasp how the child's initial development of self arises. Through narcissism generated in contact with the mother, the child establishes an image of itself as perfect, confirmed by the mirroring mother. The idealizing selfobject, by contrast, confers worth on the emerging self through an investment in the object itself, an object experienced as seductive and all-powerful. To achieve such identification involves fusing the self with this separate, and hence Oedipal, other. The ego bolsters its identity through identification with the idealizing parental image, thus finding meaning in surrounding persons and objects. For Kohut, both mirroring and idealizing selfobjects can provide for psychological satisfaction and the creation of meaning. Either can be used in the making of the self, and for creative involvement with others. A failure to invest in either type of selfobject, however, leads to psychological crisis, to chronic depression or schizophrenia.

What Kohut calls 'transmuting internalization' belongs to the kind of stable psychic structure, the self, which is derived from either mode of selfobject. What this means, in effect, is that the subject transmutes mirroring and/or idealized selfobjects into a coherent self-identity, which gives rise to trust in the external world. The subsequent involvement in interpersonal relations and the social network depends on this core sense of self, which is connected in an essential way to purposeful adult life. If, however, parents fail to provide positive experiences necessary for the development of self, then the child's internal world never receives the positive colouring it requires in order to establish stable self-identity. The rejection of narcissistic desire and idealization, severe disapproval, or uncaring letdowns all carry fragmenting tendencies into the later life of the individual. According to Kohut, such damage to self-esteem leads to emotional pathologies, especially narcissistic disturbances. Core emotional connections cannot be forged because the infant experiences itself as under attack. In this respect, narcissistic inclinations are never realistically incorporated into the interpersonal world, and are squeezed to the sidelines as buried unconscious feelings. Kohut makes the unconscious, in short, identical with failures or disturbances in the self's relational landscape. In the words of Greenberg and Mitchell: 'Kohut stresses that drives are disintegration products that appear *only* as the result of the frustration of healthy narcissistic needs. Sexual and aggressive impulses are not fundamental human motivations, but distorted, disintegrated fragments.'[26]

This severing of all necessary links between creative living and unconscious passion, however, is deeply problematic. Kohut's argument that the unconscious is a secondary phenomenon, the outcome of a breakdown in the relations of the self to selfobjects, echoes the object relational work of Fairbairn, Guntrip, Balint and others. The unconscious, according to this view, is a subjective *distortion* which psychoanalysis seeks to undo. However, as I previously argued, such a standpoint can have no proper grasp of unconscious desire as deeply inscribed in everything we do, as intimately interwoven with constituting, reproducing or transforming our conditions of personal and cultural life. Such a view fails to recognize that anxiety, depression, conflict and shifting identifications are part and parcel of personal life; it fails to see that, far from always being a blockage to self-realization, they are also a wellspring for productivity, creativity and reflexivity.

Rather, Kohut's original and lasting contribution to psychoanalysis lies in his unpacking of narcissism, especially how narcissism affects self-experience. Kohut's analysis discloses that unmediated infantile grandiosity and idealization poses acute problems in securing a realistic sense of self-esteem. He shows that the desire for empathic mirroring and parental idealization is fundamental in the making of a positive self-image. Because the narcissistic self develops in and through relational configurations, Kohut makes it necessary to think that intersubjective relations are always at the root of narcissistic pathology. Like Lasch and Kovel, Kohut extracts from narcissism a disturbing picture of interpersonal relations in modern culture. In this respect, Kohut discovers a world of uncertainty and risk, a world of such rapid social and cultural change that nothing has the feel of durability any more. In our present-day world, Kohut says, it is increasingly difficult to find a stable relational configuration to guard against the various splitting and displacing operations of the self. The internalization of selfobjects that are built upon shifting and unstable forces can only hamper self-constitution. In the face of the more lifeless dimensions of modernity, narcissism for Kohut represents a last-ditch struggle for the survival of the self.

Against the fragmentation of modern culture, Kohut's work can he read as a modernist defence of our collective need for expansive identity and secure self-boundaries. The mobile world of modernity means that individuals require identity and stable selfobjects in order to create a rich and meaningful life.

Table 3.1   Object relations, Kleinian theory, self-psychology

Theoretical model	Self–society link	Key terms
Object relational theory		
Erikson	Self-organization through basic trust and ideological adaptation	Basic trust Ego-identity
Winnicott	Personal continuity created through transitional space of culture and symbolization	Transitional space True self/false self
Giddens	Self-identity forged via trust mechanisms and routinization	Trust mechanisms Bracketing anxiety Protective cocoon
Kleinian theory		
Klein	Self embedded in fantasy scenarios, structured by mechanisms of projection and introjection	Paranoid–schizoid and depressive positions Projective/introjective Identification
Rustin Alford	Selfhood as intrinsically social; connected to alternative futures	Society as relational context Moral capacities of self
Self-psychology		
Kohut	Relational world affects self-experience	Selfobjects Transmuting internalization

CHAPTER 4

Poststructuralist Anxiety: Subjects of Desire

From Lacan to Laplanche

We left psychoanalysis at the end of Chapter 3 after examining the cultural climate of the late modern age, and looking critically at the quality of interpersonal relations realized in the contemporary social world. The guiding thread in object relational, Kleinian and self-psychological theories outlined so far concerns the extent to which social arrangements enhance or restrict the relational capacities of the self. In these psychoanalytic standpoints, the human subject is seen as self-interpreting, other-related and creatively interactive; qualities that might be either bolstered or stunted by modern institutions and social relations. In the branch of psychoanalysis which is influenced by the French theoretical currents of structuralism and poststructuralism, however, this relational capacity for self-constitution is powerfully subverted and overturned. Devoid of any fixed reference point, the human subject, in French psychoanalysis, is radically 'decentred' through endless slippages of language, caught in narcissistic mirror images, indeed dispersed and outstripped by the insatiable force of desire itself. In this chapter, I outline and discuss authors writing in a Lacanian and poststructuralist psychoanalytic vein. My starting point is with the issue of the self, paying special attention to the thesis of *decentred subjectivity*. After this, I turn to examine Lacanian and poststructuralist discussions of the self and cultural experience in the late modern age.

Jacques Lacan: returning to Freud

Perhaps more than anyone, the psychoanalyst who has most influenced the direction of contemporary social and cultural theory is Freud's French interpreter, Jacques Lacan. In an infamous 'return to Freud', Lacan set about rereading the core concepts of psychoanalysis – the unconscious, repression, infantile sexuality and the transference – in the light of modern linguistics and poststructuralist theory. The result, though much debated, has been nothing short of a complete transformation in the psychoanalytic conceptualization of the constitution of the individual subject in social and historical terms. For with great intelligence and intellectual candour, Lacan shows that the psyche cannot be mapped unproblematically on to the social world; any projected marriage between psychoanalysis and social theory for Lacan is one doomed to failure – since, always, there is conflict, tension and ambivalence between the psychic and social spheres. The reason he holds this view is perhaps best brought out in his aphoristic maxim: 'The unconscious is the discourse of the Other.' What this means, essentially, is that human passion is constituted with reference to the desire of others: both internal otherness, the unconscious, and external otherness, language. Our deepest unconscious feelings and passions are always expressed, as it were, through the 'relay' of other people. For Lacan, psychoanalysis does not need to be 'related' to social and political matters (as with, say, Marcuse or Fromm) since it is already a theory about the fabrication of the individual subject as refracted through language and thus the social world. Human desire, says Lacan, is expressed in language. Yet desire for Lacan is not pre-given; and it certainly does not just magically fit with language for its own particular ends. On the contrary, it is in and through language that the human subject and the intersubjective space of desire are interwoven with cultural forms. In this sense, language and unconscious desire are for Lacan coterminous.

'Jacques Lacan', writes his biographer Elisabeth Roudinesco, 'sought to bring plague, subversion, and disorder to the moderate Freudianism of his time.' To understand Lacan's radicalization of psychoanalysis, it is necessary to reflect a little on his remarkable life and eccentric personality. He was born in 1901 in France, the year after Freud published *The Interpretation of Dreams*. The eldest of four, he grew up in a Catholic family steeped in conservative religious tradition, which he found stifling. The favourite child of his mother, Lacan clearly enjoyed his preferential family treatment, and developed tendencies towards egoism that would blossom into his trademark style as France's leading Freudian psychoanalyst. 'At quite an early age', writes Roudinesco, 'he was already wilful and domineering, constantly asking for food or money or presents on the grounds that he was the eldest.' Such egoistic self-absorption throughout childhood and after appears to have been particularly important to Lacan's personal history; this, it is true, is speculative, but it seems plausible if only for the reason that narcissism was a theme that Lacan returned to time and again in his theoretical papers – so much so, in fact, that he has thoroughly revised the contemporary understanding of the impact of self-love upon the construction of identity.

Lacan was educated at the prestigious college Stanislas. After completing his secondary education, he studied medicine in Paris, and went on to do clinical training in psychiatry. He wrote his first published articles in the late 1920s and early 1930s while training as a psychiatrist and these mostly concentrated on neurological topics. In 1932, he had his doctoral thesis published, 'Paranoid Psychosis and Its Relation to the Personality' – a copy of which he sent to

Freud. The thesis was primarily a study of a female psychotic, and Lacan developed a detailed overview and classification of her mental disorder. There are several interesting aspects about this thesis and Lacan's early work, one of which is his attempt to move beyond the understanding of paranoia as constitutionally based to a broader psychic contextualization of various mental syndromes. In particular, Lacan was especially interested in his patient's disorders of language, and in examining the form and structure of delusional language. Though Lacan's psychiatric training roots him firmly within a medical tradition, it is perhaps important to stress that his work sought to question the ways in which psychological phenomena are related to the social order and the reproduction of the cultural system. That is to say, Lacan's main theoretical concerns from the beginning of his career concerned the nature of the relationship between the psyche and broader cultural forces, social traditions and political norms.

This can be illustrated by briefly looking at a scandalous murder that gripped much of France in the early 1930s, a crime that greatly interested Lacan and which led him to develop a novel interpretation of the relationship between the psyche and society. The essential details of this case can be set out as follows. In the town of Le Mans in north-western France, two maidservants of humble origins viciously murdered their wealthy employers. The celebrated crime of the Papin sisters radically shocked the French public and press: the attack and murder were reported as a tale of class hatred, of social tension and even of hysteria and madness. On the day of the crime, a power failure had prevented Christine Papin from conducting her normal household duties; when her employer, Mme Lancelin, returned home she firmly rebuked her employee for failing to carry out her duties. The sisters were deeply upset by this rebuke, and lashed out and attacked the Lancelins, gouging out their victims' eyes and then cutting up their bodies. Lacan, as I have already noted, was fascinated by the case of the Papin sisters, and suggested that while the crime was undertaken against a backdrop of increasing economic, social, racial and national hatreds, another – perhaps more structural – psychic force was at work: that of paranoid delusion and alienation. 'Lacan', writes Elizabeth Roudinesco in her biography of the French psychoanalyst,

> set out to show that only paranoia could explain the mysteries of the sisters' act. The episode of insanity seemed to arise out of a seemingly everyday incident: a power failure. But this incident might well have had a unconscious significance for the Papin sisters. Lacan suggested it stood for the silence that had long existed between the mistress and the maids: no current could flow between the employers and their servants because they didn't speak to one another. Thus the crime triggered by the power failure was a violent acting out of the non-dit: something unspoken, of whose meaning the chief actors in the drama were unaware.[1]

Though prior to his original rereading of Freud, we can nonetheless glimpse in Lacan's emphasis on speech between the mistress and the maids in this criminal drama a hint of his later preoccupations with language and structure. Lacan sets the crime of the Papin sisters primarily in terms of the interweaving of language, symbolism, the unconscious and paranoid alienation.

In order to develop his central hypothesis about the centrality and subversiveness of language in psychical life, Lacan undertook a radical engagement with Freud and psychoanalytic theory. But in order to trace out the interconnections between the individual subject, language and speech, Lacan was drawn to many other conceptual and theoretical currents also. In widening the frontiers of Freudian theory, Lacan drew from various traditions, including the avant-garde, the surrealists, Bataille and the works of Nietszche. Through his engagement with the philosophers, Alexandre Koyre and Alexandre Kojeve, Lacan engaged with and drew from various currents in European philosophy, and in particular reworked philosophical notions from Hegel, Husserl and Heidegger. Moreover it was through a sustained engagement with the linguistic departures of Ferdinand de Saussure, following the researches of Roman Jacobson, that Lacan – together with Michel Foucault, Roland Barthes and Jacques Derrida – was led to advance the novel thesis of the centrality of structures in the constitution of human experience and in the subversion of the individual subject. Finally, as we will see later in this chapter, Lacan also drew extensively from the structural anthropology of Claude Lévi-Strauss, and in doing so enlarged considerably the Freudian conception of the Oedipus complex and the triangular structure of the individual's relation to society and history.

Lacan's version of psychoanalysis is based upon a powerfully original reading of Freud's texts. Yet it is important to emphasize that Lacan's interpretation of Freudian psychoanalysis is of a rather special brand, concerned mostly with the development or extension of Freud's early theoretical innovations – from *The Interpretation of Dreams* (1900) through to the metapsychological papers of 1915 – in novel directions. For Lacan, this period of Freud's work is radical and subversive since it uncovers the strangeness of unconscious desire and the trauma of infantile sexuality – concepts scandalous to the Western philosophical tradition. Freud's early writings are said to show how the individual subject becomes 'other' to itself, split and fractured through the disruptive effects of unconscious repression. In Lacan's view, this perpetual fragmentation wrought by the unconscious is *the* discovery of Freudian psychoanalysis. However, the implications of this discovery – that subjectivity is radically divided between the conscious ego and unconscious desire – have been watered down, or at least this is so in Lacan's reckoning. The troubled waters of unconscious desire have been sidestepped, both in Freud's late metapsychological revisions and in mainstream American psychoanalysis. To combat this tendency, Lacan repeatedly criticizes versions of psychoanalysis, such as ego-psychology, which portray the ego as socially adaptive. By contrast, he seeks to craft new psychoanalytic terminology, a language that will not easily be incorporated within orthodox notions about mental health or psychic development. He seeks, in short, a radical language for psychoanalysis, a language that cannot be flattened.

Lacan's self-appointed project, then, is to return psychoanalysis to its most revolutionary insight, the disruptive power of the unconscious. To do this, Lacan in his *Écrits* reinterprets Freud in the light of a dazzling array of Continental theoretical traditions – including Saussurian linguistics, structural anthropology and poststructuralist theories of discourse. Moreover, to decipher the mute realm of repressed desire, Lacan fashions his own writing as fully shot through by the distortions of the unconscious itself – as an opaque discourse of metaphors, puns and contradictions. This, in itself, makes reading Lacan a difficult endeavour, perhaps more akin to reading James Joyce or Gertrude Stein than to reading the sort of psychoanalytic criticism we have considered thus far. However, whatever the difficulties of Lacan's own prose, it is necessary for us now to consider his unique blending of psychoanalysis and poststructuralist theory.

We have seen that, in classical Freudian theory, the human infant begins life in a symbiotic relation to its mother's body. It is precisely because human beings are born 'prematurely', argues Freud, that the small infant is fundamentally dependent on others for the satisfaction of his or her biologically fixed needs. According to Freud, as discussed in Chapter 1, the key feature of this dyadic child/mother relation is that the infant makes no distinction between self and other, itself and the outside world. At this point, the infant's world comprises a kind of merging of itself and the maternal body, a body that provides satisfaction, pleasure. Lacan calls this pleasurable state the 'imaginary order'. The imaginary for Lacan is a pre-linguistic, pre-Oedipal state of being in which desire slides around an endless array of part-objects. Prior to differentiation and individuation, the imaginary is a peculiar realm of ideal completeness, merging all that is inside with that which is outside. It is within this imaginary realm of being, Lacan insists, that the first part-objects of the mother's body – such as breasts, lips, gaze, skin surface and so on – are given an emotional investment by the child.

According to Lacan, this deeply imaginary mode of being provides an essential basis for the first drafting of selfhood. Lacan discusses this early construction of the self by returning to Freud's theory of narcissism, and focuses especially on the impact of mirror images in identity construction. In the essay 'The Mirror Stage as Formative of the Function of the I' (1949), Lacan describes the infant's moment of recognition of itself in a mirror, with specific reference to how this generates a narcissistic sense of self-unity. What happens when the infant sees itself reflected in a mirror, Lacan contends, is that he or she makes an *imaginary identification* with this reflected image. The mirror provides the infant with a gratifyingly coherent image of itself as *unified*; the stage of development provides the infant with psychic relief from the experience of fragmentation, by granting an illusory sense of bodily unity through the mirror's reflecting surface. Perhaps not surprisingly, the child reacts to this image of the self with fascination and jubilation. Watching its reflected gestures in the mirror, the child gleefully celebrates its newly found sense of selfhood and wholeness.

But this mirroring of self is not at all what it seems. For Lacan, the key feature of the reflecting surface of the mirror is that it distorts, deforms. For what the mirror filters out of view is that the child is, in fact, still dependent upon others for its physical security and well-being; and that its body is still fragmented, its movements uncoordinated. The mirror stage is profoundly 'imaginary' for Lacan because the consolingly unified image of selfhood generated is diametrically opposed to the multiplicity of drives and desires experienced by the child. In a word, then, the mirror *lies*. The reflecting image, because it is outside and other, leads the self to *misrecognize* itself. Imaginary misrecognition, says Lacan, 'situates the agency of the ego, before its social determination, in a fictional direction'.[2] In Lacan's theory, then, the mirror stage is a narcissistic process in which human beings construct a *misrecognized* image of self-unity.

There is, then, a distinctly negative ring to Lacan's account of the imaginary order. In this account, it is through misrecognition of the self that the essential seeds of subjectivity are planted. Imaginary misrecognition shapes both self-perception as well as fantasy-generated images of others. For Lacan, however, mirror misrecognition is not simply some phase of human development, a phase transcended by subsequent individuation. On the contrary, this imaginary realm of traps and distortions is in ongoing relation to subjectivity; it is continually rerun and played out with other persons. In this connection, Lacan's theory of the mirror stage is profoundly evocative of the narcissistic bent of much contemporary culture. Lacan's theory of the imaginary underscores the power of seductive media images and glossy commodities to draw on, and refashion, illusory desires. Advertising, television, pop iconography, as well as the media commodification of politics itself, all play a key role in structuring the identities, gender patterns and aspirations in which society reproduces itself on an imaginary plane. Hence Lacan's work, as we shall examine in the following section, has much to contribute to the study of contemporary capitalist commodification, media image production, and social, cultural and political forms.

The imaginary order in Lacan's work can thus be described as a kind of archaic realm of distorted mirror images, a spatial world of indistinction between self and other, from which primary narcissism and aggressivity are drawn as key building blocks in the formation of self. Yet if the imaginary is already an alienation of subjectivity – the small infant becoming an 'other' to itself in the act of contemplating its reflecting image – then the same is certainly true of what Lacan calls the 'symbolic order'. The symbolic order is that domain of received social meanings, logic and differentiation – in and through which the infant begins to represent desire and is thus constituted as a human subject. Reinterpreting Freud's theory of the Oedipus complex, Lacan argues that the break-up of the imaginary child/mother dyad arises through symbolization. What this means, essentially, is that the infant's imaginary unity with its mother is torn apart due to the intrusive impact of wider cultural and social processes. For Lacan, as for Freud, this happens with the entry of the father into the psychic world of the child. In disturbing the libidinal relation between child and mother, the father effectively drives a wedge into this blissful, imaginary union; and thereby refers the infant to the wider cultural network and the social taboo on incest. Lacan's innovation, however, lies in his emphasis on the underlying symbolic relations here which order social life. According to Lacan, there is a good deal more at stake than just sexual prohibition with the advent of the Oedipus complex. What Lacan terms *nom-du-père* (Name-of-the-Father or Law of the Father) is the cornerstone of his structural revision of the Oedipus complex. In contrast to a reductive focus on the immediate family situation, Lacan contends that the father intrudes into the child/mother dyad in a symbolic capacity, as the representative of the wider cultural network and the social taboo on incest. Not only is the child severed from the imaginary fullness of the maternal body, it is now inserted into a structured world of symbolic meaning – a world that shapes all interactions between the self and others. Finding itself excommunicated from the imaginary, the infant must gradually learn to represent itself within this social network.

But how does this act of self-constitution come about? How, exactly, does this shift from imaginary plenitude to the pre-structured symbolic network arise? Not just by the entry of the father, says Lacan, but by the acquisition of language itself. For Lacan, language is the fundamental medium in which desire is represented, and through which the subject is constituted to itself and to others. Language, he describes, as an intersubjective order of symbolization, an order embedded within patriarchal culture, and thus a force that perpetuates that which he calls the 'Law of the Father'. Drawing from the linguistics of Ferdinand de Saussure, Lacan argues that language is a system of signs. Signs, for Lacan as for Saussure, are made up of a signifier (a sound or image) and a signified (the concept or meaning evoked). In line with structuralist linguistics, Lacan argues that the relationship between signifiers and signifieds is arbitrary and based on convention. The meaning of signifiers – 'man', for example – is defined by difference, in this case by the signifier 'woman'. Meaning is created through linguistic differences, through the play of signifiers. 'If a signifier refers to a signified', write Laplanche and Leclaire, 'it is only through the mediation of the entire system of signifiers; there is no signifier that does not refer to the absence of others and that is not defined by its position in the system.'[3] The relation between sign and object is thus always provisional and arbitrary, and its usage depends upon historical and cultural convention.

Lacan's innovation is to apply Saussure's strucutral linguistics to the Freudian unconscious. Whereas Saussure places the signified over the signifier, however, Lacan inverts the formula, putting the signified under the signifer, to which he ascribes primacy in the life of the psyche, subject and society. For Lacan, the position of each of us as individual subjects is determined by our place in our culture's system of signifiers. The signifier represents the subject for Lacan; the primacy of the signifier in the constitution of the subject indicates the rooting of the unconscious in language. Let me sketch in what this provocative and dense argument implies. According to Lacan, the individual subject, once severed from the narcissistic fullness of the imaginary order, is inserted into the symbolic order of language. Within this order, the subject attempts to represent itself, to give expression to desire through language. Yet this proves to be a far from easy task, since the subject has become an 'effect of the signifier', inserted into the spacings or differences that constitute language. Language and interpersonal communication are therefore necessarily subterfuge, a façade covering over the impossibility of representing desire. The unconscious, then, is less a realm 'inside' the human subject, than an *intersubjective space between people*, as desire sinks or fades into the gaps which separate word from word, meaning from meaning. As Lacan puts this: 'the exteriority of the symbolic in relation to man is the very notion of the unconscious'. Or, in Lacan's infamous slogan: 'the unconscious is structured like a language'.

To illustrate how the infant is constituted as a 'subject' in the symbolic order, let us briefly consider Freud's famous discussion of the *fort-da* game in *Beyond the Pleasure Principle* (1920) – a game often cited by Lacan in respect of the ordering power of language. Watching his grandson playing with a cotton-reel toy one day, Freud observed that the infant alternatively threw the toy away, uttering an expressive *fort*! (gone), and would then pull the reel back, exclaiming *da*! (here). Freud analysed the *fort*! *da*!, 'gone', 'here', game as the child's emotional attempt to deal with the recurring disappearance and reappearance of his mother. It was through the repetition of this game of presence and absence that the child sought to separate itself out from the mother. In this connection Freud points out that the game enacts several symbolic interventions into the world of sexuality. It allows the child to express its libidinal renunciation of the mother; in turning a passive experience into an active one, it represents a symbolic 'mastery' over the unpleasant fact of the mother's absence; and the game also gives expression to the child's wish for revenge – 'all right, then go away! I don't need you I'm sending you away myself.'

Lacan's commentaries on the *fort-da* game focus on the child's shift from the imaginary world of fantasy to the new horizon of language. Stressing that subjectivity and sexualization are defined in terms of linguistic differences, Lacan argues that the phonematic opposition, 'gone', 'here', signals the child's entry into speech – into the symbolic field of culture. For Lacan, however, and in contrast to Freud, the child is not the agent of this symbolization. Instead it is the child that *receives* desire from the other, in this case the mother, who implants signifiers at the heart of the child's psychic world. 'The child,' Lacan says, 'begins to involve himself in the system of the concrete discourse of his surroundings by reproducing, more or less approximately, in his *Fort!* and his *Da!*, the vocables he receives from it.'[4] What the child receives, in short, is the whole field of received social meanings. The *fort-da* game, in springing the child into language, leads him to recognize that meaning outruns the mother/child relation. Language and speech now constitute the child in relation to others; and this is a relation which is pre-structured by social, cultural and sexual codes. The child, now severed from its full imaginary relation to the mother, must move along this linguistic chain in order to be part of the communicational situation of the social network itself.

Let me briefly summarize Lacan's doctrines. The imaginary order, emerging out of the child/mother dyad and forged in the mirror phase, is a fantasized realm of wholeness and plenitude. For Lacan, ego-formation is profoundly imaginary since it is based upon narcissitic misrecognition – and hence involves a denial of loss, fragmentation and difference. It is the symbolic order which actually breaks up this imaginary hall of mirrors – without which the subject would enter into psychosis – by instituting differentiation, logic and meaning. The Law of the Father, symbolized by his phallus, breaks up the imaginary child/mother dyad through the prohibition of desire. The space of unconscious desire is thus born into this pre-structured linguistic/sexual setting. Subjectivity and the unconscious are structured linguistically within the cultural and social Law.

Contributions and limitations of Lacan's theory

Lacan's theories rank among the most significant contributions to modern psychoanalysis. His emphasis on language in the construction of psychic life, and its intimate connection with unconscious sexuality, has been original and provocative. Lacan's placing of the subjective 'self' at the centre of imaginary experience has served as a balance against other psychoanalytic theorists, particularly those influenced by American ego-psychology, which argue that the ego is at the centre of rational psychological functioning. Lacan, by contrast, has emphasized that the self is always alienated from its own history, is formed in and through otherness, and is inserted into a symbolic network which is on the outside. Lacan continually emphasizes that the 'I' is an alienating screen or fiction, a medium of misrecognition which masks the split and fractured nature of unconscious desire.

He has added to our understanding of the intertwining of desire and language, showing that the communicational situation is itself a process of division, in which human subjects constantly repeat that elusive search for the missing object of desire. He depicts the unconscious as created by language, and locates the open-ended nature of desire within the linguistic interstices of the cultural framework. Moreover, his account of language powerfully deconstructs traditional theories of representation which presume that mind and reality automatically fit together. Lacan's analysis is in part radical since it shows that the production of meaning is embedded in the signifying chain itself. In Lacan's theory, the meanings engendered within language would not exist if it were not for the impact of the other upon the self in the symbolic register. Language, as that which is outside and beyond, constitutively mediates our relation to the social and cultural world.

Lacan's articulation of a psychoanalytic theory of subjectivity within a linguistic framework has been greeted by many as of central importance to cultural enquiry. (We shall examine the Lacanian interpretation of modern societies, culture and politics in the following section of this chapter.) The decentring of the subject; the loss, lack and impossibility of unity in psychical life; the primacy of signifiers over what is signified in the unconscious; our fragile and always precarious relation to the other: these are, in Lacanian psychoanalysis, issues of core importance. Lacanian analysis seeks to deconstruct the narcissistic illusions of the self, allowing the lack and fragmentation which the symbolic register ordains for the human subject to resurface.

However, Lacan's comprehensive reconceptualization of Freud has also come under fire. Lacan's linguistic doctrines have been severely criticized on a great number of grounds, both inside and outside psychoanalytical circles. The key conceptual difficulties in Lacan's work seem to me to be twofold: the first concerns the general way in which sexuality and the unconscious are theorized, and the second concerns the inadequacy of linguistics for the critical analysis of subjectivity.

To begin with, consider the Lacanian proposition that the imaginary contours of self-identity are traversed by illusion or misrecognition. Lacan himself was in no doubt, as we have seen, that the constitution of the self through reflection involves an inescapable alienation of the subject. From this angle, the imaginary is a *distorting trap*. It constitutes the infant as a unified self through consoling mirror images and thus screens out the dismal truth that subjectivity is, in fact, fractured and dispersed. However, there are serious conceptual difficulties with this standpoint. The argument that the 'mirror' distorts fails to specify the psychic processes interior to the individual subject which makes any such misrecognition possible. For example, what is it that leads the infant to (mis)recognize itself in its mirror image? How, exactly, does the individual cash in on this conferring of selfhood, however deformed or brittle? The central dilemma here is that surely for an individual to begin to recognize itself in the 'mirror' it must already possess a more rudimentary sense of self. For, to take up a reflected image as one's own must no doubt require some general capacity for emotional response.

Cornelius Castoriadis has argued that Lacan's theory of the mirror stage can offer no solution to this conundrum of how identity is derived from self-reflection. For Lacan's theory only makes sense if, according to Castoriadis, we recognize the profoundly *creative* nature of the imaginary register, a psychic creativity that is the precondition for the 'mirror' itself and its possible reflections. Castoriadis thus draws attention to a central limitation in Lacan's doctrine about the human subject: namely, its failure to theorize how the 'mirror' is perceived as real. In contrast, Castoriadis suggests that to understand how the individual subject responds to and recognizes itself and others requires an account of our emergent capacities for representation and identification. As Castoriadis writes, a critical psychoanalytic conception of subjectivity must presuppose the subject's 'emergent capacity to gather meaning and to make of it something for him/herself'.[5]

Equally serious is the criticism that Lacan's work actually suppresses the subversive implications of Freud's discovery of the unconscious by structuralizing it, reducing it to a chance play of signifiers. From this angle, Lacan's theory effectively represses unconscious sexuality and desire. This complaint is aimed not only at Lacan's use of poststructuralist theory, but focuses more generally upon his claim that the unconscious is naturally tied to language. Many critics – including Paul Ricoeur, Jean-François Lyotard, Cornelius Castoriadis and Jean Laplanche – have argued the Freudian point against Lacan that the unconscious is resistant to ordered syntax.[6] These critics, in differing theoretical ways, have argued that the repressed unconscious is a primary, scenic field of representational forms, drives and affects; a field which certainly intrudes upon language but one that cannot simply be equated with it. Malcolm Bowie has expressed this well:

> It is our lot as speaking creatures to rediscover muteness from time to time – in rapture, in pain, in physical violence, in the terror of death – and then to feel a lost power of speech flowing back. One may be ready to grant that these seeming suspensions of signifying law are themselves entirely in the gift of the signifier, yet still wish to have them marked off in some way as events of a special kind. A long gaze at the Pacific may be taciturn at one moment and loquacious the next. Language offers us now a retreat from sensuality, now a way of enhancing and manipulating it. Yet to these differences Lacan's theory maintains a principled indifference.[7]

Significantly, the unconscious is in some ways even more refractory to language than this characterization suggests. For the unconscious, as Freud said, is completely unaware of contradiction, time or closure. For Freud, language is explicitly located in the preconscious system and the secondary processes that characterize it. In so far as certain unconscious representations are structured by the force of repression, they have the power to stabilize the secondary processes of language. But it is the unconscious which is the precondition for language and not the reverse. As such, Lacan's reformulation of the conscious/unconscious dualism as a linguistic relation does not correspond at any meaningful level with Freud's theory.

There are also important political implications raised by Lacan's assimilation of the unconscious with a linguistic structure. A central problem left in the wake of Lacan's 'linguistic revolution' concerns the status of human agency, above all the subject's capabilities for critical self-reflection and autonomy. One reading of Lacan holds that, in presenting a model of desire as disembodied and pre-structured linguistically, the human subject is effectively stripped of any capacity for creative identity, change or autonomy. This charge, however, is in fact aimed more appropriately at those poststructuralist thinkers that champion the 'death of the subject' than at the Lacanian school. For, in contrast merely to celebrating the disintegration of the subject, Lacan posits a 'subject of the unconscious', a subject located in the spaces of language itself. Another reading of Lacan is that although the 'subject of the unconscious' is constituted in terms of difference – oppositions that are structured linguistically – no theoretical room is given in this account to practical agency. In my view Lacanianism does indeed face a real problem in this respect, casting off the most vital questions of self and self-identity on to an abstract theory of language.

There are also important criticisms to be made of Lacan's account of culture. Most importantly, Lacan's equation of language with cultural domination grotesquely downplays the importance of power, ideology and social institutions in the reproduction of the cultural, political framework. In Lacan's account, the structure of subjectivity is determined by the cultural Law. Yet although language certainly pre-exists us as individual subjects, it is surely wrong to suggest, as Lacan does, that the business of everyday talk in social life – the communicational situation of the symbolic order – is singular and authoritarian. The human subject is not constituted as 'self-divided' merely because of its insertion into language. Rather, the traumatic divisions and splits which people experience via the whole field of the socio-symbolic order are intimately linked to concrete relations of power and ideology. To understand this requires a theoretical framework more sensitive to the articulation of subjectivity as embedded in the social context – to the complex, contradictory ways in which selfhood is defined in the contemporary age of mass communication, global economic mechanisms, the risk of nuclear or ecological catastrophe and the like. It is, of course, true that there must always be a mode of discourse to encode social interests such as these; but the critical point is that Lacan's work fails to consider what the cultural and political determinants of that code might be. Instead of focusing on the political forms of specific, socially created interests and institutions, Lacan dissolves their importance into some undifferentiated, ahistorical category of the signifier itself. This is a problem which has been addressed by post-Lacanian cultural theorists as well as psychoanalytic feminists in the analysis of contemporary social relations, and we shall examine certain responses to this problem later in the book.

Finally, these problems involve broader epistemological dilemmas. The Lacanian narrative which we have traced – that the self is narcissistic, the imaginary a specular trap, the law omnipotent, and the symbolic a mask for 'lack' – would appear to undo its own claims to critical status. For surely any political project concerned with enhancing freedom and autonomy must also be caught in the same imaginary networks of illusion as subjectivity itself? But if this is so, then perhaps the whole Lacanian framework might be deconstructed. For example, how can Lacan's discourse evade the distorting traps of the imaginary domain? Surely Lacan does not seriously believe that the only way of overcoming imaginary distortion is through comic wordplay, puns and irony? In failing to grasp that human subjects are capable of critical self-reflection and self-actualization, the issue of individual and collective autonomy remains repressed in Lacan's work. Yet it is precisely this pessimistic determinism about the self and the intersubjective world that will be taken over and extended in Lacanian and post-Lacanian cultural theory.

Lacanian and post-Lacanian contexts

At first sight Lacan's interpretation of Freud might seem unpromising for critical social research. To say, with Lacan, that we are prisoners of our own desire, caught within the distorting traps of the imaginary order, and unable to advance beyond symbolic Law, is surely to undermine what is most vital to the radical political imagination. Yet it is precisely this sense of political resignation that has been used by Lacanian-inspired cultural critics to put the skids on such notions as Self, Truth, Freedom and Meaning. In Lacanian terms, to believe that these words might hold some absolute value necessarily involves accepting the world as it is. By contrast, Lacanian thought attempts to show that identity and meaning are inherently unstable, and that the oppressive function of social discourse lies in occluding the multiplicity of unconscious desire itself. Here it is not fanciful to detect similarities between Lacanian cultural criticism and the psychoanalytic criticism of Fromm, Marcuse, Lasch and others, as discussed in Chapter 2. For like Lacan, these psychoanalytic critics draw on Freud to uncover the repressive forces at work in the construction of the ego. In contrast to Lacan, however, the recovery of the unconscious for these authors also holds out a promise for social emancipation. In Lacanian and post-Lacanian thought, a radically different tack is taken. Lacanian-inspired cultural theorists do not evaluate society in terms of psychoanalytic theory, but rather explore the logic of desire as a social index. From this standpoint, subjective distortions, displacements and repressions are treated as symptoms of the social and cultural field itself.

Consideration of the implications of Lacan's work for social, political and cultural analysis has led to a number of fruitful approaches and strategies. The characteristic emphasis on problems of language and communication in Lacan's thought has made Lacanianism highly relevant to a variety of theoretical projects. Above all, Lacan's thought has been enormously important to feminist concerns with our unequal socio-sexual world. (Lacanian feminism, as well as the feminist critique of Lacan, is discussed in Chapter 5.) Lacan's thought has also greatly influenced debates in areas such as social theory, cultural studies, film theory and criticism, and literary and Marxist theory. In order to approach some of the ramifications of these debates, I shall trace the trajectory of Lacanian and post-Lacanian psychoanalysis which has had the greatest impact on general theorizing about modern culture and politics.

Althusser and after: imaginary mirrors, ideological traps

In his 1957 essay 'The Agency of the Letter in the Unconscious or Reason since Freud', Lacan tells the following story, a story about the relation of a word to its image. 'A train arrives at a station. A little boy and a little girl, brother and sister, are seated in a compartment face to face next to the window through which the buildings along the station platform can be seen passing as the train pulls to a stop. "Look," says the brother, "we're at Ladies!"; "Idiot!" replies his sister, "Can't you see we're at Gentlemen."'[8] How much can we glean about sexuality and gender from this image of everyday life? Lacan says that language assigns to individuals the signifier of their sexual difference. What this means, essentially, is that language has a certain productivity in the construction of individuals as subjects. As the little boy and the little girl gaze out at the station platform, the cultural signifier *carves out a difference* between the identical doors, inscribing each child on one or the other side of the imaginary domain of gender, Ladies or Gentlemen. Ultimately, there is no sexual relation according to Lacan. Instead, there is only each individual's relation to the Law and to language, a relation that enables social relations to persist.

It is just this imaginary inscription of the subject within social and political meanings that Louis Althusser uncovers as the principal function of ideology. Althusser, a French Marxist who had been in personal analysis with Lacan, develops the project of integrating Marxism and Lacanian psychoanalysis in order to understand the positioning of the subject in ideology. In 'Ideology and

Ideological State Apparatuses' (1971), Althusser traces how ideology functions by leading the subject to understand itself in a manner which supports the reproduction of dominant class relations. How is this achieved? The chief effect of ideology is that it provides an imaginary centring on everyday life, it confers identity, and makes the subject feel valued within the interpersonal world. 'Ideology', says Althusser, 'interpellates individuals as subjects.' Interpellation here is to be understood as the establishment of an imaginary relation to the social network, such that the individual comes to recognize himself or herself as a 'subject'. Like Lacan, Althusser insists that the cultural forms of ideology are produced, not so much in the public space of politics and history, as in the private realm of day-to-day life. In this respect, Althusser offers the following example of a person being 'interpellated' through a closed door: 'We all have friends who, when, they knock on our door and we ask, through the door, the question "Who's there?", answer (since "it's obvious") "It's me". And we recognize that "it is him", or "her". We open the door, and "it's true, it really was she who was there".'[9]

How are these imaginary dimensions of ideology to be understood? Echoing Lacan, Althusser uses the notion of the mirror stage to deconstruct ideology. For Althusser, there is a duplicate mirror structure at the heart of the ideological process, a structure which possesses all the unity and plenitude of Lacan's imaginary order. In fact, ideology is doubly specular, according to Althusser, since it grants to the individual an ideological mirror in which it can recognize both itself and others. What the mirror of ideology essentially does is to implant received social meanings at the centre of the imaginary relationship of individuals to their real conditions of existence. Thus, in constituting the self in relation to discourses of class, race, sexuality, nationalism and the like, the individual comes to *misrecognize* itself as an autonomous subject, believing itself to be legally free and self-legislating. This misrecognition, Althusser says, is rooted in Ideological State Apparatuses, institutions such as the mass media, schools, trade unions and the like, whose function is to interpellate subjects to different social positions in the terrain of class struggle. That human subjects should come to overlook the nature of their own *decentred subjectivity* is precisely the function of ideology, thus serving to reinforce the dominant power interests of late capitalism.

Althusser's linking of psychoanalysis and Marxism had a significant impact upon the human sciences at the time of its reception. His central thesis that ideology is an indispensable imaginary medium for the reproduction of social life was original and provocative, and it did much to discredit the notion of ideology as mere false consciousness. Like the unconscious for Freud, ideology for Althusser is eternal. However, it is now widely agreed that there are numerous problems connected with this theory of the subject of ideology. To begin with, Althusser's argument about the specular structure of ideology runs into the same kind of theoretical dead end as does Lacan's account of the imaginary. That is, in order for the subject to recognize itself in and through ideological interpellation, surely it must already possess certain affective capacities for subjective response. As Paul Hirst notes: 'the "individual"', who is prior to ideology and whose pre-ideological attributes of subjectivity are necessary to its becoming a subject, cannot be erased in Althusser's text'.[10] But if there is a 'real' subject hiding behind the ideological effects of interpellation, then perhaps individuals are not as passively centred within received social meanings as Althusser leads us to believe. Consideration of the Lacanian imaginary and symbolic orders underscores the point that there is a fundamental instability at the heart of selfhood. The problem here, in short, is that Althusser downgrades the split and fractured nature of repressed desire, and thus displaces the concept of the unconscious. Consequently, the place of the subject is left so empty in Althusser's theory that it is rendered fruitless for critical analysis. Subjects are serenely inserted into the process of interpellation, and the possibilities for individual and political agency in turn vanish. As such, Althusser is left unable to account for the complex interplay between split, desiring subjects and social and political relations in the modern age.

Nevertheless, whatever the limits of these theoretical dead ends, Althusser's work enabled a more sophisticated psychoanalytic articulation of subjectivity with theories of the social and culture. Those that embraced the framework of the Althusserian/Lacanian system included Etienne Balibar, Pierre Machery, Stuart Hall, Fredric Jameson, Paul Hirst and Barry Hindess. In this theoretical work, the Althusserian model was more finely developed, or reconceptualized, in order to address a range of cultural and political issues, such as race, ethnicity, nationalism, social class and the like. Yet perhaps the most important meeting point of psycho-analytical and cultural theories occurred in film and media studies in the late 1970s and 1980s, as represented in the French journal *Cahiers du Cinéma* and the British journal *Screen*. This discussion of cinema and ideology proceeded from the conceptual cocktail of Lacanian psychoanalysis, Althusserian Marxism, semiotic poststructural theory and certain aesthetic discourses. The most notable psycho-analytic thinking produced about film can be found in the work of Christian Metz, Stephen Heath, Laura Mulvey, Raymond Bellour, Teresa De Lauretis and Mary Ann Doane.

Film is analysed by these theorists as a process of ideological production. What is studied is not so much the latent unconscious thoughts of movie spectators, but rather the *ideological framing* of the film itself. This framing is imaginary. As Christian Metz puts it: 'More than the other arts, or in a more unique way, the cinema involves us in the imaginary: it drums up all perception, but to switch it immediately over into its own absence, which is nonetheless the only signifier present.'[11] Metz's reference to absence here refers to the manner in which film represses the production of its own making, the way in which it passes itself off as natural, the presentation of complex image constructions as simply the reality of day-to-day life. In this respect, the psychoanalysis of cinema is an attempt to decode the ideological images produced in film, and to trace out how these images construct the spectator-subject. The construction of the subject in film, however, is not a fixed or stable affair. Instead, it is suggested that films *order and reorder* the subject in relation to cinematic images. Whether we are watching the evening news, or the fantasy exploits of *Batman,* the point is that we are always caught up within a complex process of ideological framing, linked to the implicit assumptions and ways in which reality is being shaped before our eyes.

The role of ideological framing, though ambiguous, functions in two central modes. The first is *structurally closed.* Imagine a typical Hollywood film which dramatizes its narrative through the reality of the image, recording action as the simple unfolding of what is happening. Here spectators are invited, as it were, to identify with actors in a closed imaginary space, something akin to the mirror stage. Cinema, in this sense, is fully imaginary, constructing spectators as unified, centred subjects who 'control' the image-object before their eyes. Yet cinema in this structurally closed mode can only present such symbolic scenarios by bracketing off its active involvement in narrative construction. That is, film represses its own framing and selective definition of social reality. The second mode of film is *structurally reflexive.* Imagine a film, perhaps an avant-garde film, which constantly frustrates spectator-subject identification; a film in which action and events are presented always from different cinematic angles, including an incorporation of the role of the camera itself in the shooting of the narrative. Through such reflexive techniques, the spectator-subject is made aware of the active role of cinema itself in ideological representation.

If the selective definition of images is the very function of mainstream cinema, it is possible to imagine that film is itself a socially dominant machine of the imaginary, seeking to master reality at a stroke. This, in essence, was the view offered by theorists associated with *Screen* and *Cahiers du Cinéma* in any case. Following Lacan and Althusser, it was argued that the nub of representation in film is the way in which spectator-subject positions are fixed, and rearticulated, in relation to systems of meaning. However, there are several difficulties with this account of the relation between subjectivity, cinema and ideology. For one thing, it is not at all clear that psychoanalysis, even in its Lacanian form, is compatible with the idea of a socially determined consciousness or misrecognition. If the unconscious is the site of our fragile and precarious relation to the Other, a treacherous terrain of multiple, exploding desires, then how might subjectivity ever be 'fixed' through the image production of film? Are not the illusions of generalized mass communication in some sense connected to the phantasmagoria of the unconscious itself? Significantly, it is not at all clear what is meant by the notion of fixation in broader social and political terms. Is the fixation of the spectator-subject, for example, simply to be equated with imaginary misrecognition? Does such fixation imply false consciousness or ideological distortion? And what does it mean to say that truth lies on the other side of ideology? At this point, the Lacanian analysis of film reaches its limits.

Slavoj Zizek: ideology, identity, antagonism

Slavoj Zizek, a member of the Slovene Lacanian school (whose practitioners include Miram Bozovic, Renata Salecl and Mladen Dolor), speaks in *The Sublime Object of Ideology* (1989) of going 'beyond interpellation', to the unconscious core of libidinal enjoyment around which every cultural network is structured. Reconceptualizing the Lacanian–Althusserian framework, Zizek looks at the ambivalence of unconscious desire, and specifically the impact of fantasy, in contemporary social and political life. For Zizek, as for Althusser, ideology is an imaginary domain that always implies a shared relationship to socio-symbolic forms, such as class, race, gender and the like. In contrast to Althusser, however, Zizek contends that ideology can never be reduced to the cultural reproduction of meaning as such – to the signifying network of language alone. On the contrary, ideology always outstrips its own social and political forms; it is a realm *beyond* interpellation or internalization. In this respect, Zizek attempts to underscore the radical involvement of the self in the social context. Ideology, he says, is not something which just magically goes to work on individuals, assigning social identities and roles in the act of producing itself, but is rather an overdetermined field of passionate assumptions and commitments. The whole network of ideology, for a psychoanalytic critic like Zizek, is reproduced through the fantasy identifications of human subjects, identifications which bring into play the troubled waters of the unconscious. 'The function of ideology', writes Zizek, 'is not to offer us a point of escape from our reality but to offer us the social reality itself as an escape from some traumatic, real kernel.'[12]

Zizek's writing, stranded somewhere between high modernism and postmodernist pastiche, can be viewed as an attempt to develop a psychosocial diagnosis of the self in its dealings with the global capitalist economy. From Zizek's Lacanian standpoint, the self is marked by lack, gap and antagonism; the subject, in this view, is alienated through self-blockage or internal trauma, all knowledge of which is displaced at the level of society and history. The notion of a constitutive antagonism or lack at the heart of our personal and social lives is for Zizek the key to grasping the influence of political fantasies of complete power, control and domination. Politics, he says, vainly tries to build upon the desires that people find too painful to acknowledge.

Zizek is widely considered one of the most influential cultural theorists to have drawn from psychoanalysis in the past decade or so. He has been described as 'the most scandalous thinker in recent memory', 'the Giant of Ljubljana' and 'rein-ventor of what was genuinely exciting and revolutionary about the Lacanian school'. Certainly his eclectic approach to cultural theory, peppered with playful-ness and wit, helped to make some of his early writings both readable and enjoyable. Readability is perhaps the last thing that springs to mind when contem-plating Lacanian cultural theory; yet Zizek's mastery of Lacanian theories of ideology is so forceful that his work is comprehensive and challenging. It is against this backdrop that Zizek has cast his theoretical net uncommonly wide – from film studies and feminism to philosophy and political theory. His work in recent years has been an intriguing mix of Hegel and Hitchcock, Spinoza and science fiction, Marx and the Marx Brothers. Moreover, his output has been prolific: *For They Know Not What They Do* (1991), *Looking Awry* (1991), *Everything You Always Wanted to Know About Lacan (But Were Afraid to Ask Hitchcock)* (1992), *Enjoy Your Symptom* (1992) *Tarrying with the Negative* (1993), *The Metastases of Enjoy-ment* (1994), *The Invisibile Remainder* (1996), *The Plague of Fantasies* (1998) and *The Ticklish Subject* (1999). For reasons that I try to draw together here, Zizek's work powerfully illustrates the continuing significance of psychoanalytic inquiry for cultural theory.

If *The Sublime Object of Ideology* is a provocative reconstruction of critical theory from Marx to Althusser, reinterpreted through the frame of Lacanian psycho-analysis, Zizek's *Looking Awry* presents a complimentary account of the political underpinnings of Lacan's 'return to Freud', in which a multiplicity of discourses (communitarianism, universalism, feminism, postmodernism) are traced out and deconstructed. Zizek untangles secret libidinal investments at work in everything, from ideology and international relations to perverse sexualities and detective thrillers. Enjoyment, says Zizek, lies at the core of identity; the enjoyment of which Zizek speaks, however, cannot be given a wholly positive gloss, if only because in Lacanian psychoanalysis enjoyment is always intricately interwoven with lack. The individual subject, once ripped away from the plenitude of the imaginary order, is *itself* constituted as internally blocked, marked by lack, alien-ated through fruitless searches for meaning and unity whose sole purpose is to repair this essential nothingness. It is here that Zizek describes fantasy as a compensation for lack. Fantasy is the very dimension of libidinal enjoyment, spinning off in both pleasurable and painful directions, covering over the empty space of the self. From this angle, fantasy is at once connected to the *ideological* and *pre-ideological*, the latter being a realm of non-meaning which for Zizek is the source of the power and failure of social signification. In *Looking Awry*, Zizek discusses, among other films, Terry Gilliam's *Brazil* as demonstrating fantasy's fundamental ambiguity in ideology. *Brazil* is a black comedy about life in a crazed, totalitarian society. Zizek analyses the ideological manipulation represented in *Brazil* in the following way:

'Brazil' is the stupid song from the 1950s that resounds compulsively throughout the film ... it seems that the idiotic, intrusive rhythm of 'Brazil' serves as a support for totalitarian enjoyment, i.e., that it condenses the fantasy frame of the 'crazy' totalitarian social order that the film depicts. But at the very end, when his resistance is apparently broken by the savage torture to which he has been subjected, the hero escapes his torturers by beginning to whistle 'Brazil!' Although functioning as a support for the totalitarian order, fantasy is then at the same time the leftover of the real that enables us to 'pull ourselves out', to preserve a kind of distance from the socio-symbolic network.[13]

Enjoyment thus lies at the root of ideology, driving the imagination of the self within the framework of received social meanings. Yet enjoyment is also something which *cannot* be fully incorporated into the symbolic; it is a hard kernel of desire, traumatic irrationality, the ultimate displacement at every point of ideological identification.

The political thrust of all of this is to demonstrate that ideological discourse, which operates in and through fantasy, provides a lining or support to the lack or antagonism that marks the self. Ideologies of, say, nationalism, racism or sexism structure the fantasy coherence of cultural formations, with unconscious forms of libidinal enjoyment erupting as symptoms of antagonism. Significantly, Zizek sees recent eruptions of neo-nationalism and ethnic xenophobia across Europe in these terms; racism, he says, is an outer displacement of what we cannot accept within. The projection of a 'surplus of enjoyment' on to denigrated others, the dumping of distressing and painful affect on socially valorized objects of antagonism, lies at the heart of the psychic dimension of racism and strategies of political exclusion. This eruption of excess enjoyment, directed at the Other, represents an unbearable kernel of desire; such excess is alleviated solely through its translation into an ideological symptom. The collapse of Soviet totalitarianism in Eastern Europe unleashed a surplus of fantasy, antagonistic desire that was too painful to acknowledge within certain cultural formations. Ideological xenophobias, such as nationalist or racist desires, thus involved the projection of pain on to something perceived as strange and Other.

What is perhaps most striking here is not so much the length to which Zizek has gone (following Althusser) in translating Lacanianism into an explicit social theory, but rather his reformulation and reworking of psychoanalysis in order to grasp the cultural determinations of all desire. 'The Real', 'antagonism', 'beyond interpellation', 'symbolic destitution', 'pre-ideological kernel of desire': Zizek's neologisms abound throughout the language of post-Lacanian cultural criticism. Certainly the frenetic urgency with which Zizek has pursued political matters concerning the self and its symbolic identifications has been dramatic, if only because it is evident that he believes something sinister lies at the centre of capitalist consumer culture. The postmodern development of the consumer age, according to Zizek, has struck at the core of our psychic worlds, producing deformation, disfigurement and disillusionment. There are few signs of any remedy for this, except perhaps a vague sense that postmodern irony, cynical distance or engaging with the negative is the best for which we might hope, both individually and socially. Not all of Zizek's followers read him this way, however. 'The rhetorically distinctive wittiness of Zizek's works', write Elizabeth and Edmond Wright, 'slyly transforms the apparently uncompromising bleakness of his politico-philosophical psychoanalyses into a buoyantly ironic political program.' This in turn raises the vexed question of whether ironic philosophical programmes can produce concrete political transformations.

It is perhaps because of such nagging worries about how best to connect psychoanalytic critique with political activism that Zizek, in his most recent writings, has turned to more abstract, philosophical issues. 'A spectre is haunting Western academe,' writes Zizek in *The Ticklish Subject*, 'the spectre of the Cartesian subject.' Rejection of the Cartesian subject lies at the core, says Zizek, of contemporary 'radical' thought. Poststructuralists, postmodernists, deconstructionists, feminists: all are united in their disowning of the Cartesian heritage. Psychoanalysis, too, is often thought to join in this denunciation; after all, it is with Freud that rationalist claims to consciousness, knowledge, understanding and self-control have been subverted. Yet Zizek thinks this is a misreading of Freud. His remarkable claim, fleshed out in detail in *The Ticklish Subject*, is that radical politics requires a 'philosophical manifesto' of Cartesian subjectivity. 'The point', writes Zizek, 'is not to return to the cogito in the guise in which this notion has dominated modern thought (the self-transparent thinking subject) but to bring to light its forgotten obverse, the excessive, unacknowledged kernel of the cogito, which is far from the pacifying image of the transparent Self.' Here we are back to the terrain of subjective excess, an excess of passion through which people channel their dreams and anxieties within the context of society and political history; it is this excess – the other scene of Cartesian self-transparency – which Zizek sees as troubling individual and political life.

Zizek contends that, in conditions of postmodernity, we inhabit spaces of 'post-politics'. Post-politics does not mean that politics is dead. On the contrary, contemporary politics is ideological through and through. Zizek says that, notwithstanding the collapse of communism and the rhetoric of the advanced capitalist societies to be non-ideological, globalization has unleashed an insidious inner colonization of human subjects, one that penetrates to our most intimate selves and deepest libidinal recesses. Postmodern culture, says Zizek, is jaded. Alongside changes in technology and communication, the functioning of self and society has undergone an implosion of signs, symbols and significations. Meaninglessness – the sense that nothing has value – is increasingly prevalent. As a result, Zizek argues, the self develops various fetishes relating to political and public life: 'I know what I'm doing is meaningless, but still I do it nonetheless.'

Like his other books, *The Ticklish Subject* has done much to generate interest in psychoanalysis within the social sciences and humanities. As the fullest exposition yet that Zizek has provided of the philosophical foundations of his psychoanalytic cultural theory, the work is an engrossing account of some of the conditions and curves of postmodern political life. However, like several other critics, my own sense is that Zizek's key thesis – that the culture of advanced capitalism is contaminated by a fetishistic logic of disavowal, masochistic deception and psychic fragmentation – is faulty. Not only does this approach reproduce some of the most questionable assumptions in Althusserian theory (do we really want to return to the political dead ends of Althusser!), but many of Zizek's theoretical conclusions enter into an embarrassing contradiction with his progressive political goals. To begin with, if loss and pain are fundamental anchors for desire as enmeshed in ideological forms, their composition would seem to be more internally differentiated than Zizek recognizes. According to his interpretation, ideology is a fantasy scenario, the sole purpose of which is to 'fill in' or 'cover over' in terms of lack. Yet the problem with this view is that it flattens out the complex, contradictory reception of ideological forms by individuals. Whether one is in the grip of identity politics, reading philosophy or watching Oprah Winfrey, these are – for Zizek – all pieces of ideological fantasy aimed at effacing the sour taste of lack, gap and antagonism. Lack, and the partial erasure of such subjective destitution through fantasy, simply becomes the uniform measure of cultural domination. Yet, in advancing this view, Zizek strikes the ideological world empty of meaning. The 'impossible kernel of desire' of which Zizek speaks, though offering a potential space for critical political resistance, ultimately drains away the core emotional, unconscious connections through which human subjects interact in daily life. It offers no basis for understanding the richly ambiguous links between desire and social action, nor any basis for discriminating between the differentiated ideological formations of the contemporary epoch. Social differentiation and cultural discrimination are lost in this approach, as Zizek simply passes over the multiplex ways in which people come to challenge or resist political ideologies.

It is perhaps strange that, similar to several major social theorists who have turned to psychoanalysis this century, Zizek thinks we live in an age in which establishment culture destroys all creative ways of living. Much like Marcuse's vision of the 'one-dimensional society' or Lacan's account of the timeless symbolic, Zizek believes we lack the necessary individual and collective agency to creatively confront the disorder of global capitalism. In this judgement, he may well be proven correct – though psychoanalysis, as I have argued throughout, provides other ways of thinking about both self-development and possible trajectories of social development.

Jean Laplanche: seductive presences

Lacanian social theory has exacerbated classic Freudianism's tendency to read the complexities of power and culture off from the contradications of repressed desire. Lacan's account of the individual subject operates on a fairly global level, tracing the repressed unconscious within a structure of linguistic interrelationship, whereas the contemporary French psychoanalyst Jean Laplanche is more concerned with examining the complexities of desire in relation to parental sexual signification. The problem of desire – where does the unconscious come from? – is theorized by Laplanche as a series of conflictual sexual messages sent by parents to the pre-Oedipal child. These sexual messages, misread and even then only partly digested, are pressed deeply into the child's emotional world. In terms of the philosophical premises of Lacanian psychoanalysis, parental sexual messages, glossed by Laplanche as core defining moments in which otherness intrudes into psychic life, construct the structure of the unconscious and the psyche in general. In other words, desire is ignited through multiple excitations or penetrations of the psyche, stirred by behavioural gestures of the parents in the process of caring for the infant. Laplanche calls this 'primal seduction', the process by which the other comes to dwell within the self.

Having trained with Lacan, Laplanche's early writings indicate a strong conceptual debt to his former analyst. Indeed, the book for which Laplanche is perhaps best known in the Anglo-American world is *The Language of Psychoanalysis* (1967), co-authored with J. B. Pontalis – an encyclopedic coverage of core psychoanalytic concepts through the lens of French Freudianism. Further works of psychoanalytic exposition and critique followed, including the influential tract *Life and Death in Psychoanalysis* (1976), in which Laplanche struggled to remain faithful to the Lacanian modifications to psychoanalysis, principally through expressing his general suspicion of structural theory. It seems likely that Laplanche's lasting contribution to contemporary psychoanalysis will be his reflections on otherness in the formation of human subjectivity, as developed in his 'general theory of seduction', set out in the five-volume *Problématiques* (1980–87). A summary of Laplanche's post-Lacanian theory of seduction has quite recently appeared in English, in the volumes *New Foundations for Psychoanalysis* (1987) and *Essays on Otherness* (1999).

In typical Lacanian vein, the term 'signifier' is central to Laplanche's work. However, Laplanche deploys the term in a radically different fashion from that of Lacan. He postulates not a language, but verbal and non-verbal human expression as lying at the root of unconscious childhood experience. Enigmatic sexual messages, or seductive signifiers, form for Laplanche an emotional backdrop to everyday relations of childcare and nurturing. Through adult dispositions and behavioural gestures, the child is lent, as it were, an unconscious framework of meaning in order to naturalize his or her place in the world. 'The *enigma*', says Laplanche, 'is in itself a *seduction* and its mechanisms are unconscious.... The "attentions of a mother" or the "aggression of a father" are seductive only because they are not transparent. They are seductive because they are opaque, because they convey something enigmatic.'[14] Signifiers are enigmatic for Laplanche in the sense that adult messages outstrip the child's capacity for emotional understanding and response, and also as such messages are shot through with parental unconscious signification. In interacting and caring for the child, notes Laplanche, the parent, in sending out enigmatic messages, is 'compromised by his own unconscious sexuality'.[15] The mother and the father, in short, routinely present to the child that which they do not know about their own sexuality. What is on the outside, adult sexual messages, creates an inaccessible world of signification on the inside, the repressed unconscious.

Laplanche gives as an example of such enigmatic signifiers the child's exploration of the breast. According to Laplanche, the breast is a site for transmission of various opaque sexual messages to the child. As Laplanche puts this:

> Can analytic theory afford to go on ignoring the extent women unconsciously and sexually cathect the breast, which appears to be the natural organ for lactation? It is inconceivable that the infant does not notice this sexual cathexis.... It is impossible to imagine that the infant does not suspect that this cathexis is the source of a nagging question: what does the breast want from me, apart from wanting to suckle me, and come to that, why does it want to suckle me? (p. 126)

In other words, the child receives a sexually loaded message from the mother, a message which founds desire and cements the child's emotional relation to the intersubjective world.

Psychoanalytic theorists divide between those like Lacan and Laplanche who, through complex conceptual systems, view the construction of the unconscious in terms of the intrusion of outside forces and especially otherness, and those like Freud and the Cornelius Castoriadis of *The Imaginary Institution of Society* who insist, in a more isolationist fashion, that unconscious imagination emanates from the singular primacy of the psyche's capacity to generate fantasy. Laplanche's originality is not just to see strangeness or foreignness as traumatizing to the narcissistic closure of the psyche, but to the otherness of the unconscious in general. Strange seductive messages or intrusive enigmatic signifiers cut to the core of the origins of sexuality, and Laplanche's boldest move here is to recast the dialogue between self and other as a series of complex libidinal piercings, closures and reopenings. So much is clear from his general theory of seduction; though some critics worry whether 'seduction' is, in politically strategic terms, the most apt terminological choice. Current controversies over Freud's so-called neglect of child sexual abuse loom large here. Indeed, it is interesting to note that Laplanche's general theory of seduction was attracting attention within the psychoanalytic community in France at roughly the same time that Jeffrey Masson was attempting to destroy the intellectual and political credentials of psychoanalysis in America. In *The Assault on Truth: Freud's Suppression of the Seduction Theory* (1984), Masson claimed that Freud had seen into the terrible truths of patriarchal society, particularly the shocking psychic consequences of child sexual abuse and incest, but had closed his eyes to this by downgrading his patients' stories and reinterpreting them as unconscious fantasies. Sexual abuse, says Masson, was recast as the product of children's sexual imagination. Masson's attack on Freud, however, entirely missed the point that what is at stake in the psychoanalytic perspective is *psychical reality* – that is to say, the disordered and conflictual forms of fantasy that infuse all constructions of self-experience and affective investments in the intersubjective world. Neither Freud, nor Laplanche after him, denies the existence of child sexual abuse, nor the destructive consequences of such trauma within our culture. As Laplanche has rightly claimed, however, Freud's seduction theory was an attempt to deal with a more general theoretical problem, namely the ways in which otherness and difference present themselves to the psyche.

Suggestive as it is, Laplanche's work is not without its problems. Lacanian critics have noted that Laplanche's general theory of seduction fails to adequately account for the break-up of primary narcissism. What is meant by this charge is that Laplanche offers no third term or agent to whom the child is referred as regards Oedipal anxiety or symbolic identification. Failing to specify the complex process in which the child becomes enmeshed in the triangular structure of family relations, Laplanche instead concentrates only on the singular child/parent relation – and this is a failing in the eyes of various Lacanians and neo-Lacanians. More troubling, perhaps, is Laplanche's conceptual stress on passivity. In Laplanche's work, people appear as essentially passive in relation to enigmatic signification. Indeed, there is almost a complete separation of the world of enigmatic signification from the actual responses of individuals. As Jacqueline Rose has argued, Laplanche's reinterpretation of repression means that the 'child receives everything from the outside', with desire inscribed in the internal world via the deformations of parental sexuality itself.[16] There is another way of putting this point. Laplanche, like Lacan, presents us with a structural model of the conditions of possibility for unconscious desire. Both theorists betray a poststructuralist distaste for individual subjectivity; and both in their different ways develop an inadequate account of psychic interiority, creativity and imagination. Otherness, in short, is elevated over and above the individual subject. Yet important as others are in the constitution of the self, otherness, strangeness and foreignness will always be internally processed and given shape at the level of fantasy by the unconscious imagination of individuals.

Whatever these limits, Laplanche has constructed a valuable theory within which the primacy of otherness in the formation of the unconscious is given its due. His work as a whole underscores the inescapable imprint of otherness upon self-identity and structures of intersubjectivity.

Table 4.1   Poststructuralist anxiety: subjects of desire

Theorist	Subjectivity and the unconscious	Key terms
Lacan	Self as narcissistic misrecognition, represented through symbolic order of language	Mirror stage Imaginary Symbolic Unconscious structured like a language
Althusser	Individual as subject of ideological misrecognition	Interpellation Hailing
Zizek	Self decentred through pre-ideological lack of desire	Enjoyment Antagonism
Laplanche	Self constituted in and through primal seduction, an opaque realm of sexual messages from the Other	Enigmatic signifiers Seduction

CHAPTER 5

Psychoanalytic Feminism

From Chodorow to Butler

'The greater part of the feminist movement', wrote Juliet Mitchell in her pioneering book *Psychoanalysis and Feminism* (1974), 'has identified Freud as the enemy ... [but] a rejection of psychoanalysis and of Freud's works is fatal for feminism.'[1] From the intellectual context of the 1970s, Mitchell's foray into the convergences between psychoanalysis and feminism signalled an important departure for the resurgent women's movement. As 1960s radicalism gave way to the political resignation of the 1970s, and as memories of the 'sexual revolution' of the preceding years faded, it became all too clear that sexism and oppressive gender ties were still deeply entrenched in modern societies. According to Mitchell, the women's movement needed to supplement a sociological and economic focus on women's oppression with a more specific focus on sexual ideology, examining the symbolic forms through which patriarchy and gender roles are internalized. For if our unequal sexual world is replicated through oppressive social practices – such as the socio-economic conditions of mothering, job discrimination and unequal wages – it is also profoundly shaped by an ambivalent emotional structure involving fear, envy, aggression and hatred in gender relations. For Mitchell, and indeed for contemporary feminist politics, such sexual ideologies – which powerfully shape gender relations in contemporary culture   urgently demand practical examination. In doing so, it is argued, the women's movement will be better placed to understand polarized sexual roles and to rethink the possibilities for restructuring gender relations.

Psychoanalytic feminism is today more intellectually fertile and robust than ever before. In fact, the encounter between feminism and psychoanalysis has proved to be of crucial importance in transformations of gender power, sexual practices and sexed identities. Broadly speaking, the major division in psychoanalytic feminism is between Anglo-American object relations theory on the one hand, and French Lacanian and post-Lacanian theory on the other. Through the object relations lens, feminist theorists analyse sexuality and gender against the backdrop of interpersonal relationships – with particular emphasis on the pre-Oedipal child/ mother bond. Poststructuralist feminists indebted to Lacanian psychoanalysis, by contrast, deconstruct gender terms with reference to the structuring power of the symbolic order, of language as such. In theoretical terms, the differences between these approaches to understanding women's oppression are considerable. In practical terms, however, the issues addressed involve various points of convergence. For example, both Anglo-American and French theories examine the forces inhibiting women's agency and autonomy in contemporary culture; the relationship between maternal and paternal power in infant development; the connections between sexuality, the body and its pleasures; and the recontextualization of psychoanalytic concepts in feminist, political terms. In this chapter, I shall review these emphases in Anglo-American and French psychoanalytic feminism, concluding with an examination of current possibilities for greater dialogue between these theoretical standpoints.

Phallic power: sexuality and psychoanalytic theory

For Freud, as discussed in Chapter 1, the notion of 'castration' is of key importance to the structuring of the small infant's representation of sex and gender difference. It is with reference to the presence or absence of the phallus, under the sign of the castration complex, that masculinity and femininity are constructed. Freud's starting point is that libido is 'masculine'; it is this proposition that leads him to speculate that 'the little girl is a little man'. Secondly, Freud contends that the Oedipus/castration complex affects boys and girls differently. In the case of the boy, it is the father's possession of the mother's body, coupled with a fantasy about the little girl's lack, which gives meaning to the threat of castration – a narcissistic wound that dissolves the Oedipus complex. Once negotiated, the boy learns that his possession of a penis can be used to express desire. In the case of the girl, castration is imagined as already inflicted, as she learns that both herself and mother lack a penis. This experience of 'penis envy' actually produces Oedipal desire in the small girl, causing her to reject her mother as a love object and turn to her father in the hope of winning the missing phallus. According to Freud, both the boy and the girl must undergo a violent separation from the mother's body – and to this extent both are 'castrated'. However, the psychical distinction between the sexes, as Freud describes it, is negative in a more profound sense for the girl than for the boy. Female 'castration' involves the repression of the girl's earlier active sexuality.

Given Freud's account of female sexuality in terms of penis envy, what possible attraction might psychoanalytic theory hold for feminists? For surely to define human sexuality as resting upon a male norm, with the feminine cast as supplementary and derivative, is only to raise phallocentrism to a higher power. For some feminists, this is precisely the ideological effect of psychoanalysis. Freudian theory, according to this view, is used to deny active agency to women. The discourse of psychoanalysis is itself repressive, reinforcing the patriarchal insistence on heterosexuality by 'adapting' or 'reinscribing' women within oppressive sexual norms. As Mary Daly argues, the word 'therapist' should be read as 'the/rapist'.[2] In this account, then, Freud is the enemy, the patriarchal father of normalizing discourse.

Instead of taking such an anti-psychoanalytic line, however, the great bulk of contemporary feminist theory has acknowledged, and made use of, the (partial) truth(s) of Freud's account of sexuality – however ideologically suspect this account may be in some respects. Here feminists, of divergent theoretical backgrounds, claim the accuracy of Freud's linkage of masculinity with individuation, agency and desire on the one hand, and of femininity with passivity and lack on the other. In general terms, feminists recognize that cultural processes of individuation pose key problems for a feminist transformation of gender power. But Freud's theory of sexual difference, it is argued, shows the profound desexualization to which women must submit in order to take up gender roles of femininity in contemporary culture. Whether we speak of the desexualized images of motherhood which circulate through the mass media, or even Madonna-inspired representations of seductive femininity, the essential point remains the same: an object-like status, which at best only allows women a certain pleasure in being desired, is taken as the central attribute of the feminine.

This much of Freud, then, is widely accepted: modern culture enforces a brutal desexualization of female subjectivity – a desexualization which can make women submissive, passive, envious and sometimes ill. But it is here that we also find the beginnings of a feminist engagement with, and critique of, Freud. Psychoanalytic feminists say that Freud is descriptive, not prescriptive, about gender and sexuality. Feminist theorists stress that the psychic structures which underpin patriarchy are not pre-given; these structures can be altered and transformed. From this angle, the view that castration denotes femininity itself depends on a series of suppressions and displacements of the social and political forces that structure gender difference.

Contemporary psychoanalytic feminists have gone far in tracing how asymmetrical relations of power impact upon sexuality. Through an in-depth political critique of the primacy of the phallus in the construction of personal identity, feminists have powerfully shown that anatomy is not destiny. Perhaps the most significant emphasis here concerns the political links between male power and the status of the phallus in psychoanalytic theory. Broadly speaking, attention has focused on the power of culture as regards the father/phallus, as the necessary third term which disrupts and divides the child/mother relationship. A number of differing factors are linked to the reproduction of gender asymmetries in this respect. Lacanian feminists highlight links between language and the phallus as the signifier of difference par excellence, a signifier which cannot be captured or contained and is thus deconstructed as illusory. Post-Lacanian feminists focus attention on the child/mother dyad, tracing the subterranean influence of patriarchy upon the child's sexual desires. Alternatively, other developments in feminist thought have concentrated less on the role of the father, focusing instead on the impact of mothering in the reproduction of gender asymmetries. This approach, which has produced fruitful feminist interventions and strategies, is generally associated with object relations theory in psychoanalysis – and it is this version of psychoanalytic feminism that I first want to discuss in detail.

Reversing Freud: object relations feminism

The object relations approach in feminist theory accords prime importance to the early mother/child bond, or to what psychoanalytic theorists term the pre-Oedipal period. The starting point here is that the pre-Oedipal stage is fundamental to the infant's psychic structure and emerging sense of self. Unlike Freud's theory, in which sexual difference and gender identity are constituted only with the passing of the Oedipus complex, object relations theory posits a core sense of gender identity. Challenging Freud's account of Oedipally organized gender difference, the object relations school of psychoanalysis underscores the infant's primary, erotic connection with the body of the pre-Oedipal mother – a connection conceptualized as the central organizing axis for all human social relationships. The role of the father, accordingly, shifts into the background in this theory. It is the pre-Oedipal mother who structures and cements the child's basic sense of self-hood and gender. Love and desire are born through an erotic union with the mother, a primary love that exerts a profound influence throughout life.

This upgrading of the role of the pre-Oedipal mother in infant development, however, cannot be given a wholly positive gloss. For if the child begins life under the sign of maternal devotion, this is also a relationship that generates feelings of intense helplessness, fear and even hatred. The small infant experiences intense ambivalence in relation to the pre-Oedipal mother, ambivalence that swings between states of idealized love and fears of engulfment. It is precisely from this focus upon pre-Oedipal ambivalence that feminists drawing on object relations theory attempt to trace dominant social constructions of femininity in contemporary culture.

The view that our earliest experiences of an omnipotent mother lead to a general fear and loathing of anything female is given powerful expression in the work of the American cultural theorist, Dorothy Dinnerstein. In *The Mermaid and the Minotaur* (1976), Dinnerstein examines the psychic impact upon the sexes of societal nurturing arrangements. Her claim is that, given exclusive female mothering in late capitalist societies, children of both sexes encounter a social context that violently deforms gender. Female mothering, Dinnerstein says, leads us inevitably to fear women. Both sexes fear the power that mothers wield over them as infants, a fear which leads children to betray the 'engulfing mother' by turning to the father in search of emotional security. Paternal authority offered by the father offers an escape route from ambivalence, involving infantile helplessness, rage and hate felt towards the mother. As Dinnerstein writes: 'It is as we leave infancy that the possibility of transferring dependent, submissive feeling to the second parent – whose different gender carries the promise of a new deal, a clean sweep – entices us into the trap of male domination.'[3] In other words, patriarchy is the outcome of a denial of emotional ambivalence: unconscious anguish in connection to the mother is denied, coupled to an idealization of paternal authority. The psychic costs of this denial are severe. Men and women remain haunted by the memory of maternal dominance. For while infantile helplessness may have been repudiated, the return of the repressed continually threatens to outstrip masculinist culture. Significantly this situation, says Dinnerstein, is worse for women than for men. Associated with the power of mothering, women are doubly denigrated – as mother and as wife or lover – within the contemporary gender system.

Situating her analysis of the mother/child relationship within a Kleinian framework, Dinnerstein contends that socially predominant ideologies of gender are marked by a failure to work through persecutory and depressive anxieties about women, especially women's role as mothers. Instead of gaining a sense of the mother as an independent agent, fantasies proliferate about women as all-powerful and thus as objects of fear. In this context, Dinnerstein locates some of the most pathological features of contemporary culture: man's need to control and humiliate women; woman's collaboration in denigrating her own sex; the domination of nature; sexual violence; and the cultural denial of human fragility. The way forward to a transformation of gender, says Dinnerstein, is through shared parenting. 'So long as the first parent is a woman,' writes Dinnerstein, 'women will inevitably be pressed into the dual role of indispensable quasi-human supporter and deadly quasi-human enemy of the self.'

Dinnerstein's work offered one of the first psychoanalytic challenges to mainstream feminist accounts of gender relations. Society, for Dinnerstein, is not something external, which then 'goes to work' on people by imprinting gender power. Rather, society is a force that penetrates to the deepest emotional roots of sexual experience, engendering anti-female feelings in the very act of constituting the self. As such, her work raises important issues about the connections between sexuality, power and culture. Significant as it is, though, Dinnerstein's critique of gender is severely limited by several major flaws. She assumes, for example, that the avoidance of psychic pain in early life connects with the devaluation of women in a universal, mechanistic way. What this overlooks, however, is that motherhood is situated in a social, political and economic context – a *patriarchal* context which distorts the social organization of parenting and child-rearing. In other words, what Dinnerstein's model cannot adequately accommodate is the impact of ideology: those complex, contradictory political forms through which society influences the feelings, thoughts and aspirations of individuals. This is a serious omission, and it is one which causes Dinnerstein to ignore the point that men, as well as women, can be idealized, envied, feared and hated. Moreover, Dinnerstein's account of the contemporary gender system runs into a kind of theoretical brick wall since she cannot comprehend resistances to, or transformations in, gender power. Women and men are simply deemed dependent on patriarchy as a way of sidestepping their neurotic, paranoid reactions to motherhood, child-rearing and nature.

A theory of gender that does discriminate between the lived experience of males and females can be found in the approach taken by the American psychoanalytic feminist Nancy Chodorow. Chodorow, like Dinnerstein, is interested in the political ramifications of exclusive female mothering. She employs psychoanalytic theory for analysing the reproduction of gender asymmetries in modern societies and for tracing paths to social change. Yet unlike Dinnerstein, Chodorow argues that a mother's love is profoundly different for sons and daughters – a difference that leads to socially structured psychological processes of gender power. In her pioneering book *The Reproduction of Mothering* (1978), Chodorow argues that mothers experience their daughters as doubles of themselves, through a narcissistic projection of sameness. Chodorow calls this pre-Oedipal bond between mother and daughter *narcissistic object-attachment*; such attachment means that the mother relates to her daughter as simply an extension of her own life, and not as an independent person. As Chodorow puts this:

> A mother is likely to experience a sense of oneness and continuity with her infant. However, this sense is stronger, and lasts longer, vis-à-vis daughters. Primary identification and symbiosis with daughters tend to be stronger and cathexis of daughters is more likely to remain and emphasize narcissistic elements, that is, to be based on experiencing a daughter as an extension or double of a mother herself, with cathexis of the daughter as a sexual other usually remaining a weaker, less significant theme.[4]

From this pre-Oedipal merging, daughters develop a strong capacity for empathy, sensitivity and intimacy with other people. Yet because daughters are perceived as the selfsame as mother, differentiation of the self is beset with emotional difficulties. The female child, in brief, finds it painfully difficult to disengage from the mother's love. Locked within maternal narcissism, the daughter is, in effect, emotionally hindered in the task of establishing a sense of independence and individuality. From this perspective, Chodorow reinterprets Freud's concept of 'penis envy' not as biologically pre-given, but as a sign of the daughter's desire for autonomy. The daughter turns to her father, through an awareness of the social privilege that the phallus symbolizes, in the hope of achieving a sense of independence from the mother. Yet because fathers are emotionally distant and absent (for reasons which we will soon examine), daughters are unable to break with the power and authority of the pre-Oedipal mother.

The emotional sensitivity and intuitive concern which are often taken as the hallmark of womanhood – so Chodorow contends – is a direct outcrop of these socio-structural patterns embedded in the early pre-Oedipal mother/daughter bond. Daughters grow up with a powerful sense of emotional continuity with their mothers, a continuity which provides the basis for a strong relational connection in women's adult life. However, this relational component of feminine identity is achieved only at a severe personal cost. Since mothers do not perceive daughters as separate, girls remain without adequate affirmation of their sense of personal identity and agency. This results in a confusion of ego boundaries, coupled with a wider estrangement from personal needs, aspirations and desires. Feelings of inadequate separateness, lack of self-control, and a fear of merging with others thus arise as prime emotional problems for women. Related to this is the socially devalued gender category of the feminine. For Chodorow, women's 'core gender identity' (weak ego boundaries, immersion in narcissism, etc.) comes to mirror a culturally devalued social position. One common way out of these difficulties for women, says Chodorow, is through a defensively constructed set of personal boundaries: denying what is needed within, focusing on what is needed by others – particularly, the needs of men.

In similar fashion, Chodorow argues that a distinctly masculine form of personality structure, or core male identity, exists. Reversing Freud through the object relations lens, Chodorow argues that masculine identity is forged against the backdrop of a primary identification with the mother. Such love for the mother, says Chodorow, makes the achievement of maleness much more difficult than was originally presumed by Freud. For what boys must at all costs repudiate, in order to forge a masculine sense of selfhood, is their emotional intimacy with the mother. Boys must deny their primary bond to female eroticism, repressing their own femininity permanently into the unconscious. The originating cue for this repression, somewhat paradoxically, comes from the mother. Chodorow argues that boys are assisted in the developmental task of making their maleness through the mother's perception of gender difference. From the start of life, Chodorow says, mothers propel their sons towards differentiation and autonomy, prizing assertiveness in interpersonal relations. Chodorow calls this pre-Oedipal mother/ son bond *anaclitic object-attachment*; this is a kind of attachment by which mothers relate to their sons as different and other from themselves. Mothers thus lead their sons to disengage emotionally from care and intimacy. This prepares boys for an instrumental, abstract attitude towards the world, an attitude which will be expected from them in the public sphere of work and politics.

The gendered self for Chodorow is therefore constructed relationally. Like Dinnerstein, Chodorow argues that sons and daughters seek to escape from the engulfing pre-Oedipal mother by turning to paternal authority. Yet unlike Dinnerstein, Chodorow claims that feelings of powerlessness – feelings which produce the emotional break with mother – are handled differently by the sexes. Sons are better placed to establish boundaries, separation and autonomy because they are recognized as sexually different and distinct by the mother. Daughters, by contrast, develop their emotional life around relationships, nurturance and care, primarily due to a narcissistic identification with the mother. Significantly, one consequence of this re-evaluation of the role of the pre-Oedipal mother is that the function of the father in psychic differentiation diminishes. Although fathers come to be idealized as representatives of the outside world, they have only a shadowy emotional existence for sons and daughters, even after the passing of the Oedipus complex. In this account, paternal authority is viewed as a uniform, repressive 'last-ditch escape from maternal omnipotence'.[5]

What this account of gender relations suggests, therefore, is that exclusive female mothering produces an ideology of male domination. The absence of any primary attachment to males in pre-Oedipal childhood leads to an idealization of men and a devaluation of women. The only way out of this self-reproducing gender system, Chodorow argues, is through shared parenting. The inclusion of men in early parenting activities should lead to a break-up of established gender polarity. Both parents would be available to establish a caring, nurturing connection with their children. In this context, children of both sexes would be able to forge emotional intimacy and autonomy through a primary relatedness to mother and father. As Chodorow theorizes such gender transformation:

> Masculinity would not become tied to denial of dependence and devaluation of women. Feminine personality would be less preoccupied with individuation, and children would not develop fears of maternal omnipotence and expectations of women's unique self-sacrificing qualities. This would reduce men's needs to guard their masculinity and their control of social and cultural spheres which treat and define women as secondary and powerless, and would help women to develop the autonomy which too much embeddedness in relationships has often taken from them. (p. 218)

Let me sum up the main threads of Chodorow's theory. Exclusive female mothering is posited as central to the reproduction of gender asymmetries in modern societies. Exclusive female mothering produces social relations split between connected, empathic female identities on the one hand, and isolated, instrumental male identities on the other. Masculine identity is built on a denial of primary maternal identification resulting in a fragile sense of self, defensively structured by an abstract attitude to the world. Feminine identity is grounded in a strong sense of gender, but limited in capacity for autonomy and individuality. The only viable route out of contemporary gender asymmetries, says Chodorow, is through shared parenting.

There has been considerable debate in feminist circles regarding the general applicability of Chodorow's perspective on gender identity, with some feminists disclaiming the universalist bent of her work, while others have questioned whether strong generalization about the shaping of gender was what Chodorow's sociology actually produced. I will discuss this controversy in some detail shortly; but it is worth noting that there are other ways of understanding the tension in feminist politics between the universal impact of phallocentrism and the individuated particularism of gender identities. Indeed Chodorow has, since the writing of *The Reproduction of Mothering*, sought to examine in detail the complex fantasies, projections and introjections through which individual depth and creativity reflect the imprint of more common interests and cultural discourses. In *Femininities, Masculinities, Sexualities* (1994), for example, Chodorow argues that meaning is fashioned at the intersection of a particular, socio-historical psyche and a particular, socio-historical culture. Psyche and culture, she insists, cross and tangle – with neither reducible to the other.

Such a position, in my view, provides for a richer, more complex understanding of questions pertaining to human sexuality than that offered in Chodorow's earlier contributions. This is perhaps especially clear in Chodorow's discussion of sexual diversity in *Feminities, Masculinities, Sexualities*, specifically the enormous fluidity of fantasies, projections and introjections that support and structure each individual's internal history. Arguing against the flawed universality of Oedipal fixation in traditional psychoanalysis, particularly the repressive insistence on a fixed dichotomy between 'gay' and 'straight' sexed identities, Chodorow restates her belief in the fluidity of sexuality and fantasy. She argues that Freud's account of the Oedipus complex is less concerned with privileging so-called normative heterosexuality (as is commonly assumed), and instead maps the terrain of psychic traumas as related to gender. In presenting this plea for an acceptance of sexual diversity, Chodorow contends that sexual identity, whether straight or gay, is always a kind of defence, symptom or compromise formation.

Chodorow's work presents a powerful and compelling account of those psycho-social forces that distort gender relations. Her theoretical model has exercised enormous influence in feminism, sociology, cultural theory and psychoanalytic studies.[6] Her claim that there is a stable gender identity for males and females has proved attractive to many wishing to understand the persistence of patriarchal domination. In this respect, Chodorow's claims about female psychology are illuminating. Of key importance here is Chodorow's assertion that women want to have children in order to recapture the primary bond of the mother/daughter relationship. The reasoning here is surely clear. Women's lives are emotionally drained because men are cut off from sexual intimacy and interpersonal communication. From this angle, the desire to have a child is actually rooted in distortions of the current gender system. Conversely, the abstract traits of male selfhood described by Chodorow provide a direct purchase on the anxieties that many men experience in relation to intimacy. Masculinity, says Chodorow, necessarily involves the adoption of intolerance, insensitivity and emotional coerciveness. From this angle, male sexual dominance, often involving the use of violence towards women, has its roots in the damaged, fragile and precarious nature of masculine identity.

Nevertheless, Chodorow's theory has limitations. To begin with, there is something too neat and comfortable about Chodorow's claim that exclusive female mothering produces asymmetric gender roles. Chodorow presents us with a model of woman as mother, as primary caretaker, with maternal desire fixed into either narcissistic or anaclitic modes of identification. But is the institution of mothering really so strongly delimited to these psychic categories? What of mothers who encourage 'feminine' modes of expression in their sons? What of mothers who foster 'masculine' aims of autonomy, independence and achievement in their daughters? What of the increasing phenomenon of single-parent, mother-led families? The difficulty is that Chodorow ignores the vast complexities of family life in modern societies, and privileges instead a traditionalist style of mothering that today is rapidly in decline. As Lynne Segal writes: 'I have found everywhere evidence of the amazing diversity buried within the ideology of the familial: fathers who were present and caring, 'working' mothers who were strong and powerful within the home, daughters who bonded tightly with fathers or older brothers, mothers who could not love their sons, mothers who never accepted their daughters, mothers who identified with their sons, and so on.'[7] I agree with Segal, but it is important to press this point further. The reason that such emotional diversity in the parent/child bond remains missing from Chodorow's work stems from her overconcentration on maternal desire – that is, on how the mother relates to her child. This focus, when used in isolation from psychoanalysis, means that the emerging infant is viewed only as a cipher in the construction of selfhood and gender. Yet it seems more likely, and certainly more in keeping with psychoanalytic theory, that identity construction also arises from the infant's internal world.

Following directly from this, Chodorow's use of object relations theory has been criticized for misreading core tenets of psychoanalysis. According to some critics, her concept of 'core gender identity' returns us to a *pre*-Freudian view of subjectivity, one that altogether brackets the psychoanalytic discovery of pre-Oedipal bisexuality and instead affirms the consoling unity of personal identity. Consequently, instead of exploring the problematic construction of sexual difference and gender, Chodorow can only describe how culturally dominant sex-roles become interwoven with core masculine and feminine identities. Her whole model, in other words, is a functionalist version of how sexual identities are generated to mirror gender power in patriarchal modern class society. As Jacqueline Rose notes, Chodorow's psychoanalytic feminism fails to get beyond a basic socio-logical notion of 'gender imprinting'.[8] Related to this is the criticism that, in diverting attention from the split and conflict-ridden 'subject' of psychoanalytic discourse, Chodorow collapses the dynamic interplay between the psychic and social fields. Lost are the vital psychoanalytic concepts of unconscious desire, anxiety, trauma, condensation and displacement – all of which suggest that gender roles are provisional, always in the process of dispersion, dismantling and recon-struction. Instead, sexual difference is replaced by an unproblematic version of sanitized sex-roles.

Finally, there are substantive problems with the emancipatory claims of this theory. Chodorow argues that, under conditions of shared parenting, men would develop the kind of relational qualities that women possess, while women would be free to develop personal autonomy. But if one considers the terms of Chodor-ow's analysis – that gender identity is powerfully shaped in negative and polarizing forms – it is not at all clear how women and men might liberate themselves from the destructive gender identities that currently preoccupy them. Is Chodorow, then, simply too optimistic about shared parenting? From a feminist angle, the answer is surely yes. Chodorow offers no convincing psychoanalytic reasons as to why shared parenting would eradicate male domination or transform gender power. Neither does she consider that her account of gender transformation fits neatly with dominant cultural fantasies which idealize fathers as figures of separ-ation and agency, while devaluing mothers as models for gender autonomy. The problem, then, is not that increased male participation in child-rearing fails to bring greater intimacy into the parent/child relationship – clearly, it often does. Rather, the difficulty is that there is no reason to suppose that shared parenting will, of itself, alter power relations between men and women. Chodorow's theory, in other words, fails to consider the structural, symbolic forms of gender hier-archy. Instead, her account (at both the descriptive and prescriptive levels) re-duces the social to familial ideology – thus screening from view the wider social, cultural and political forces constitutive of patriarchy.

Feminist issues in contemporary object relations theory

Object relations theory of the kind advanced by Chodorow and Dinnerstein is unable to grapple with the structural determinants which underpin asymmetric gender relations. Recent approaches in object relations feminism, however, do focus on the symbolic forms of gender constitution, and, unlike Chodorow, have not concentrated exclusively on maternal behaviour. Indeed, attention has turned to the emotional world of the developing infant, as related to the structural positioning of mother, father and the ideological complexities of contemporary gender relations. Though there are many theorists that might have been examined, I have chosen in what follows to concentrate briefly on the conceptual departures of Jessica Benjamin, Madelon Sprengnether and Jane Flax.

A critical theory of gender, argues Jessica Benjamin in *The Bonds of Love* (1988), should focus on women's lack of agency within the wider social context of power relations. Like Chodorow, Benjamin sees the contemporary gender system as locating the mother at the pole of biological regression on the one hand, with the father at the pole of progressive agency on the other. Yet unlike Chodorow, Benjamin refuses to view the psychic world of the developing child as simply mirroring gender asymmetry. On the contrary, Benjamin contends that it is necessary to tackle head-on 'the problem of desire': that is, the identifications and cross-identifications through which the infant establishes basic differences between itself and other people. To do this, Benjamin develops the concept of 'identificatory love', which is a pre-Oedipal phase of rapprochement in which the child seeks to establish a sense of attachment *and* separation with parental figures. Emotional continuity is central here. Through identification, the small child is able to separate out a sense of self while remaining emotionally connected to others.

According to Benjamin, if one examines the roles of the sexes in modern culture it becomes evident that pre-Oedipal identificatory love is routinely denied and displaced. Children of both sexes cannot maintain their identificatory love for the mother since she is devalued by current sexual ideology. This leads Benjamin to adopt a similar position to Chodorow. The core of her argument is that, while boys can identify with the father and his phallus to separate from the mother and establish autonomous individuality, the same path to psychic individuation is denied to girls. An alternate, empathic relationship with the exciting father, says Benjamin, is usually refused, the result being women's 'lack' of desire and its return as masochism in idealizations of male power. For Benjamin, what this means is that the tension between dependence and independence, which underpins healthy emotional relationships, breaks down within culture at large. Moreover, sexual relations between men and women grow diseased and deformed into master/slave patterns.

In *Like Subjects, Love Objects* (1995) and *The Shadow of the Other* (1998), Benjamin explores in more detail the range of multiple identifications that women and men forge or discover through sexual object choice as well as the negotiation of personal identity. In this interpersonal feminist psychoanalysis,

Benjamin elaborates upon post-Oedipal constructions in which the self accepts multiplicity and difference, owns complementary erotic fantasies or gender ideals, and tolerates oscillating and alternating identifications. Benjamin's arguments in these works are highly complex, though she starts from the relatively uncontentious position that traditional psychoanalysis has been too father or masculine-centred. She forcefully questions Freud's construction of gender identity along the lines of splitting and polarization – masculinity versus femininity, activity versus passivity, same versus other. Oedipal theory, says Benjamin, too neatly divides the sexes around the notion of anatomical difference, foreclosing the myriad psychic paths through which individuals identify with, as well as emotionally own, both masculine and feminine ideals within the self.

Against the Oedipal construction in which object love and identification are polarized, Benjamin focuses instead on the murky, indistinct emotional identifications with both mother and father, stressing throughout that interpersonal relationships and fantasy always coexist. Perhaps what is most important here is Benjamin's stress on the bisexual or polymorphous identifications of the most primitive stage of psychosexual development, the pre-Oedipal position. According to Benjamin, pre-Oedipal bisexuality suggests that the defensive repudiation of opposite sex identifications in the Oedipal stage depends upon a denial of bisexual identifications as well as the adoption of mutually exclusive gender positions. Such substitution of paradox for polarity, argues Benjamin, may be an accurate portrayal of dominant forms of gender relationship in masculinist culture. However, her critical point is that the recuperation of the pre-Oedipal phase can be revisited throughout life, and indeed cross-identifications of the pre-Oedipal stage, with tolerance for difference and multiplicity, inform what she terms the 'post-Oedipal' configuration, in which a more playful and creative approach is taken to identity, sexuality and gender. Benjamin distinguishes between the Oedipal and post-Oedipal constellations of identity in the following manner:

> It is possible to distinguish between two forms of complimentarity. The earlier Oedipal form is a simple opposition, constituted by splitting, projecting the unwanted elements into the other; in that form, what the other has is 'nothing'. The post-Oedipal is constituted by sustaining the tension between contrasting elements, so that they remain potentially available rather than forbidden and so that the oscillation between them can be pleasurable rather than dangerous.[9]

Expressed in this way, Benjamin's argument carries interesting implications for the analysis of gender, particularly as regards the development of boys. According to Benjamin, the psychological task of replacing splitting and polarization with the sustaining of psychic tension and the ability to manage opposing emotional dispositions towards self and other results from fluid boundaries between Oedipal and post-Oedipal configurations. For the boy, inclusion of denied feelings or blocked identifications depends upon regaining contact with multiple identifications of the pre-Oedipal period, in particular experience of the mother as a creative subject.

What of the possibilities for change? Benjamin differs sharply from both Chodorow and Dinnerstein in her evaluation of gender transformation. Paternal identification, Benjamin says, can play a positive role in the achievement of autonomous female subjectivity. According to Benjamin, however, any identification with the father is likely to prove counterproductive as long as the cultural devaluation of women remains in place. In this context, an alteration of parenting arrangements – as proposed by Chodorow and Dinnerstein – is itself an insufficient basis to transform gender structures. Non-repressive gender relations, Benjamin argues, depend rather on replacing the cultural split of progressive, autonomous father against regressive mother with new sexual identifications that permit a less rigid set of sexual roles. This would involve the repudiation of defensive modes of separation – that is, the father's phallus would no longer be used as the dominant medium to beat back an engulfing mother. Instead, children might construct more fluid sexual identifications – expressing both masculine and feminine aspects of identity – in relation to a socially and sexually autonomous mother, and a more empathic, caring father. Two figures of love and idealization – mother and father – are thus located as necessary for the creation of non-patriarchal patterns of socialization.

Pursuing these themes, Madelon Sprengnether in *The Spectral Mother* (1990) contends that psychoanalysis has itself devalued female subjectivity. The phallocentrism of psychoanalysis, according to Sprengnether, is evident in Freud's own ambivalence towards the mother, an ambivalence that at once makes the maternal the centre point of emotional experience and receptacle of the projection of desire. This romanticization of maternity, Sprengnether says, is reinforced throughout post-Freudian psychoanalysis, from postulations of 'good-enough mothering' in object relations theory to the rich maternal splendour of the imaginary order as described by Lacanians. For Sprengnether, as for Benjamin, assumptions which negate the complexity of women's subjectivity must be rejected and overturned. In this connection, the question for psychoanalytic feminism becomes how to reconceive of the maternal in a manner that does not result in the exclusion of the feminine from society and culture. The answer Sprengnether offers is that the 'body of the mother' – in light of the multiple trajectories of desire – represents an alternative paradigm for the constitution of an elementary form of selfhood. Taking aim at the patriarchal, theoretical gestures of Oedipus and the holy phallus, Sprengnether contends that the mother's body is fluid and plural, a foundation for the emergence of difference and estrangement, the site of an originary, non-violent separation between self and other. The maternal body is thus opposed to the fixed boundaries of Oedipal significations, and functions as a creative source in the replay of non-identity. Ultimately, the maternal body, Sprengnether contends, is a locus of otherness and familiarity, difference and identity. Since all human beings enter the world through the body of a woman, maternal subjectivity is a presence always coloured by absence. As Sprengnether puts this: 'Rather than fleeing, condemning, or idealizing the body of the (m)other, we need to recognize her in ourselves.'[10]

This raises the vexed question, much debated in feminist theory, as to whether the lifting of repression can be directly connected to the achievement of equality in gender relations. This is an issue which has been taken up in recent times by the American psychoanalytic feminist Jane Flax, who argues that the object relational goals of interpersonal communication and dialogue are of central importance to gender transformation.[11] Flax criticizes the tendency in feminist politics to generalize gender roles – as in the commonplace view that women are in touch with their feelings, whereas men repudiate their capacity for intimacy. According to Flax, it is important to recognize that there are different modes of gender constitution, and that each mode is harnessed to power interests in different ways. In the plural sexual domains of postmodern culture, says Flax, gender is continually dislocated and dispersed. Difficulties with sexuality, love and intimacy are as common to women as to men. In this context, Flax underscores the object relational focus on emotional communication as essential to interpersonal equality and democracy. Recovering emotional communication with the self and with others is crucial to transformations of gender. The development of autonomy and respect between the sexes, informed by emotional links of self and other stretching back to the pre-Oedipal stage, is the basis for an open-ended restructuring of gender. What is being stressed here is the capacity of both sexes to re-eroticize interpersonal relations. It is not a question of which of the sexes is better placed to undertake the emotional work of gender struggle. Rather, the human capacity for emotional connection is something that has to be worked at by men and women.

At this point, we can summarize the key issues raised in object relations feminism in the following terms:

1. Psychical organization is constituted in relationship with the pre-Oedipal mother; this is a relation which forms internalized object relational patterns essential to selfhood and gender identity.
2. Contemporary sexual divisions, especially exclusive female mothering, is pivotal to analysing the reproduction of male-dominant gender relations.
3. Contemporary family arrangements produce male identities with isolated, instrumental relations to the world, and female identities with empathic, caring connections to others.

4. Sexual divisions, as currently constituted, fuse to reproduce asymmetrical gender relations of power; such relations are directly bound up with technical frameworks involving economic, social and political institutions.
5. Gender transformation presumes a recovery of the feminine and female sexuality, rooted in reflexively negotiated relations of care, respect and emotional communication between the sexes.

Lacanian feminism

In recent years within psychoanalytic feminism, attention has turned to Lacanian theory in order to advance political debate on subjectivity and sexuality. Feminists who defend, and those that recontextualize, Lacanian psychoanalysis stress the role of symbolic forms in the structuring of desire – even that primary bond between child and mother, a bond so dear to object relations theorists. In contrast to object relations feminism, Lacanians argue that there can be no experience of sexuality and gender not generated through the symbolic codes of contemporary culture. To hold otherwise – Lacanians contend – is to read back into the pre-Oedipal stage sexual distinctions which do not arise until after the symbolic law of the Oedipus complex impacts upon the child. In Lacanian feminism, subjectivity and sexuality are by definition tied to language and culture. The symbolic, language, the Law of the Father, the phallus as transcendental signifier: these are, in Lacanian feminism, key mechanisms through which asymmetrical power relations between men and women are reproduced.

In order to understand Lacanian claims about our current gender system, it is necessary to situate Lacan's doctrine in relation to older psychoanalytic debates about female sexuality. Very broadly speaking, these debates revolve around the following, opposing claims: those that rely on traditional Freudian theory, and assert that sexuality is constituted through the effects of 'castration'; and those that derive their theoretical base from post-Freudian clinical work, focusing on the pre-Oedipal development of sexuality and gender.

Let us recall some pertinent features of the traditional Freudian view of sexual difference, previously discussed in Chapter 1. Bisexuality, says Freud, is at the bedrock of psychic organization for both sexes. The very persistence of unconscious, infantile sexuality in human development (that is to say, variability in sexual aim and contingency of object choice) means that identity and gender are precarious constructs. Freud's point here is that unconscious dimensions of sexuality continually undercut any consistent form of identity. Sexual identity thus involves repression, and as such is fractured in expression. But how is sexual identity constituted? For Freud, sexual subjectivity is organized phallically. The psychical distinction between the sexes takes place in a social context which gives it its meaning. That context is patriarchy; in psychoanalytic terms, the paternal institution of sexual prohibition in the Oedipus complex. This complex initiates sexual division, a division in relation to language, power, cultural processes and social institutions. This is a division that places man closest to the machinations of power, and excludes woman.

By contrast, many psychoanalytic theorists have expressed dissatisfaction with Freud's sexual monism, and have endeavoured to introduce greater complementarity into the psychoanalytic understanding of sexual development. In this connection, the view that femininity arises from a failed sense of masculinity has been firmly rejected by many post-Freudian theorists. Instead, a core sense of gender identity is presupposed for both sexes from the beginning of life. Much more weight is accorded to the infant's developing awareness and experience of gender, which in turn becomes the primary determinant of sexual difference. (The work of Dinnerstein, Chodorow and others in the object relations school presuppose such a pre-Oedipal gendered subject.) Accordingly, there is a shift in focus here away from the father and Oedipus towards the mother and pre-Oedipal relations.

Casting a careful eye over the complexities of these positions, Lacan's innovation is to develop a language-centred rereading of Freud's Oedipus complex – the crucial moment of psychic individuation – while incorporating elements of post-Freudian revisionism. What Lacan does, in effect, is to redescribe the primary mother/infant bond as a realm of imaginary desire, while simultaneously shifting gears to the structuring of Oedipal desire, described at the level of the symbolic order. The key term in Lacan's work which explains this division between imaginary unity and symbolic differentiation is the phallus. For Lacan, as for Freud, the phallus is the marker of sexual difference par excellence. The phallus smashes the incestuous unity of the mother/infant relation, and thereby constitutes the identity of a subject. The fundamental difference between Freud and Lacan, however, is that the latter claims to disconnect the phallus from any linkage with the biological penis. The phallus, says Lacan, is illusory, fictitious, imaginary. The phallus exists less in the sense of biology than in fantasy, merging desire with power, omnipotence and wholeness.

But what role, exactly, does the phallus play in psychic individuation? According to Lacan, the desire of the child – of either sex – is to *be* the exclusive desire of the mother. The child, however, soon learns that the mother herself is lacking. The child becomes aware that the mother's desire is invested elsewhere: in the father and his phallus. Significantly, the child's discovery that the mother is lacking occurs at the same time that it is discovering itself in language and culture, as a separate individual identity. This situation arises, says Lacan, with the entry of a third person (the father) or term (language). It is the symbolic function of the father, as possesser of the phallus, to prohibit Oedipal desire – a prohibition which at one stroke constitutes the repressed unconscious. Lacan argues that the sexes enter the symbolic order of language as castrated. The moment of separation from imaginary plenitude is experienced as loss, the loss of connection with the imaginary, archaic mother. The pain of this loss *is* castration. The child imagines the phallus as the source of the mother's desire, and from this perspective both males and females experience loss, depression and a profound sense of emptiness.

While lack transcends gender, Lacan says that to enter the symbolic order is to enter the realm of the masculine. That is to say, while both male and female children are castrated (the pain that neither can be everything for the mother), the phallus in modern culture comes to be identified with the penis and with male power. Gender identity is formed through a privileging of the visible, of having or not having the phallus. Males are able to assume phallic privilege since the image of the penis comes to stand for sexual difference. As Lacan puts this: 'It can be said that the [phallic] signifier is chosen because it is the most tangible element in the role of sexual copulation ... it is the image of the vital flow as it is transmitted in generation.'[12] Masculinity is constructed around the sign of the phallus, a sign which confers power in most social contexts. By contrast, femininity is constructed through exclusion from the symbolic realm of power. Femininity is outside language, culture, reason and power. 'There is no woman,' says Lacan, 'but excluded from the value of words.'[13] Lacan's interpretation of sexuality and gender thus underwrites current stereotypes – male sexuality as active and striving, female sexuality as essentially passive. This account of sexuality has been greeted as descriptive, not prescriptive. Women have been excluded, brutally and violently, from masculinist culture and discourse. Yet Lacan's description of how one is constructed as masculine or feminine seeks also to destabilize dominant images of sexuality. Beyond his bleak Oedipal reinforcement of the rule of the phallus, Lacan's self-appointed task is to unmask the 'fraud' of sexual identity. According to Lacan, though sexuality is articulated around the phallus, human subjects remain fundamentally split at the core. Desire lurks beneath the very signifiers that structure sexuality. Gender fixity is thus always open to displacement. Woman as the excluded Other is certainly consistent with the gender structure of modern societies; but it is this absence of the feminine which also threatens to outstrip the very foundations of sexual division.

The broader implications of the preceding discussion can now be expounded upon. For Lacan, the phallocentric organization of sexual subjectivity cannot be divorced from the discontinuous nature of unconscious desire. It is within the terms of sexual difference, the symbolic order and language that subject positions of masculinity and femininity are constituted. Yet gender organization is in turn outstripped by the fractures of the unconscious. Sexual subjectivity and loss are inextricably linked for Lacan, and the phallus just *is* that transcendental signifier which represses or covers over the missing object of desire at the level of gender division. Exactly why this loss of imaginary plenitude, and the subsequent impinging of symbolic reality, must be organized in such a one-sided masculinist fashion is not something that unduly concerns the phallocentric Lacan – indeed, this is a point which has been taken up by many feminist critics of Lacanian theory. Nevertheless, Lacan's language-centred account of the function of the phallus is important since he demonstrates that sexual difference is not a mere reflex of anatomy. Rather, sexual difference is staged through fantasy, its effects dramatized at the level of the symbolic order.

Lacan's theory was taken up enthusiastically by the feminist critic Juliet Mitchell in her *Psychoanalysis and Feminism* (1974) – a widely read book in which the author employs Freudian and Lacanian psychoanalysis as a means of fusing a discussion of gender power with an Althusserian–Marxist account of capitalism. In Mitchell's view, Lacan's analysis of the phallic organization of sexuality and language deconstructs gender hierarchy in a way that feminists cannot afford to ignore. Lacan provides an account of sexual difference not according to some pre-given essence, but according to the phallocentric organization of modern culture. 'If psychoanalysis is phallocentric,' Mitchell writes, 'it is because the human social order that it perceives refracted through the individual human subject is patrocentric. To date, the father stands in the position of the third term that must break the asocial dyadic unit of mother and child.'[14] Mitchell argues that definitions of masculinity and femininity are constituted via the symbolic order – with man as a self-determining, autonomous agent, and woman the lacking Other, the cause of sexual desire. The political implications of such cultural fantasy, Mitchell argues, is that man imagines himself unified, projecting his sense of lack and otherness on to woman.

Employing the Lacanian concept of the symbolic order to deconstruct gender inequality is, however, politically problematic.[15] Mitchell's work examines how the inscription of gender power in language can be traced to social reproduction. For Mitchell, the patriarchal symbolic order constructs polarized sexual identities, which in turn leads to the reproduction of gender asymmetry. Apart from preaching the obvious (that is, that gender power is reproduced), however, Mitchell's analysis mistakenly assumes that the production of gender is a stable affair. But what of conflictual sexual ideologies? What of more fluid identities, in which gender difference is traversed by new heterosexual, gay and lesbian sexualities? It is true, of course, that any form of identity is situated within the parameters of a male-dominant socio-symbolic order. Yet different lifestyle choices and sexual orientations highlight the gross limitations of a socio-symbolic reductionist approach to issues of gender power. Such difficulties have their roots in broader theoretical impasses. In Mitchell's reading of Lacan, the symbolic order is all-enveloping, constituting polarized gender identities in a universal fashion. In this privileging the Lacanian account of the symbolic order, Mitchell disregards the turbulent and precarious terrain of unconscious sexuality and passion. She ignores the ways in which the unconscious often disrupts repressive gender categories. The issue of gender construction is thereby inserted into a conceptual straitjacket.

Not all Lacanian feminists take the symbolic order as a description of the fixity of gender identity. Jacqueline Rose, who worked with Mitchell in developing a powerful feminist reading of Lacan, contends that psychoanalysis explores the failure of sexual identity as much as its consolidation. As Rose puts this: 'If psychoanalysis can give an account of how women experience the path to femininity, it also insists, through the concept of the unconscious, that femininity is neither simply achieved nor is it ever complete.'[16] What might it mean to say that feminine identity, in some sense, fails? Since woman is consituted through the symbolic order as a sign of lack or otherness, says Rose, femininity constantly escapes language and cultural categorization. Put simply, women do not slip into feminine roles easily or painlessly. The 'feminine' in contemporary culture is associated with denial and repression. But it is also associated with resistance, in both the personal and institutional spheres. For example, the refusal to adopt 'feminine' passivity has been regarded by the medical establishment as a mark of hysteria – a kind of resistance to patriarchy.

As lack, as absence, as what is repressed within the male-dominated symbolic, feminine sexuality is always outside (and possibly beyond) the regulation of the phallic economy. Here Rose takes her cue from Lacan's late work on female sexuality. In his Seminar 'Encore' in 1972–3, Lacan articulates the concept of *jouissance*, a mysterious state of sexual joy, an erotic satisfaction which dissolves the boundaries of self and other. According to Lacan, women hold a special relationship to *jouissance*, an emotional state not contaminated by patriarchal discourse. In Rose's Lacanian gloss:

> woman is implicated, of necessity, in phallic sexuality, but at the same time it is 'elsewhere that she upholds the question of her own *jouissance*'. . . Lacan designates this jouissance supplementary so as to avoid any notion of complement, of woman as a complement to man's phallic nature (which is precisely the fantasy). But it is also a recognition of the 'something more', the 'more than *jouissance*'. . . . Woman is, therefore, placed *beyond* (beyond the phallus).[17]

In brief, women's *jouissance* threatens a disruption to the phallic organization of language and culture, even though little can be said directly of this libidinal condition which remains excluded from symbolic representation.

The work of Rose represents an evocative blending of Lacanian theory and feminist politics, a politics that casts the feminine as a problem of desire itself. Her work is not, however, without difficulties. To begin with, what might a transfiguration in *jouissance* actually look like, outside individuals demonstrating, in some sense, libidinal pleasure or enjoyment? What of a critical interrogation of the feminine? Does this simply consist of a potential disruption to the socio-symbolic order, or might it involve a transformation of gender power itself? The problem here, in other words, is that if *jouissance* cannot articulate itself at the level of the symbolic, it is difficult to understand how significant changes in gender relations may come about. Yet it is precisely this issue of the specificity of female sexual subjectivity that will be taken up by post-Lacanian feminists, a version of feminist theory which leads to quite different conclusions about sexuality and culture.

Feminism beyond Lacan

In recent years, there have been numerous attempts to articulate an alternative vision of sexual subjectivity in feminist thought. This re-evaluation of femininity is generally referred to as post-Lacanian feminism, and it has a number of different theoretical manifestations. This branch of feminist psychoanalysis is 'Lacanian' because it adopts a broadly structural interpretation of masculine and feminine gender categories, viewing woman as the excluded Other of masculine discourse and culture. But it is also 'anti-Lacanian' since it opposes the view that woman can only be defined as the mirror opposite of the masculine subject, and thus never escape the domination of a rigidly genderized discourse. Instead, post-Lacanian feminists evoke a positive image of femininity, an image that underscores the multiple and plural nature of women's sexuality.

Julia Kristeva: the politics of subversion

One of the most influential sources for this kind of feminism is the work of the internationally renowned psychoanalyst Julia Kristeva. Kristeva is a Professor of Linguistics at the University of Paris VII, who did her psychoanalytic training with Lacan. A literary critic and novelist, Kristeva's work blends together psychoanalytic theory, structural linguistics and European philosophy to produce a suggestive account of the relations between repressed desire, human sexuality and contemporary culture.

In *Revolution in Poetic Language* (1984), Kristeva contrasts Lacan's account of the symbolic order – the social and sexual system of the Law of the Father – with those multiple psychic forces which she terms 'semiotic'. The semiotic, according to Kristeva, is primarily prolinguistic – semiotic processes include libidinal energies and bodily rhythms experienced by the child during the pre-Oedipal relationship with the mother. For Kristeva, these pre-Oedipal forms undergo repression with entry to the social and cultural processes of the symbolic order. That is to say, the flux of semiotic experience is channelled into the relatively stable domain of symbolization and language. However, Kristeva contends that the repression of the semiotic is by no means complete; the semiotic remains present in the unconscious and cannot be shut off from culture.

Against this psychoanalytic backdrop, Kristeva explicitly connects her analysis of femininity with the maternal. According to Kristeva, our semiotic longing for the pre-Oedipal mother is part and parcel of selfhood, making itself felt through tonal rhythms, slips and silences in everyday speech. These semiotic forces, she insists, are subversive of the symbolic order, primarily since they are rooted in a pre-patriarchal connection with the mother's body. Hence, the subversive or disruptive potential of the semiotic is closely interwoven with femininity. But it would be a mistake to say that the semiotic belongs exclusively to women. On the contrary, the semiotic is a pre-Oedipal realm of experience that comes into being prior to sexual difference – or so says Kristeva. If the semiotic is 'feminine', this is a femininity always potentially available to women and men in their efforts to transform identity and gender power. As children of both sexes initially belong to women – that is, to a woman's body – all individuals are faced with the emotional task of establishing a relation with the feminine. Femininity cannot be discussed, argues Kristeva, without confronting the impact of the maternal.

Kristeva sees artistic creation and literary expression as possible containers for unspoken experience, in particular giving symbolic form to the semiotic. It is in the cultural products of the artist or the writer, says Kristeva, that the semiotic may impress itself upon symbolic structures, thus threatening established meaning. She finds such a poetics of the semiotic in the writings of various avant-garde authors, principally Mallarmé, Lautreamont, Artaud and Joyce. While all male authors, Kristeva makes much of the aesthetic structure of such poetic language, especially the shifting field of semiotic forces that unlinks obvious meaning. Here Kristeva stresses that the energy of the pre-Oedipal semiotic ushers in a 'feminine articulation of pleasure', a realm of secret desires which defies patriarchal culture and language. In other writings, Kristeva attempts to give the idea of semiotic subversion further empirical content through the study of motherhood. In pregnancy, Kristeva says, woman can recover a repressed relation to the semiotic maternal through the profound emotional experience of giving birth. Pregnancy involves a kind of pleasurable, creative linking with otherness. In her essay 'Women's Time', for instance, she argues that pregnancy reproduces 'the radical ordeal of the splitting of the subject: redoubling of the body, separation, and coexistence of the self and of an other, of nature and consciousness, of physiology and speech'.[18] This mode of relating, Kristeva says, involves a potential reconstruction of human social relationships, one in which a new relation to the semiotic body, its pleasures, and its dismantling of fixed oppositions (self/Other, man/woman) can overturn existing masculinist culture.

Kristeva further expands her account of the complex interplay of semiotic and symbolic orders with the concept of the 'abject'. The abject for Kristeva is a kind of startling, disturbing fantasy that provides an imaginary lining to self-experience and, therefore, allows the infant to separate itself from the pre-Oedipal mother. More specifically, Kristeva argues that the pre-Oedipal mother becomes abject, an object of horror, distaste and fear. Like Dinnerstein and Chodorow, Kristeva contends that the infant fears the omnipotent powers of the pre-Oedipal mother, and thus expels or abjects her in order to create a separate psychic space. Related to this is the intervention of the 'father of personal pre-history', or pre-Oedipal father, which the infant identifies with in order to break with the omnipotent mother. The imaginary, pre-Oedipal father is understood in Lacanian terms as the mother's desire for the phallus. Yet the crucial point about these psychic processes for Kristeva is that they indicate a profound mixing of maternal and paternal power in infant development. According to Kristeva, desire of the archaic mother is not fully repressed with entry to symbolization and culture – as Lacan tends to suggest. On the contrary, there is a continual shuttling between the semiotic and symbolic, maternal fragmentation and paternal structuration.

In her most recent work, especially *Tales of Love* (1987), *Black Sun* (1989) and *New Maladies of the Soul* (1993), Kristeva examines the psychic turmoil produced by contemporary culture with reference to the themes of depression, mourning and melancholia. In depression, says Kristeva, there is an emotional disinvestment from the symbolic power of language. The depressed person, overwhelmed by sadness (often as a result of lost love), suffers from a paralysis of symbolic activity. In effect, language fails to fill in or substitute for what has been lost at the level of the psyche. The loss of loved ones, the loss of identity, the loss of pasts: as the depressed person loses all interest in the surrounding world, in language itself, psychic energy shifts to a more primitive mode of functioning, to a maternal, drive-related form of experience. In short, depression produces a trauma of symbolic identification, a trauma which unleashes the power of semiotic energy. In the force field of the semiotic – rhythms, changes in intonation, semantic shifts – Kristeva finds a means to connect the unspoken experience of the depressed person to established meaning, thereby permitting a psychic reorganization of the self. It is against this background that Kristeva stresses the deeper political implications of psychoanalysis: she contends that psychotherapeutical work with her patients is more likely to produce lasting personal and political changes than is political activity on a more institutional level. In Kristeva's rendering, psychoanalysis *is* radical political activity.

Kristeva's theory of the feminine semiotic, as a mode of experience available to women and men in the restructuring of gender power, has been fiercely contested, both inside and outside feminist quarters. For example, it has been claimed that, in collapsing the feminine with unconscious experience, Kristeva argues for a political pluralism without feminist content.[19] In this critique, women's actual experiences of both oppression and active gender struggle are displaced in favour of an abstract, male model of semiotic (literary) practice. From the other side of the coin, Kristeva has also been charged with essentialism and sexual separatism – with reducing semiotic subversion to the biological conditions of motherhood, and thereby erasing the capacity of men (and also of women who choose not to be mothers) to partake in radical gender struggle.[20] Neither of these criticisms is, in my view, accurate. It is important to see that Kristeva is not claiming the semiotic realm as the exclusive province of either women or men – even if there may be an essentialist slippage in her account of motherhood. Rather, Kristeva teaches us to see that, as split, desiring subjects, we all have a pre-Oedipal, feminine connection with the mother, a connection which is potentially subversive of patriarchal logic and thought. There is indeed a problem, though, in Kristeva's account of the political implications of semiotic subversion. Kristeva assumes that semiotic displacements in language and culture are, in some sense, equivalent to overturning and transforming social and political relations. However, it seems to me that this is a hazardous connection at best. How, exactly, might semiotic silences and displacements be used to overcome repressive gender relations? How, for example, might semiotic subversions transform or eradicate gender tensions, sexual violence or pornography? Kristeva's theory in this respect needs more specification. The possible links between the semiotic and critical self-reflection are sidestepped in her analysis, thus leaving little possibility for a meaningful psychic reorganization of the self.

Luce Irigaray: representing the feminine

There may, however, be compelling psychological or emotional grounds for supposing that feminine sexuality is disavowed within the symbolic order of contemporary culture. According to the French philosopher Luce Irigaray, the feminine cannot be adequately symbolized – in discourse or in theory – under patriarchy, as femininity is the repressed or hidden support structure upon which phallocentric social relations depend. Irigaray, taking her cue from Lacan, proposes the feminine as permanently excluded from language in the symbolic order. She writes of the corrosive personal consequences for women of the process of 'specularization'; women, she says, reflect back to men particular phallocentric ideals concerning masculinity, such that the feminine is defined not in its own terms, but always as mirror, reflection or object. From maternal devotion to sexual masquerade, the seductive presence of the feminine frames the illusions of masculine desire.

More concretely, Irigaray argues that the pre-Oedipal mother/daughter relationship remains on the 'outside' of symbolic boundaries – an outside that leaves women in a state of 'déréliction', undifferentiated from maternal space. As she puts this, 'there is no possibility whatsoever, within the current logic of socio-cultural operations, for a daughter to situate herself with respect to her mother:

because, strictly speaking, they make neither one nor two, neither has a name, meaning, sex of her own, neither can be "identified with respect to the other" '.[21]

In contrast to Lacan, however, Irigaray contends that the idea of woman as outside and Other always threatens subversion, thus transforming the dominant masculinist social order. The feminine, says Irigaray, threatens subversion to patriarchal language and culture. Here Irigaray's position has affinities with Kristeva's notion of the semiotic. However, Irigaray goes further than Kristeva as regards the disruptive impact of female sexuality, proposing a direct link between women, feminine sexuality and the body. In line with other feminists of the 'écriture féminine' movement, such as Hélène Cixous, Irigaray grounds the feminine in women's experience of sexuality and the body, an experience which is plural, dispersed and multiple. Women, says Irigaray, need to establish a different relationship to feminine sexuality, affecting a range of displacements to patriarchy through writing as a cultural practice. Speaking the feminine, says Irigaray, can transform the constricted and constricting sexed identities of patriarchy. In her more recent work, from *An Ethics of Sexual Difference* (1993) to *To Be Two* (1999), Irigaray locates the renegotiation of identities in the frame of ethical practice, specifically the recognition of the otherness of the other sex. An ethics of sexual difference, she argues, would respect the Other in her or his own right, with regard or sensitivity to finitude, mortality, creation and the divine.

Irigaray's psychoanalytic feminism, especially her early writings, has been sharply criticized as biologically essentialist. Here it is suggested that Irigaray's direct appeal to feminine specificity or the material female body assumes that there is an unchanging, transhistorical female sexuality subversive of all social contexts. This critique of Irigaray's essentialism has been forcefully developed by both Moi and Segal. Other feminists have questioned this essentialist critique, and have instead argued that Irigaray's work seeks to theorize the reproduction and transformation of feminine specificity in terms of the broader cultural force of sexual difference. While Irigaray is certainly concerned to trace the impact of distorting socio-symbolic forces upon the pre-Oedipal mother/daughter relationship, it does seem that her appeal to feminine specificity is problematic to say the least. Juliet Mitchell sums up the difficulty with this position: 'You cannot choose the imaginary, the semiotic, the carnival as an alternative to the symbolic, as an alternative to the law. It is set up by the law precisely as its own lurid space, its own area of imaginary alternative, but not as a symbolic alternative. So that politically speaking, it is only the symbolic, a new symbolism, a new law, that can challenge the dominant law.'[22]

Judith Butler: gender as performance

Like Kristeva and Irigaray, the writings of the feminist critic Judith Butler also problematize the notion of essential 'female' identity as necessary for feminist politics and radical political action. Butler, a Professor at the University of California, Berkeley, quickly established herself with the publication of *Gender Trouble: Feminism and the Subversion of Identity* (1990) at the forefront of feminism, women's studies, lesbian and gay studies, and queer theory. Indeed the core idea expounded in *Gender Trouble* – that gender is a kind of improvised performance, a form of theatricality that constitutes our sense of identity – came to be read by many as foundational to the project of queer theory and the advancing of dissident sexual practices during the 1990s. Indeed, the book was used to question both the 'naturalness' of gender and also the fictions that support compulsory heterosexuality and polarities of gender (heterosexual/homosexual, masculine/feminine, active/passive, etc.). Interestingly, Butler herself has been reluctant to define her work solely in terms of the project of queer theory; she has described herself primarily as a feminist philosopher, whose work combines cultural theory, psychoanalysis and modern European thought. What is perhaps most suggestive about her writings, at least from a psychoanalytic perspective, is the deft manner in which she argues that sex and sexuality cannot be separated off from, or contained by, the category of gender; her problematization of whether sexual or gender difference is preferable as a category for feminist analysis; and her detailed critique of psychoanalytical perspectives on sexual difference, primarily through a dialogue of Freudian–Lacanian psychoanalysis and Foucaldian theory.

In questioning traditional divisions between 'sex', 'sexuality' and 'gender', Butler contends that biology is not, in itself, a neutral foundation on which culture inscribes different categories of sexual identity. The biological realm for Butler is itself culturally gendered; there is no biological foundation at the heart of gender. Sex, sexuality and gender are cultural constructs, fully emotionally invested, performed and policed according to the dictates of a power that works in part to both establish and destablise individual subjects. As Butler writes:

> If sex and gender are radically distinct, then, it does not follow that to be a given sex is to become a given gender; in other words 'woman' need not be a cultural construction of the female body, and 'man' need not interpret male bodies.[23]

How is it, Butler seems to be asking, that culture limits our sexual repertoires. Here Butler questions the philosophical and political tie between anatomy, sex and gender. The search for foundations, she suggests, has made our sexual repertoires less imaginative than they might otherwise have been, partly because this search has been an attempt to guarantee meaning, and has been at the cost of displacing the theatricality integral to the making of sexual identity. 'Gender', writes Butler, 'is not to culture what sex is to nature; gender is also the discursive/cultural means by which "sexed nature" or "a natural sex" is produced and established as "prediscursive" prior to culture, a politically neutral surface on which culture acts' (*Gender Trouble*, p. 11).

Having questioned the entrenched idea that gender is an expression of biological sex, Butler turns to psychoanalysis to probe the psychic constellations that underpin gender identification. Here Butler invokes the notion of *performance*. She argues that the self is constituted in the act of performing sexuality, the enacting of desires, the doing of gender. Psychoanalysis is used by Butler in a profoundly interesting manner to probe the complex ways in which men and women establish identifications with masculinity and femininity; in our performative acts, says Butler, we are copying images of sexuality in order to create the effect of the natural, the original and the actual. But if this is true of our sexual identity, there is no gender performance more authentic than any other reckoning of gender. In what Butler calls 'the imaginable domain of gender', the stylized self imitates or copies the cultural representations of masculinity and femininity that individuals see routinely in the mass media. The performance of sexuality – straight, gay, transsexual – thus comes close to caricature, the imitation of enforced cultural codes, the copying of erotic copies. In giving psychoanalytic flavour to this notion of performance, Butler suggestively reworks Freud's concept of identification – the notion that the ego frames itself on the basis of objects once loved. The constitution of sexual identifications, according to Butler, is based upon the fantasized imitation or incorporation of lost loves, coupled with an acting out or performative display of erotic or gender signs. In this connection, Butler draws not only from Freud, but also Lacan, especially his provocative notion of the mirror stage. Sexuality, in Butler's appropriation of Lacanian psychoanalysis, is reproduced through performative display, by literalizing imaginary projections and recasting them as idealizations which secure sex and gender binaries.

Butler's account of the theatrical making and remaking of sexuality has been sharply criticized for its political voluntarism; the suggestion that individual subjects can construct or deconstruct sexual identities as they choose can only be maintained as long as one continues to ignore issues of social power, cultural context and political domination. This criticism, while accurate in some respects, misses the broader cultural context in which Butler views the crafting of dominant forms of sexuality; the production of sex and gender, says Butler, arises not as a matter of free choice, but rather as a result of the subject's embeddedness in a range of discourses available for delineating the self, all of which are overdetermined and invested with cultural norms, and thus contoured by heterosexual normative gender framings. However, Butler does see possible radical transformations in performative enactments of gender which may expose the constructed or artificial markers shaping dominant gender categories. Transgressive perform ances – such as drag – may, under the appropriate social context, undermine patriarchal discourses and the coercive power of heterosexuality.

More and more, Butler's writings in the late 1990s focused on gender identifications and attachments as theorized in psychoanalytic scholarship, specifically through the theorization of loss, suffering and melancholia. It is this focus on grief and sadness in particular, as explored in *The Psychic Life of Power* (1997), which provides a bridge between her earlier idea that the performances of sex retroactively produce the effect of core gender identities and her provocative notion that at the heart of gender lies unacknowledged grief. In contemporary society, according to Butler, recognition of, and engagement with, such disavowed grief accounts for our increasing cultural anxiety about masculinity and femininity.

In 'Melancholy Gender/Refused Identification', a chapter in *Psychic Life* that expertly wraps psychoanalysis within the concerns of contemporary feminist theory, Butler analyses gender performance as a kind of melancholy. In particular she examines Freud's reflections on loss, mourning and grief. Freud's argument that there is a deep and lasting emotional tie between love and loss on the one hand and identification and identity on the other is reconfigured in terms of feminist theory and sexuality studies. In Freud's theory, the loss of a loved person is at once painful and traumatic, to such an extent that the self incorporates aspects of the lost love as a means of (a) keeping at bay the pain of loss, and (b) gradually detaching from the lost love. In melancholia as opposed to normal mourning, Freud notes, the self fails to break from the lost love, and instead preserves love in the psyche by failing to mourn, by failing to use language or engage in symbolic activity. Butler agrees with the core thread of Freud's analysis, and notes that melancholic identification is not a means of breaking attachment with lost love, but rather a way of preserving objects internally.

Melancholic identification, says Butler, is highly consequential for gender. Reflecting on loss from a psychoanalytically informed feminist point of view, Butler stresses that people fashion identity against the emotional backdrop of unacknowledged suffering, grief and melancholia. She develops this standpoint in the following way:

> It seems clear that the position of 'masculine' and 'feminine' which Freud, in *Three Essays on the Theory of Sexuality* (1905), understood as the effects of laborious and uncertain accomplishment, are established in part through prohibitions which demand the 'loss' of certain sexual attachments, and demand as well that those losses not be avowed, and not be grieved. If the assumption of anonymity and the assumption of masculinity proceed through the accomplishment of an always tenuous heterosexuality, we might understand the force of this accomplishment as mandating the abandonment of homosexual attachments or, perhaps more trenchantly, pre-empting the possibility of homosexual attachment, a foreclosure of possibility which produces a domain of homosexuality understood as unliveable passion and ungrievable loss. This heterosexuality is produced not only through

implementing the prohibition on incest but, prior to that, by enforcing the prohibition on homosexuality.[24]

Here Butler refers to the ways in which gender is constituted through the repudiation of homosexual attachments, theorized in psychoanalytic doctrine through reference to the Oedipal conflict. For example, the little girl adopts a disposition towards femininity through her subjection to a prohibition that bars the mother as an object of desire, the result of which is to install a melancholic identification with such prohibited homosexual desire. This repudiated identification with the mother as an object of desire, and in particular the disavowal of her various loves and pleasures thus results in a rejection of love for one's own gender. Similarly, the consolidation of masculinity entails the repudiation of femininity as essential for the heterosexualization of male desire.

If gender identifications, accomplishments and performances are the result of an ungrieved loss, emotional sensitivity to suffering is made all the more difficult in a culture that Butler terms 'compulsory heterosexuality'. Heterosexuality is compulsory for Butler in the sense that it depends on the rigorous repudiation, foreclosure or exclusion of difference and otherness. Butler has discussed the prevalence of homophobia in the military and armed forces in the United States in an interview, where she commented 'that crafting a sexual position, or reciting a sexual position always involves becoming haunted by what's excluded. And the more rigid the position, the greater the ghost, and the more threatening it is in some way.'[25] According to Butler, homosexuality *panics* heterosexuality because it represents a return of the repressed; homosexual desire threatens the repudiated and unresolved knot of grief at the core of gendered identities.

Butler's most remarkable contribution to feminist thought has been her revelation of how refused identifications – repudiated, unresolved and disavowed – become literalized as gender certainties and thus infuse as fantasies the making of identities. Loss that is refused, says Butler, not only shapes – in a deeply emotional sense – the performance of sexuality, but structures gender idealization and the illusions of fantasy. The political purpose of Butler's psychoanalytic reflections, it seems, is to ask what it would be like to inhabit a culture that recognized and sanctioned discourse about such loss – that is to say, the provision of a public, political discourse which permitted mourning of disowned or repudiated gender identities. As a result, Butler's interrogation of psychoanalysis is politically compelling, uncovering the psychic sources of our discontent with sexuality and gender, while keeping open a space for more open and fluid gender possibilities. That being said, some critics worry that the voluntaristic emphasis that seemingly defines her notion of performance is at odds with her psychoanalytic understanding of loss, grief and melancholia. Butler, one might claim, is a kind of proto-postmodern feminist, advocating the power of emotional attachment as a consequence of melancholia, while dreaming of the transcendence of gender norms through improvisational theatrics for remaking sexuality. There may well be some truth to this charge, especially as regards the manner in which Butler's work has been taken up in sexuality studies for the analysis of queer or non-normative gender framings. My own view is that Butler anticipates no such transcendence (in the sense of utopian transformation) of the power of feelings within gender relationships; her own project, by contrast, is to trace forms of power as deeply interwoven with the emotional terrors and traumas of all gender identities.

Psychoanalytic feminism and sexual emancipation

What do current versions of psychoanalytic feminism suggest about gendered asymmetric relations of gender power? Most significantly, psychoanalytic feminism highlights the profound yet subtle links between unconscious desire and gender identity – thus raising subjectivity and sexuality as a problem for political debate. Focusing on the unconscious construction of sexual difference, psychoanalytic feminists (from diverse theoretical backgrounds) stress that socio-political change is a difficult and painful endeavour, and that there can be no easy paths to gender transformation. From this angle, psychoanalytic feminism is concerned with tracing the reproduction of gender hierarchy and women's subordination; or, as Mitchell puts this, psychoanalysis 'describes' rather than 'prescribes'. As it stands, however, it seems to me that such a descriptive approach to women's oppression cannot really address those issues that are most theoretically and politically difficult today. I have in mind here the horrific rise of sexual violence (ranging from sexual harassment to rape and body mutilation), underpinned by the cultural implosion of totalitarian and apocalyptic sexual fantasy. In such a political climate, the language of 'gender internalization' is no longer adequate (if, indeed, it ever was) to understand the social reproduction of sexual identifications and identities. The imaginary and symbolic forms constitutive of gender power need to be addressed in a different fashion, one that focuses on the imbalances and discontinuities of sexual identification as much as on the reproduction of gender significations. We need to know more about the psychic processes of sexual identification, and of how existing identifications interact, conflict and reinforce one another in the current gender system. We need to know more about the potentialities of such variations for subjectivity, sexuality and gender differentiation. And we need to know more about the enabling aspects of sexualities, enquiring at what point fantasy structures outstrip themselves and marshal human subjects into active forms of gender struggle and commitment.

In my view, if we are successfully to confront such issues, it will be necessary to develop a more open dialogue between competing theoretical approaches in psychoanalytic feminism. A more flexible conceptual approach to sexuality and gender, in particular, will need to tackle head-on the question of linking interpersonal analysis with a consideration of the broader symbolic forms that constitute and reproduce our unequal sexual world. In this respect, the consequences of the restructuring of family life is a good example of the need to overcome theoretical polarization. For the transformation of parenting – as the post-structural Lacanian critique highlights – cannot of itself change the symbolic force of the phallus in determining the meanings of sexual difference. However – and this is where the claims of Lacanian feminists are vulnerable – this does not mean that current transformations in familial ideology are not altering the domain of personal life – from which more wide-ranging social changes might spring. Clearly, we need to know more than we currently do about how the reorganization of the family in late modernity intersects with the reproduction of sexual difference. Is it producing more or less gender-divided identities? This is an area, I argue, that demands sustained theoretical and empirical consideration, not vague polemic.

Finally, what of the possibilities for sexual emancipation? Again, psychoanalytic feminism shows that this is not just some utopian dream. Rather, our liberation from gender oppression is already in process, discernible in the active struggles of women and men to reconstruct the links between personal life and the socio-political world. Sexuality and identity are being continually reforged in modern societies. The women's movement, men's groups, gay and lesbian forums: these are critical engagements with the ideological apparatus of patriarchy and the limits of sexual dualism. No one knows how far, or with what consequences, the psychic restructuring of gender may be practically effected. What can be said, however, is that psychoanalytic feminism has a crucial and ongoing role in helping to illuminate and guide the emotional processes by which polarized gender can be transformed.

Table 5.1 Psychoanalytic feminism

Theory	Sexuality and gender asymmetry	Key terms
Object relations feminism (Dinnerstein, Chodorow)	Exclusive female mothering constitutes gender power; transformed through shared parenting	Core gender identity Pre-Oedipal sexuality
Contemporary object relations feminism (Benjamin, Sprengnether, Flax)	Gender asymmetry structured within interpersonal relations	Mother as subject Intersubjectivity
Lacanian feminism (Mitchell, Rose)	Sexuality and gender constituted through socio-symbolic order	Patriarchal symbolic Sexual division
Post-Lacanian feminism (Kristeva, Irigaray, Butler)	Pre-Oedipal sexuality distorted by patriarchal symbolic; subversion through feminine imaginary	Semiotic Dereliction Female imaginary Melancholic identification

CHAPTER 6

The Dislocating World of Postmodernism

Identity in Troubled Times

We have seen that the concept of identity undergoes a significant transformation as a consequence of conceptual developments in contemporary psychoanalysis. How we view the identity of the self alters considerably depending on which version of psychoanalytic theory we turn to for instruction. In Freudian terms, selfhood can be thought of as a direct outcrop of the unconscious itself. In object relational theories this Freudian subject-centred analysis is overturned in favour of a more interpersonal approach. Object relational theorists, with differing descriptive accounts, argue it is more useful to think of self-identity as constituted within intersubjective relations, which may either facilitate or disrupt the psychic underpinnings of self-organization. Kleinians share this intersubjective focus, but critically underscore the internal world of fantasy which connects paranoid destructiveness and reparative despair to self-development. In Lacanian psychoanalysis, this potential for self-integration is deconstructed as an imaginary concealment of the absence and lack which haunts personal identity. Rather than bolstering the narcissistic illusions of the ego, Lacanians trace the subject as repressively inscribed within a symbolic network of unstable signifiers.

It can be argued, however, that all such attempts to theorize the 'subject' are themselves imaginary fictions. To divide the inner world into so many agencies or functions is, in fact, to engage in an act of conceptual house-tidying, a kind of repressive closure of the complexity and ambiguity of human experience itself. From this angle, the term 'subject' is just a shorthand way of designating at the level of theory the complex, contradictory elements of emotional life. Yet there really is no 'individual subject', as the sum total of psychical traces, elements and parts. All there is are fluid and multiple forms of libidinal enjoyment. The indeterminancy of desire, *jouissance*, the death drive, signifiers, bodily zones, intensities: there is only the pure multiplicity of unconscious pleasure unfolding endlessly.

With this vision of desire as decentred and desubjectivized we have entered the era of postmodernity – characterized by its suspicion of grand narratives and totalizing concepts, its deconstruction of all interpretative significance as

ideological closure, its debunking of the 'self-identical subject', its euphoric celebration of the particular, the fragmented, the indeterminate and the multidimensional. 'Postmodernity', Zygmunt Bauman writes,

> is modernity coming of age: modernity looking at itself at a distance rather than
> from the inside, making a full inventory of its gains and losses, psychoanalysing
> itself, discovering the intentions it never before spelled out, finding them mutually
> cancelling and incongruous. Postmodernity is modernity coming to terms with its
> own impossibility; a self-monitoring modernity, one that consciously discards what
> it was once unconsciously doing.[1]

Postmodernism, in this sense, exists as a *radicalized tendency* of modernity. The
postmodern is, as Jean-François Lyotard comments, a kind of 'working through
... operated by modernity on itself'.[2] Significantly, this postmodern self-monitor-
ing operates most powerfully at the level of ideas and theory, in and through a
critique of the conceptual realm as traversed by random libidinal intensities and
forces. Postmodernism, as Samuel Weber argues, proclaims that the 'self-dissimu-
lating distortions' uncovered by Freudian psychoanalysis saturate the entire field
of theoretical understanding; and to this, we might add, one field which cannot
escape such scrutiny is psychoanalytic discourse.[3]

The postmodern theories examined in this final chapter develop powerful, and
sometimes radical, readings of psychoanalysis. Postmodern theories deploy and
refashion psychoanalytic concepts, perhaps somewhat paradoxically, to launch a
sustained critique on the theoretical operations of psychoanalysis. Through a
discontinuous presentation of theory, the standpoints considered trace the inter-
relation between self and society in an age of pervasive globalization.

Deleuze and Guattari on capitalism and schizophrenia

In their celebrated work *Anti-Oedipus* (1977), Gilles Deleuze and Félix Guattari
elaborate a vision of schizophrenic desire as the basis for an account of postmodern politics and culture. *Anti-Oedipus*, a book that scandalized French psychoanalysis and generated heated disputes among intellectuals, develops a
postmodern psychoanalysis from two main perspectives. First, through using
psychoanalytic theory against itself, tracing how the repressive inscription of desire
within language is reinforced by the practice of psychoanalysis. Second, through
the dismantling of grand theory in favour of a multiple, desubjectivized account of
desire; this is a reading of psychoanalysis that constantly threatens to undermine
its own internal coherence. Deleuze and Guattari proclaim that schizophrenia is
the most promising guide to understanding the nature of desire in contemporary

culture. They propose a celebration of the fluid and multiple intensities of schizophrenic desire, intensities which they celebrate to oppose the repressive functioning of social norms and cultural traditions. To this end, they develop the notion of
a 'subjectless machine', a kind of schizophrenic overflowing of desire that produces and reproduces itself in aimless circulation. Against the Oedipalizing logic
of capitalist discourse, where desire is channelled into prescribed pathways under
the sign of the commodity, Deleuze and Guattari speak up for the impersonalized
flows of schizoid desire, a productive network of libidinal articulations which
potentially might short-circuit the symbolic order of capitalist production.

Deleuze and Guattari configure the social world as a mix of libidinal and
symbolic forms that continuously displace one another. Against this backdrop,
they present a speculative account of the historical development of capitalist
production. In its early stages, capitalism is said to have severed the economic
realm from symbolic forms such as kinship systems, customs, religious beliefs and
the like. Capitalist production, at this historical point, was embedded in a more or
less stable collectivity, with pre-given social roles and identities. The emergence of
monopoly capitalism, however, radically transforms the social world: it sweeps
away traditional social forms, as economic forces bite deeply into the symbolic
realm itself. The creation of an international capitalist system, it might be said,
breaks down the symbolic framework of the local community and of tradition.
Deleuze and Guattari refer to this process as the 'deterritorialization' of social
codes. What this means, roughly speaking, is that capitalism ruthlessly dismantles
bourgeois cultural forms and moral codes, replacing these with the exchangeability and anonymity of the commodity form. Deleuze and Guattari argue that the
logic of capitalist economic relations is deeply interwoven with the discontinuities
of schizophrenic desire. Like the indifference of the commodity itself, schizophrenia knows no symbolic limit, no constraint of reality, no high-minded guilt born of
the superego. Instead, schizoid desire produces itself in fragments of pleasure,
slicing capitalist temporality into the fluidity of the moment. 'The order of desire',
write Deleuze and Guattari, 'is the order of *production*; all production is at once
desiring production and social production.'[4]

Capitalism, however, not only deterritorializes outmoded social forms, but
constantly 'reterritorializes' in radically new ways. Against capitalism's dismantling of pre-existing social boundaries, Deleuze and Guattari point to a proto-
fascist, paranoiac tendency, a tendency at the heart of modernity, that restructures
schizoid flows into unified forms and cultural meanings. What is being emphasized here is the oppressive nature of late capitalist society, its recoding of desire
into the ordered, conventional world of international banking, stock markets and
insurance companies. Schizophrenic and paranoiac desire: both forms of production are to be found at different levels of the social system. Global capitalism
produces a profound deterritorialization of social forms into schizoid flows on the

one hand, while simultaneously recoding these flows into the symbolic circuit of culture on the other. From Perrier water to *Playboy* magazine: the schizophrenic signals of desire are endlessly recoded to support the economic logic of capitalism.

Like several psychoanalytic approaches we have looked at in earlier chapters, Deleuze and Guattari see the familial structure of Western culture as the key institutional mode of repressing desire in capitalism. Central to their interpretation of the Oedipus complex is the notion of a 'subjectless machine'. Desire prior to Oedipus, Deleuze and Guattari contend, is multidimensional, discontinuous and shifting. Desire just is the production of 'machine parts', spilling out across libidinal surfaces, pluralized in its operations through contact with other human 'machines'. As Deleuze and Guattari reconceptualize the pre-Oedipal moment: 'The breast is a machine that produces milk, and the mouth a machine coupled to it' (p. 1). Desire is thus schizoid and subjectless, an impersonal force of production. But not so after the effects of Oedipalization. The impersonal force of schizoid desire, according to Deleuze and Guattari, is repressively codified through Oedipus. That is to say, the Oedipus complex works to *personalize desire*, referring all unconscious productions to the incestuous sexual realm of the family network. Oedipus, then, is a prime instance of the capitalist recoding of desire. Deleuze and Guattari argue that psychoanalysis functions as a repressive force which projects desire into the personalized, neuroticized structures of 'daddy–mummy–me'.

It is worth noting that Deleuze and Guattari are by no means suggesting that this paranoiac process of capitalist reterritorialization is complete. For them, the schizoid nature of desire constantly escapes the well-ordered structures of capitalist production, at which point there is a dismantling of received social meanings. The schizoid tribulations of desire, argue Deleuze and Guattari, are transgressive, polymorphous and fragmenting. In its anarchic, heterogeneous lines of libidinal intensity, schizophrenic desire offers, paradoxically, to outstrip the centralized, unified organization of capitalist production in which it is encoded. 'Schizophrenia', write Deleuze and Guattari, 'is desiring production at the limit of social production' (p. 35). Like the Surrealist avant-garde, Deleuze and Guattari are fascinated by the notion of transgression, the breaking of limits, the undoing of rules. Smashing through the boundaries of ordinary life, schizoid desire is pure production: desire turning in upon itself to further the production of desire.

This valorization of the absolute positivity of desire is in direct contrast to the Lacanian model of the unconscious. Whereas Lacan posits unconscious desire as a product of lack, the cravings of the schizo-subject are conceived instead as pure affirmation. Lacan's casting of desire in terms of lack, absence and failure – so Deleuze and Guattari contend – is itself the projection of Oedipus into contemporary theory, institutions and affairs. Psychoanalysis, both traditional and Lacanian, constructs desire as loss for the purpose of adapting human subjects to the social order.[5] From this angle, psychoanalysis deciphers and reinscribes Oedipal compulsions for identification which are essential to the ego-centred, neurotic structures of subjecthood of late capitalism. In this manner, the signs of power constitute us as individual subjects through and through. In contrast, Deleuze and Guattari emphasize the multiple paths of desire – schizoid proliferations, openings, zigzags and flows. To designate this, they propose 'schizoanalysis', which interprets unconscious desire hydraulically as a desiring machine; unconscious flows of libidinal energy at once anchor and destabilize the social process. As they put this:

> To discover beneath the familial reduction the nature of the social investments of the unconscious. To discover under the individual fantasy the nature of group fantasies. Or, what amounts to the same thing, to push the simulacrum to the point where it ceases to be an image of an image, so as to discover the abstract figures, the schizzes-flows that it harbours and conceals. ... To overturn the theatre of representation into the order of desiring production: this is the whole task of schizoanalysis. (p. 271)

For Deleuze and Guattari, schizophrenia is revolutionary since it defies identification, categorization and differentiation. According to this view, unconscious desire represents nothing, neither representation nor the sign. It simply *is* – indeterminate, impersonal production. Hence the factory metaphor, 'desiring machines'.

A number of social and political implications arise from the foregoing analysis. To begin with, the work of Deleuze and Guattari seeks to undermine traditional conceptions of politics and revolutionary social action. Politics, embedded in desiring and social production, is not something that can be rationally refashioned, since society is caught up in the territorialization of norms. So too, blueprints for social and political transformation will be unsuccessful because such activity and planning will necessarily involve a paranoiac encoding of desire. But in what actual sense, then, is social change possible? It would seem that the only means for overcoming cultural oppression, for Deleuze and Guattari, lies in the schizophrenic process itself. Their case suggests that the best thing is to push the schizophrenic process as far as it will go, to the point where the social system is broken apart by the libidinal forces it seeks to suppress. In the words of Deleuze and Guattari's commentator Brian Massumi: 'Schizophrenia as a positive process is inventive connection, expansion rather than withdrawal.'[6] To turn the process of schizophrenia against the logic of capitalist production potentially might permit the construction of alternative social relations that permit spontaneity and intensity of desire free from cultural constraint.

Anti-Oedipus offered a timely critique of psychoanalysis and Lacanianism at the time of its publication in France. Most commentators would now agree, however, that 'schizoanalysis' itself is fatally flawed. There are at least three core objections which can be levelled against the work of Deleuze and Guattari in this connection. In the first place, there is no reason to assume, even granted that subjectivity may be usefully decentred and deconstructed, that desire is naturally rebellious and subversive. To treat the unconscious as *ipso facto* politically transgressive is to invoke a libertarian theory of the subject, one that uncritically celebrates the flows of desire in opposition to the symbolic order of representation. But this simple prioritization of schizoid processes over the socio-symbolic network fails to consider the social and political forms in which desire is embedded; this model fails to examine the ideological context in which persons attempt a psychical reorganization of the self. The fact that desire is routinely displaced and projected on to others as well as properly owned and nurtured, that fantasy objects yield pleasure and enjoyment but also disturb and terrify, is completely ignored. This perspective contains no adequate account of psychic interiority, nor can it theorize intersubjective relations. What this approach theorizes, rather than the subject and unconscious enjoyment, is the mind-shattering flux of schizoid desire. Significantly, however, no account of the emotional ramifications of this condition is offered. Deleuze and Guattari assume that desire is in some sense true to itself, that its primal positivity is damaged only when it becomes enmeshed in the socio-symbolic of modern societies. But this individualist emphasis eliminates both the concept of the unconscious (there is no primary unconscious in this perspective, since desire is a decentred product of entry into the symbolic order), and of the human subject as agent. Self-autonomy, interiority, the unconscious: these essential elements of identity are disowned. As a consequence, the individual is seen as no more than various organs, intensities and flows, rather than a complex, contradictory identity with a differentiated mode of psychic organization.

This issue might not be quite as significant if it were not for the emancipatory claims made by Deleuze and Guattari for schizophrenia, which in turn leads me to a second objection to their work. According to Deleuze and Guattari, the troubles of modernity are to be erased through the expressive disorder of schizoid desire. To grasp the limitations of this view we need to look no further than to psychoanalytic portraits of schizophrenia. What these findings reveal is a world, not of euphoric celebration, but of disintegration, fragmentation, terror and emotional devastation. In schizophrenia, Freud wrote, the individual rejects reality and turns desire back upon itself with a vengeance.[7] This destroys the self to its very core. Consequently, psychotic delirium is experienced as pure fragmentation – objects and others are randomly experienced without the structuring force of a meaningful, symbolic order. As Kovel puts this: 'The centre of schizophrenia is annihilation: the person becoming schizophrenic remains materially present and conscious, but ceases to be.'[8] This annihilation of self, perhaps not surprisingly, leads to the psychical destruction of others – that is, interpersonal relations. Having repudiated social reality, the schizophrenic is left with nothing to invest emotional energy but a substitutive fantasy world. But this fragmented world is not really any kind of 'world' at all: previous terrors and anxieties are now poured into delusions and hallucinations, which rebound upon the subject with unbearable force, producing terrifying vulnerability.

Against this backdrop, is it reasonable to assume that liberation might be uncovered in 'the glaring, sober truth that resides in delirium'? That is to say, how should we rate Deleuze and Guattari's celebration of schizophrenia? Not very highly, and it is important to outline why. Whatever the 'intensity' of schizoid desire, Deleuze and Guattari fail to consider the pain and emptiness of the psychotic experience. As such, their account of schizophrenia cannot provide any moral criterion. For example, how might an individual disconnected from subjectivity and intersubjectivity achieve critical self-reflection? If it is through the disordered flow of schizoid desire itself, is there nothing to be said about the rights of other persons? Clearly, if schizoid desire is accorded absolute entitlement we are dealing with a deep-lying potential for violence to the self, to others and to society. Here it might be argued, as some of Deleuze and Guattari's commentators have done, that to value the schizophrenic *process* in itself is not to sing the praises of schizophrenia.[9] In this reading, it is the schizophrenic process – that breakdown of symbolic forms into random flows, images and part-objects – which is potentially transformative of repressive social conditions. This case, however, still recklessly ignores the relations between psychic structure and social life. Any emancipatory theory of alternative social arrangements must provide a means for constituting the individual within socially valued forms; such structuration of the individual, psychoanalytically speaking, involves the overcoming of infantile omnipotence and the acceptance of decentred subjectivity. Deleuze and Guattari offer no such means. Their vision, even when read as a valuation of schizophrenia as process, projects the individual out of the social–historical world and into carnivalesque hyperspace.

Thirdly, serious difficulties arise from Deleuze and Guattari's work for the interpretation of contemporary culture. Their social critique hinges on the point that the expressiveness and positivity of desire are ruined through insertion into the cultural order of representation. But it might be as well to question what type of cultural order Deleuze and Guattari have in mind here. For it seems that in defending the cravings of the schizoid-subject against the repressions of modernity, Deleuze and Guattari slide into an indiscriminate rejection of institutionality as such. All political and social systems become, in effect, 'terroristic' – regardless of their modalities of power and law. But surely the claim that some orders of representation are not more repressive than others is highly problematic. What, for example, of the vital political differences between liberal democracy and fascism? What about the impact of symbolic forms and ideologies, such as religious fundamentalism, nationalism and political militancy? Surely these socio-symbolic forms affect possibilities for self-realization and autonomy in crucially distinct ways. Deleuze and Guattari's work, in this respect, is unconvincing. By flattening out the complex, contradictory reproduction of modern societies into a mechanistic account of the 'terror of norms', Deleuze and Guattari are left without any secure footing to elucidate the revolutionary political agency which they wish to see realized. Instead, Deleuze and Guattari are left with little more than a romantic, idealized fantasy of the 'schizoid hero'.

Lyotard on libidinal intensities

In the work of Deleuze and Guattari, a primary emphasis is placed on the disorder of desire. Schizoid desire signals the recovery of repressed differences, the multiplication of libido in a new era of postmodernity. Similar theoretical directions can also be found in the early work of Jean-François Lyotard, who explicitly poses the question of political society as a problem of desire in *Libidinal Economy* (1974). But whereas Deleuze and Guattari interpret the political in terms of schizoid desire against repressive desire, 'revolutionary' desire against 'fascist' desire, Lyotard turns instead to the mutual imbrication of the social and libidinal, law and desire. Ideology for Lyotard is not simply a matter of the repressive closure of desire. On the contrary, the ideological can be described as itself libidinal, inscribed always on the 'inside' of desire. What is needed is not the projection of some utopian realm 'beyond' our socio-political condition, but a reconfiguration of the libidinal intensities and singularities of social life itself.

There is an intrinsic link, Lyotard says, between the order of discourse and desire. The social order, though dependent on a repression of desire, is traversed by the libidinal sphere. A discursive repression of desire is thus always potentially open to transformation by the operations of desire itself, just as repressive political regimes, no matter how ideologically secure they may appear, are liable to be overthrown by citizens desiring alternative forms of life. Lyotard expresses this by noting that the return of the repressed 'violates the order of speech'. However, Lyotard altogether rejects the libertarian view that such violation is inherently good, and discursive repression bad. All social and political systems, he argues, negotiate networks of discourse and desire. Instead of prioritizing desire over signification, as in Deleuze and Guattari's *Anti-Oedipus*, by contrast Lyotard draws attention to differing modalities of desire and the structure of their production. Highlighting ambivalences in Freud's account of the unconscious, Lyotard discerns two aspects of desire: desire-as-wish (fantasy) and desire-as-force (libido). Desire-as-wish, the figural component of the unconscious, is the representational form impressed upon lost objects. Here the individual subject fantasizes images of the self, of others and of the world as a compensation for various lacks or exclusions. In this regime, desire operates under the sign of lack, absence and negativity. By contrast, desire-as-force, the energetic component of the unconscious, is pure energy, libido and primary process. In this regime, desire functions through the act of its own production, endlessly reproducing itself in some transcendental process of repetition.

Lyotard wishes to claim desire-as-force as inherently positive and affirmative. He advocates, in Nietzschean fashion, a celebration of unconscious intensity and power. On the basis of this vision, Lyotard speaks of the primacy of libidinal intensities. He describes the functioning of a 'libidinal band'; by 'band', he means a flux or scramble of energy cathexes, intensities lodged across surfaces of the body. How might we imagine this 'libidinal band'? Libidinal intensities are not focused upon 'objects of desire' (such as Oedipal figures), for this is the province of desire-as-wish. Libidinal intensities consist, rather, of the flux of desire itself, energy in a state of continuous nonlinear movement. Lyotard refers to a rotation of the libidinal band that constantly disrupts all intersections of self and other, of internal and external, of the differentiation of 'this' from 'not-this'. The whole notion is somewhat like the 'action painting' of Jackson Pollock, in which lines of figures interweave without end. However, libidinal intensities cannot be really understood in this way either. There is no point, Lyotard warns, of trying to capture the best image of the libidinal band, nor seeking to observe it, since we are dealing with a force that is prior to representation and conceptual thought. Indeed, conceptual thought is itself only possible through a cooling of libidinal energy, through a binding of intensities of desire. As such, it is really impossible to talk of this unconscious realm without deforming it in the act of doing so.

In Lyotard's 'libidinal band', then, we are dealing less with a domain of direct description than with a kind of fiction which at once precedes and exceeds representation, signification and meaning. Yet if it is the case that libidinal intensities constitute and account for the realm of representation, it is certainly not Lyotard's purpose simply to oppose the libidinal to the social sphere. Lyotard, to his credit, rejects as politically naive proclamations about the 'truth of desire'. As he puts this, there is no 'place where desire would be clearly legible, where its proper economy would not be scrambled'.[10] The opposition of desire and signification cannot make sense of the process of social transformation. A new vision is required to understand the structure of libidinal and social formations. For Lyotard, this involves the dissolution of representation and of theory as a *medium* of the libidinal band itself. 'The representative chamber', he writes, 'is an energetic system' (p. 11). Western knowledge, Enlightenment domination, science and technology: such discourses and practices – so Lyotard contends – are themselves libidinal. But in what manner, more concretely, might such a view-point contribute to social and political critique? Lyotard's specification of the libidinal nature of social practices, discourses and concepts is rooted in an attempt to de-legitimize the totalizing, objectivistic pretensions of contemporary affairs and institutions. By showing that desire constitutes the social through and through, Lyotard wishes to highlight that 'knowledge' is itself only one mode of libidinal intensity among others. From this angle, Lyotard's critique appeals to the singularities and intensities of desire against the repressive claims of Enlightenment reason.

To attempt to salvage the singularities of libido may not be that easy, however. If desire is split and conflictual – divided between desire-as-wish and desire-as-force – so too the intensities of the libidinal band are deeply structured by discontinuities of the unconscious. Such are the psychic implications of Eros and the death drive, a dualism which Lyotard invokes to conceptualize the limits of symbolization. This is not just, as most interpretations of Freud hold, because the death drive displaces the narcissistic unity established by Eros. It is because, as Lyotard rightly emphasizes, the disruptive, unbound force of the death drive is part and parcel of various manifestations of eroticism, or Eros. Holding this in mind, it can be said that the deathly force of the libidinal band leads to a complete annihilation of the symbolic network itself; or, as Lyotard puts it, the primary chaos of the death drive reveals 'the limit of representation and of theory'. From a psychoanalytic perspective, Lyotard is referring to symbolic, not biological, death. The disruptive energy of the death drive produces the moment of discontinuity, of rupture, at which point there is a short-circuiting of the socio-symbolic order. Here human subjects can briefly glimpse social reality in its full libidinal plenitude – heterogeneous, fluid and multiple.

At this point, we get to the heart of Lyotard's political analysis in *Libidinal Economy*. It is to trace the libidinal intensities *lodged* in cultural representations and social meanings. 'What would be interesting,' writes Lyotard, 'would be to stay where we are, but at the same time silently to grab all opportunities to function as good conductors of intensities' (p. 311). According to this view, it is simply mistaken to believe that desire does not flow freely enough in contemporary society – as Deleuze and Guattari contend. For the fact of the matter, according to Lyotard, is that desire circulates endlessly around objects, surfaces and bodies. In this connection, late capitalism for Lyotard is an immense desiring system. He describes postmodern capitalist society as a culture swamped with flashy commodities and signs, in which all social forms are colonized by the economic logic of exchange. Yet the implications of this for radical politics are not necessarily bad news. According to Lyotard, the exchangeability and anonymity glimpsed in contemporary capitalist processes parallel the aimless flux of the libidinal band itself. 'If desire is not to be opposed to capitalism,' as

Geoffrey Bennington says of Lyotard's position, 'it can be recognized *in* capitalism.'[11] Lyotard thus advocates embracing the fragmentation of desire as a way of intensifying the lived experiences of postmodern culture. The challenging and exhilarating task for postmodernism is to recognize that desire is always already realized, to extract pleasure from the fragments and surfaces in which identities are constituted.

From the standpoint of critical psychoanalytic theory, however, all of this is deeply problematic. The difficulties with Lyotard's conception of libidinal intensities relate, above all, to particular assumptions about human subjectivity and agency. Lyotard's celebration of the energetic component of the unconscious is achieved at the cost of displacing the vital role of representation in psychical life. Lyotard contends that representation is a local effect of libidinal intensities. Yet this altogether erases the fundamental stress upon representation in Freud's interpretation of the self. According to Freud, representation and desire are inextricably intertwined. Selfhood for Freud is anchored in an unconscious structure of representations, drives and desires. This creative core of the unconscious imagination lies at the basis of how men and women image themselves and each other in institutional social life. By severing the representational space of the self from unconscious desire, seeing the former as a reductive outcrop of the latter, Lyotard is able to imagine that the libidinal economy moulds all cultural productions to their roots. Yet how far is it really possible to disentangle libidinal forms of social life from the representational structures in which they are embedded? How can we disconnect the way we feel about personal and social life from the images we have of ourselves and other people? The energetic dynamics at the root of social organization cannot be unhinged from cultural representations as easily as Lyotard thinks. This is because representation and desire, signification and affect, are deeply tied together. Significantly, fixation and repetition are central issues here, and it is from this angle that some forms of cultural representation predominate over others in contemporary culture.

These ambiguities connect to deeper theoretical and political problems. Lyotard argues for a multiplication of libidinal formations in opposition to dominant forms of rationality in modern societies. Yet Lyotard's political dilemma is that the concept of libidinal intensities is cast so wide as to be effectively fruitless for critical social analysis. As Peter Dews has argued, Lyotard's position is bereft of any moral or political orientation.[12] The problem of arguing for the 'dissimulation of intensities', in short, is that such dissimulation can be ideologically marshalled by conservative political forces as well as by the Left. Indeed, intensities of affect derived from the institutionalization of a brutal, authoritarian political regime – one need only think of the political crisis between Israel and Palestine – can be as great as the libidinal intensity derived from the liberal affirmation of difference and singularity. As such, Lyotard's position really fails to pose any kind of threat to the dominant power interests of capitalist society.

The experience of postmodernity

Notwithstanding the foregoing criticisms, the work of Deleuze and Guattari, and of Lyotard, offers provocative images of how the modern world shapes and structures the symbolic identifications, ideals and illusions of individual subjects. Everyday experience, according to these images, is characterized by psychic fragmentation and dislocation. Modern culture, simply, is an immense desiring system, fracturing social space through schizoid tendencies towards deterritorialization while also managing to create unity through a depersonalized incorporation of libidinal intensities. Significantly, these fragmenting trends create new forms of personal identity, otherness, fantasy and symbolism.

Modernity has been understood as the historical trajectory of modernization. The key processes of modernization – such as industrialism, bureaucratic organization, technology and science – have unleashed profound cultural transformations. The rise of nation-states, corporate capitalism, the industrialization of war, new communication technologies: these are the central institutional features of the late modern world. For many theorists, this crisis-ridden system of global interconnectedness in which we now live is experienced by people ambivalently – as exciting adventure and terrifying risk, perpetual disintegration and renewal. Modernity is seen as an institutional setting which simultaneously empowers and constrains people, engendering their deepest hopes and fears. The modern task is creative engagement with changing forms of life, a reflexive involvement with the disorientating global world. But this is not easy. Just as a growing sense of turmoil and flux infuses social institutions and affairs, so too self-identity is recast through experiences of disorientation and discontinuity. In this context, mature and creative psychic organization depends upon an open, revisable sense of self-identity – a willingness to embrace change in the affairs of day-to-day life. In Winnicott's terms, the transitional realm of intersubjectivity is the essential condition for the development of such creative self-organization. In Giddens's picture of modernity, people handle dangers and fears through reflexive monitorings of trust.

For postmodern theorists, however, changes in social, cultural and political conditions are so far-reaching that it is deemed inappropriate to talk of self-identity at all. Changes in the proliferation of generalized communication; the dispersal of economic production and consumption; global, multinational capitalism; the multiplication of new political movements and identities; the fracturing of knowledge and information: postmodern society is a *radicalized* modernity, a world of cataclysmic change, dynamism and intensity. By a perverse kind of internal logic, postmodernity breaks up social reality into chunks of experience without reference, structure or unity. Of particular relevance in this context is the proliferation of images, messages, signs and codes disseminated through the mass media. For postmodern theorists, this proliferation of images in postmodern social space entails a radical breakdown in our sense of subjective reality. Postmodernity multiplies, dislocates and disperses the psychological forms of everyday reality. It destroys structures of time, space, history and truth, and replaces them with a celebration and pluralization of brute immediacy. Indeed, it has been suggested by some critics that it is now impossible to achieve any kind of critical distance for the illumination of social experience at all. Faced with the multiplication of social reality, the trusted distinctions between meaning and non-meaning, truth and fantasy, surface and depth can no longer be sustained.

Fredric Jameson has proposed, in what is regarded as a classic essay on post-modernism, a more direct relationship between contemporary identity and culture on the one hand, and socio-economic processes on the other.[13] Jameson interprets the fluidity and multiplicity of postmodern cultural experience as a symptom of 'multinational capital'. The globalizing tendencies of late capitalism, he argues, breaks up the fabric of culture and the personal sphere, creating 'a new and historically original penetration and colonization of Nature and the Unconscious'. This global process of commodification involves the dissolution of selfhood and psychical structure, with 'postmodern hyperspace' proclaimed by Jameson as 'transcending the capacities of the individual human body to locate itself, to organize its immediate surroundings perceptually and cognitively to map its position in a mappable external world' (pp. 83–4). Social space becomes pro-foundly imaginary, fantastical, overheating the very social imagination to which it is bound. The whole thing is something akin to the Lacanian child in its pre-mirror, imaginary phase – in which no divisions exist between self and world. For Jameson, the postmodern human subject is caught within a global, computational network of random signifiers and cultural representations which seduce and tantalize, but ultimately fail to make sense.

Jameson proposes a list of the dominant characteristics of postmodern culture. These include 'The Waning of Affect', 'Euphoria and Self-Annihilation', 'Loss of the Radical Past', 'The Breakdown of the Signifying Chain' and 'The Abolition of Critical Distance'. All of these refer to the fragmentation of subjecthood, dis-persed across the global, multinational capitalist system. In postmodern culture, according to Jameson, 'there is no longer a self present to do the feeling'. Social identity, rather, is forged in and through fragments of language, media messages and television images. Yet the press-button society of postmodernism leaves us cold, and without bearings. As cultural production becomes increasingly depthless and meaningless, so also does the self. Jameson, in a series of discussions about contemporary painting, contrasts the alienated subject of modernism with the fragmented subject of postmodernism. He points to Munch's painting *The Scream* as a cultural emblem of modernist solitude and isolation, of the 'age of anxiety', contrasting this with the postmodern depthlessness of Warhol's painting *Marilyn*, in which the repetition of the image of Marilyn Monroe demonstrates the breakdown of trusted distinctions between people and their images. In this connection, postmodernism can be said to raise commodification to the second power, using the world of late capitalism to generate new forms of cultural representation.

For Jameson, as for Deleuze and Guattari and Lyotard, there are profound links between postmodern social experience and schizophrenia. Following Lacan, Jameson contends that biographies of self-identity are written against the backdrop of a unification of past, present and future. Experiencing language as temporally linked to social life is the psychological basis upon which a sense of psychological well-being rests. Contemporary postmodern social conditions, however, profoundly derail the relationship between self and language, desire and discourse. The dislocations and terrors of postmodern experience lead to a breakdown of the signifying chain itself. The present becomes dispersed, the past and future isolated. Desire randomly connects to bits of persons, experiences and objects, as subjects live among a 'rubble of distinct and unrelated signifiers' (p. 72). In this context, the dissolution of self accompanies a transmutation of feeling. As Jameson notes: 'This is not to say that the cultural products of the postmodern era are utterly devoid of feeling, but rather that such feelings – which it may be better and more accurate to call "intensities" – are now free-floating and impersonal, and tend to be dominated by a peculiar kind of euphoria.'

Discussions about schizophrenia as a psychic metaphor for the postmodern tend to operate on different theoretical and cultural levels. In the 'schizoanalysis' proposed by Deleuze and Guattari, the schizoid tribulations of desire are given a positive gloss. Deleuze and Guattari celebrate the positivity of the flux of desire as a potential displacement to the repressive structures of late capitalism. In the work of Lyotard, a different tack is taken. The intensities of schizophrenic desire are not resistant to socialization, but already define and situate language, society and cultural politics. The emancipatory prospects for postmodernity thus depend upon a progressive reappropriation of the singularities of libidinal intensity. For Jameson, schizophrenic desire also best captures the nature of the postmodern condition. Yet according to Jameson, this fragmentation of self is not something to be celebrated, since to do so would play directly into the hands of the dominant cultural logic of capitalism. All these accounts of postmodern experience can be found in current psychoanalytic studies and cultural and social theory. The broader issue raised by 'schizophrenic fragmentation' as an emblem of the postmodern, however, is whether the term can usefully serve at this level of cultural generality. Certainly it is possible to deploy 'schizophrenic fragmentation', like Jameson, as a benchmark for the assessment of postmodernism. Yet even this approach to understanding contemporary selfhood and society contains serious problems and contradictions.

One objection to the kind of cultural analysis just discussed is that it cannot really account for its own claims. If postmodern subjectivity really is fragmented, decentred, discontinuous and schizoid in character, then how might it be possible for some cultural critics to map the psychical determinants of the contemporary world? That is to say, how is it possible to overcome the deforming, schizoid imaginary structures of the contemporary world in the act of interpreting them? It has been argued that such an objection really misses the point of postmodernism. It has been suggested that the work of Deleuze and Guattari, and of Lyotard, avoids this objection by disrupting the linear presentation of theory in favour of the displacements of desire itself. According to this view, the underlining of the flux of desire is mirrored in the discontinuous, fragmentary forms of postmodern discourse. In the postmodern world we know that all theory is necessarily partial and provisional; accordingly, any account of the postmodern condition will be bound up with the conditions of desire. There are still serious difficulties, however, with this conception of postmodern theory and practice. For one thing, to employ deconstructive strategies in critical theory, no matter how fragmentary and multidimensional, is not the same as living with psychotic or schizophrenic disturbances. For the fact of the matter is that the postmodern cultural practice under consideration uses metaphors, symbols and interpretative strategies – the very psychical processes closed down and foreclosed in schizophrenia. This suggests that postmodern cultural forms might not be as brittle and fragmented as imagined. Has the capacity for critical self-reflection and analysis been impoverished by postmodernity? Can postmodern identity only be equated with fragments of language or discourse? The complex, contradictory ways in which people search for individual and collective identity, I argue, require greater analytical depth than the foregoing postmodern theories provide.

Another objection to the postmodern celebration of schizophrenic renewal is the charge of naturalistic essentialism. In this respect, it is clear that psychoanalysis does not view psychosis as any form of emancipation. On the contrary, schizophrenia is conceived as a kind of psychical murder, an annihilation of self and of symbolic connectedness to the world. In this context, the postmodern search for schizophrenic cultural forms that would allow us to be *ourselves*, free from the constraints and limitations of the social world, is simply ill-defined. It is an approach framed upon a naive naturalism (desire as somehow, almost magically, always true to itself), and to that extent offers little space for critical examination of the changing relations between self and society. As Jacqueline Rose puts it, there is a 'sanitization' of schizophrenia in postmodern theory, a kind of cleaning up operation, in which this psychic model becomes 'strangely divested of some of the most difficult aspects of the psychic itself'.[14] So too, the social domain is also sanitized, as devoid of the realities of political change, social transformation and ideological conflict. More specifically, there is a failure to attend to the political content of self-organization, as well as social conditions structuring desire. It is important to see that schizophrenia and psychosis are not alternatives to the current social order, but painfully desperate psychical forms experienced within the organizing social, political and ideological conditions of the late modern world.

Related to this is the feminist objection that the schizophrenic metaphorization of the postmodern serves to silence issues of sexual difference and gender power. There is some agreement among feminists that the fragmentations of contemporary selfhood are themselves the product of an insipid intensification of patriarchal power. Certainly, it might be thought that this is a difficult claim to sustain in the light of recent gender transformations and the advances of the women's movement. However, many feminists argue that postmodern social, cultural and political conditions are now affecting sexuality in a dramatic way, generating violence and hatred at the heart of sexual fantasy. Significantly, much of the writing on postmodernism examined in this chapter displaces questions of sexual difference on to the general categories of fragmentation and disintegration. This is, however, a very curious displacement. For schizophrenic fragmentation is itself a disavowal of sexual difference. In schizophrenia, the psychotic denies the fact of castration, rejecting the *gendered structures of social life*. Yet the relation between sexual difference, fragmentation and new forms of gender power is not raised in the theories examined.

Postmodernism as repression: excavating the imagination

Postmodern thinking about self and society emphasizes the dislocation and fragmentation of contemporary experience. Postmodernity, as we have seen, arises at that point in which the interchangeability and indifference of economic commodification penetrate deeply into the communicational networks of modern culture itself. In the writings of the late European psychoanalyst Cornelius Castoriadis, however, this expansion of the term 'commodification' conjoins the economic realm to social experience only at the cost of displacing the creativity of the social–historical process. For Castoriadis, postmodernity is itself a cultural symptom of a society that has come to forget its own creative self-institution. Against this cultural tendency, Castoriadis is concerned with examining the psychoanalytic, social and political mechanisms by which human creation emerges in subjectivity and in history. To do this, Castoriadis develops in his path-breaking book, *The Imaginary Institution of Society* (1987), the concept of the *radical imaginary*, by which he means a purely creative architecture of representations, drives and desires through which self and society are constituted and reproduced. The radicial imaginary, as it affects personal and social life, is an open-ended stream of significations and passions; imagination is a productive core which permits human subjects to create and reproduce society anew.

The term 'imaginary', says Castoriadis, has been reductively understood in traditional thought. For the imaginary has been cast as no more than a reflection or copy of the external world. The Lacanian conception of the 'imaginary order' is a prime example. In the Lacanian imaginary, the small child receives a reflection from the mirror, a reflection which functions as a distorted image for the drafting of the self. In contrast to Lacan, Castoriadis argues that the 'imaginary does not come from the image in the mirror or from the gaze of the other. Instead, the "mirror" itself and its possibility, and the other as mirror, are the works of the imaginary.'[15] Human imagination, Castoriadis proposes, is creation *ex nihilo*. The imaginary is pure creation, the making and remaking of images and forms as an explicit self-production. This does not mean, absurdly, that human beings are unconstrained in their individual and collective activity. On the contrary, Castoriadis links the self-creating nature of cultural production to the *instituted imaginary representations* which belong to society and to history. The productive core of society, whether at the level of individual fantasy or at the level of Western global expansion, arises through such structuring of imaginary representations.

To speak of 'imaginary representations' as being at the core of the social world is certainly at odds with the bulk of contemporary theory, and it is usually from this angle that Castoriadis is criticized in poststructural psychoanalysis and postmodern circles. Such critics argue that the whole concept of representation – the idea that some transcendental signified automatically assigns a set of stable meanings to individuals – has seriously come to grief since Saussurean or post-Saussurean linguistics. This kind of criticism, however, actually targets an empirical model of representation, which posits a one-dimensional, functional connection between subjective thoughts and external reality. The imaginary dimension of representation for Castoriadis is entirely different in scope. The representational forms of the unconscious do not denote an organic bond between image and thing, idea and object. Through a brilliant reinterpretation of Freudian psychoanalysis, Castoriadis speaks of a 'representational flux' which lies at the heart of the radical imaginary and its ever-erupting significations. The unconscious, says Castoriadis, exists *as* representational flux, continually overdetermined and interwoven with the cultural fabric of society. Following Freud, Castoriadis argues that, from the beginning of life, representations are geared towards the pleasure principle. What is important here is pleasure, satisfaction and enjoyment. The hallucination of the breast by the infant is a key Freudian instance of representation as a source of unconscious pleasure.

To the radical imaginary of the individual subject corresponds what Castoriadis calls the 'social imaginary' of culture and social institutions. The social imaginary, to be sure, is not simply the sum of individual fantasies in any given society. The social imagination draws upon the affective investments of individual subjects, certainly. But through the institutionalization of social practices, the social imaginary always exceeds the domain of radical imagination. Here, as it were, there is a structuring of the radical imagination in and through symbolism, language, tradition and custom. Castoriadis explains the social imaginary as follows:

> This element, which endows the functionality of each institutional system with its specific orientation, which overdetermines the choice and connections of symbolic networks, which creates for each historical period its singular way of living, seeing and making its own existence, its world and its relation to it, this originary structuring, this central signifier-signified, source of what is each time given as indisputable and indisputed sense, support of the articulations and distinctions of what matters and what does not, origin of the augmented being of the individual or collective objects of practical, affective and intellectual investment – this element is nothing other than the imaginary of the society or period concerned.

Self and society, in brief, are constituted within the activity of the creative imagination. The imaginary dimension of personal and social life always outstrips the world of external reality. Consider capitalism, for example. Capitalism organizes personal activity, social structures and institutions in order to affirm itself as accumulation and commodification. But there is something profoundly imaginary, deeply fantasmatic, driving the imperative for accumulation and wealth. Objects, such as cars or televisions, are 'seen' in daily life. But the actual commodity 'car', or the commodity 'television', are in a sense invisible objects – invested with powerful affect, overdetermined with fantasy. Commodification exists through fantasizing, through the social imaginary.

Social life is necessarily structured by the activity of the imagination, which is manifested in what Castoriadis terms a 'world of significations'. Any such world of signification is the generation of radically different imaginary patterns, driven and overdetermined by the image-creating realm of the unconscious. What is at stake here is the essentially productive core of society. 'The imagination', says Castoriadis, 'gives rise to the newly thinkable.'[16] The philosophical systems of Kant and Hegel, the scientific discoveries of Newton, Einstein or Darwin, the institutionalization of Gods and Spirits: such world-constitution is the creative imaginary dimension of society.

Institutionalized society exists in and through these imaginary forms. Yet cultural forms can harden in such a way that the productive core of the social imaginary diminishes. Here it is as if social life becomes uncoupled from the creative imagination and its source of inspiration. From this perspective, society becomes profoundly alienated, fetishizing reality through a dull repetition of the selfsame. Such a 'retreat into conformism' is how Castoriadis describes postmodern social conditions. Ideological regression, intellectual poverty, the waning of social and political conflict, the destructive expansion of techno-science: these and other features of our postmodern age represent a flattening of the creative imagination, what Castoriadis terms our 'second-order imaginary'.

Castoriadis's work as a whole represents an original psychoanalytic contribution to the analysis of what one might call the imaginary tribulations of contemporary culture. He makes an urgent plea for the recovery of human imagination in the widest sense, at once personal and political. Charting the enormous dangers of destructive social practices in the postmodern age, Castoriadis seeks to disclose new possibilities for the contemporary imagination. As Castoriadis writes of the postmodern political condition: 'For the resurgence of the project of autonomy, new political objectives and new human attitudes are required, of which, for the time being, there are but few signs. Meanwhile, it would be absurd to try to decide if we are living through a long parenthesis, or if we are witnessing the beginning of the end of Western history as a history essentially linked with the project of autonomy and codetermined by it.'[17]

Table 6.1   **The dislocating world of postmodernism**

Theoretical model	Conception of self and society	Key terms
Deleuze and Guattari	Modernity as repressive fusion of desiring and social production; transgression through schizophrenia	Schizoanalysis Deterritorialization Reterritorialization
Lyotard	Libidinal intensities lodged in social institutions and affairs; multiplication of intensities affirmed through postmodernity	Libidinal band Desire-as-force
Jameson	Schizoid fragmentation as postmodern cultural experience	Breakdown of signifying chain Postmodern hyperspace
Castoriadis	Intersection of radical and social imaginary; postmodernism as general conformism	Radical imaginary Social imaginary Second-order imaginary

Conclusion: Psychoanalysis as Critical Theory

In the course of this book I have examined core theoretical trajectories in contemporary psychoanalytic thought and studies. Freudian theory, ego-psychology, object relations, Kleinianism, self-psychology, Lacanian and post-Lacanian theory, feminist and postmodern psychoanalysis: all of these approaches, notwithstanding divergences in basic assumptions, provide valuable insights into the difficulties of living in the late modern world. In discussing these standpoints, I have also set out a number of critical remarks concerning their readings of selfhood, unconscious desire and contemporary culture. In these concluding pages, I want briefly to develop some thoughts about the nature of psychoanalysis as a critical theory.

I began this book by arguing that psychoanalytic theory is an inherently critical, political discourse. I mean by this that psychoanalysis is a critical reflection on the central modes of feeling, valuing and caring in modern societies. Very often, the political credentials of psychoanalysis are evaluated in terms of rigidly individualist categories, notably as concerns psychotherapy. In such accounts, politics is related to psychoanalysis only in terms of therapy, which is then assessed as either conformist or radical in nature. I have tried to show throughout this book, however, that the political is part and parcel of psychoanalytic discourse at a much deeper level. I have suggested that what is at issue in psychoanalysis is the interlacing of repressed desire and power relations, unconscious passion and cultural reproduction. The variety of psychoanalytic approaches considered in this book offer complex, contradictory positions on this focus of concern. However, in all of these approaches, political and social connections of many kinds are treated as central to the very condition of human subjectivity. From Sigmund Freud to Jean Laplanche, psychoanalytic theory has been intricately interwoven with political values and ideological assumptions. Indeed, psychoanalysis places a question mark against the ideology of subjectivity itself – bringing the question of the subject back to political issues of desire, gender, language, history and society.

The political significance of psychoanalysis, therefore, lies precisely in tracing the imprint of the social, cultural network upon unconscious passion. As Herbert Marcuse puts this: 'psychoanalytic categories do not have to be "related" to social and political conditions – they are themselves social and political categories'.[1] It is characteristic of psychoanalytic discourse, as I have tried to show, to deconstruct the complex interplay between unconscious desire and social life.

What I have suggested, in sum, is that a strategy of *theoretical linkage or cross-referencing* is the most fruitful and productive way to engage with psychoanalytic doctrine. What is required is openness to differences within psychoanalytic theory, differences which I believe might serve as the medium for rigorous critical reflection. This is not to say, however, that we should attempt a synthesis or integration of psychoanalytic approaches. Any such ideal of conceptual unity in contemporary psychoanalysis is, in my opinion, misplaced. For the theoretical divergences here are simply too great. As we have seen, there is little common ground on the role of pre-Oedipal development, the wider cultural effects of Oedipus, the dynamics of splitting and the like. What I am suggesting, rather, is that the articulation of differences in psychoanalytic theory will allow us at least to make a start in comprehending the heterogeneity of unconscious desire in its relation to the self, to others and contemporary culture. Only through the articulation of differences shall we be able to set psychoanalysis within the wider social context, and to theorize the kinds of political effects which theories produce.

Theodor Adorno, one of the most astute commentators on the radical potentials of psychoanalysis, well knew the dangers of conceptual isolation or closure. For Adorno, it is quite mistaken to imagine that we might affirm a moment of psychic experience which is not, at the same time, a condensed imprint of the subject's struggles in the social and political domain. From this viewpoint, the idea that there are impartial or non-political modes of psychoanalytic criticism is simply a theoretical fantasy, a fantasy aimed at erasing contradiction, antagonism and differentiation. Commenting on the historical tendency to separate psychoanalysis from the social and political world, Adorno writes:

> The more strictly the psychological realm is conceived as an autonomous, self-enclosed play of forces, the more completely the subject is drained of his subjectivity. The objectless subject that is thrown back upon himself freezes into an object. It cannot break out of its immanence and amounts to no more than equations of libidinal energy. The soul that is broken down into its own laws is a soul no longer.[2]

Theories which are incapable of thinking through the social, historical constitution of psychic experience will be, on the whole, unable to confront contradiction and conflict – dimensions of experience implicitly distilled in their readings of selfhood and desire. Crises of identity and desire, in other words, will remain within an imaginary orbit, in which social conflict and the contradictions of modernity are wished away.

By contrast, I have argued throughout this book that it is vital to recover the central organizing role of power relations and patterns of cultural domination in the constitution of identity and repressed desire. If psychoanalysis is to remain effective as a critical theory, it must necessarily step back from the tendency to see the self solely in terms of the 'psychic', and instead confront head-on the issue of the construction of the unconscious in the field of the social and political. Only if this is achieved will psychoanalysis be able to confront issues of new political importance in social and cultural enquiry – such as the resurgence of racism and nationalism, changing cultural definitions of masculinity and femininity, problems of human agency and the like.

A critical psychoanalytic theory, in order to be reflective and encounter otherness, must display an openness about conceptual approaches and methods of study. No single theory will have the whole truth. No single theory will be able to confront the contemporary, multidimensional identities of the postmodern world. For these reasons, I have suggested that it is necessary to recognize the interlocking concerns of psychoanalytical theories, and to recognize that these doctrines are bound up with political ideologies in ways which always outstrip their modes of thinking. The variety of theories in contemporary psychoanalysis, I have suggested, are therefore better understood as images of what it feels like to live in the multidimensional world of modernity. The Freudian stress on ambivalence, the object relational discourse on connection and relatedness, the Kleinian underwriting of splitting, the Lacanian emphasis on otherness, the postmodern account of fragmentation and dispersal: these are ideological forms engendered in and through the late modern age. Yet consideration of these images does not occur in a realm closed off from the social world. Critical thinking about different psychoanalytic theories is connected in an essential way to transformations in self-identity and social relations. 'As the understanding of Freudianism is changed,' Paul Ricoeur comments, 'so is the understanding of oneself.'[3] Critically reflecting on psychoanalytical doctrines, and putting them into practical engagement with each other, might indeed help alternative subjectivities and social futures to be realized.

Notes

1 The Making of the Self

1. Dennis Wrong, 'The Over-socialized Conception of Man in Modern Sociology', *American Sociological Review*, 26 (1961), pp. 183–93.
2. See E. L. Freud (ed.), *Letters of Sigmund Freud: 1873–1939* (London: The Hogarth Press, 1970), pp. 408–9.
3. Sigmund Freud, *The Standard Edition of the Complete Psychological Works of Sigmund Freud*, tr. J. Stachey (London: Hogarth Press, 1935–74), XXIII, p. 174.
4. Sigmund Freud, 'An Outline of Psycho-Analysis,' *SE*, XXIII, p. 154.
5. Philip Rieff, *Freud: The Mind of the Moralist* (Chicago: University of Chicago Press, 1979).
6. Freud, 'Inhibitions, Symptoms and Anxiety', *SE*, XX, p. 170.
7. Freud, *The Ego and the Id*, *SE*, XIX, p. 28.
8. Freud, 'Some Psychical Consequences of the Anatomical Distinction between the Sexes', *SE*, XIX, p. 252.
9. Slavoj Zizek, *The Sublime Object of Ideology* (London: Verso, 1989), p. 49.
10. Cornelius Castoriadis, *The Imaginary Institution of Society* (Cambridge: Polity, 1987), p. 104.
11. See Heinz Hartmann, *Essays on Ego Psychology* (New York: International Universities Press, 1964).
12. Russell Jacoby, *Social Amnesia* (Boston: Beacon Press, 1975).
13. Harry Guntrip, *Schizoid Phenomena, Object Relations and the Self* (London: Hogarth Press, 1968), p. 422.
14. D. W. Winnicott, 'Ego Distortion in Terms of True and False Self', in *The Maturational Process and the Facilitating Environment* (London: Hogarth Press, 1965), p. 147.
15. Jean-François Lyotard, *The Postmodern Condition: A Report on Knowledge* (Manchester: Manchester University Press, 1986).
16 See Jacques Lacan, 'The Mirror Stage as Formative of the Function of the I', in *Ecrits: A Selection* (London: Tavistock, 1977), Ch. 1.
17. Gilles Deleuze and Félix Guattari, *Anti-Oedipus: Capitalism and Schizophrenia* (New York: Viking, 1977).
18. See Jean Baudrillard, *L'échange symbolique et la mort* (Paris: Gallimard, 1976). For a useful overview of Baudrillard's writings in English see Mark Poster (ed.), *Jean Baudrillard: Selected Writings* (Cambridge: Polity Press, 1988).

2 Modern Culture and Its Repressed

1. Sigmund Freud, 'Civilized Sexual Morality and Modern Nervous Illness', in *The Standard Edition of the Complete Psychological Works of Sigmund Freud*, IX, p. 203.
2. Freud, *Totem and Taboo*, SE, XIII, p. 74.
3. Freud, 'Analysis Terminable and Interminable', *SE*, XXIII, p. 243.
4. Paul Ricoeur, *Freud and Philosophy: An Essay on Interpretation* (New Haven: Yale, 1970), p. 307.
5. Freud, *Civilization and Its Discontents*, SE, XXI, p. 122.
6. Freud, *Civilization*, p. 145.
7. Erich Fromm, 'The Method and Function of an Analytic Social Psychology: Notes on Psychoanalysis and Historical Materialism', in A. Arato and E. Gebhardt, *The Essential Frankfurt School Reader* (New York: Continuum, 1985), p. 483.
8. This summary of the essential needs of mankind in Fromm's theory is detailed in Ch. 3 of *The Sane Society* (London: Routledge, 1991), pp. 30–66.
9. Herbert Marcuse, *Eros and Civilization* (London: Ark, 1956), p. 258.
10. Marcuse, *Eros*, p. 143.
11. For further discussion of this point see my *Social Theory and Psychoanalysis in Transition: Self and Society from Freud to Kristeva* (London: Free Association Books, 1999), pp. 94–102.
12. Frantz Fanon, *Black Skin, White Masks* (London: MacGibbon and Kee, 1968), p. 165.
13. Homi Bhabha, *The Location of Culture* (London: Routledge, 1994), p. 41. Next quotation is from p. 40.
14. Fanon, *Black Skin*, p. 110. Next quotation is from p. 177.
15. Fanon, *Black Skin*, p. 191.
16. See Ashis Nandy, *The Intimate Enemy: Loss and Recovery of Self under Colonalism* (Delhi: Oxford University Press, 1983), p. xi.
17. Nandy, *Intimate Enemy*, p. 35.
18. Joel Kovel, 'Narcissism and the Family', reprinted in his *The Radical Spirit: Essays on Psychoanalysis and Society* (London: Free Association, 1988), p. 199.
19. Christopher Lasch, *The Culture of Narcissism* (London: Abacus, 1979), p. 82.
20. Christopher Lasch, *The Minimal Self: Psychic Survival in Troubled Times* (New York: Norton, 1984), pp. 195–6.

3 Object Relations, Kleinian Theory, Self-Psychology

1. Erik H. Erikson, *Childhood and Society* (Harmondsworth: Penguin, 1965), pp. 239–41.
2. Erik H. Erikson, *Identity, Youth and Crisis* (New York: Norton, 1968), pp. 22–3.
3. Erik H. Erikson, *Gandhi's Truth* (New York: Norton, 1969), p. 433.
4. Nathan Leites, *The New Ego* (New York: Aronson, 1973). See also Mark Poster, *Critical Theory of the Family* (London: Pluto, 1978).

5. Adam Phillips, *Winnicott* (London: Fontara, 1988), pp. 29–30.
6. See Phyllis Grusskurth, *Melanie Klein: Her Life and Work* (New Haven, Conn.: Yale University Press, 1986), p. 399.
7. D. W. Winnicott, 'Primary Maternal Preoccupation', in *Through Paediatrics to Psycho-analysis* (London: Hogarth Press, 1958), p. 304.
8. D. W. Winnicott, *Playing and Reality* (Harmondsworth: Penguin, 1974), p. 83.
9. See Nancy. J. Chodorow and Susan Contratto, 'The Fantasy of the Perfect Mother', *Feminism and Psychoanalytic Theory* (Cambridge: Polity, 1989).
10. Anthony Giddens, *Modernity and Self-Identity: Self and Society in the Late Modern Age* (Cambridge: Polity, 1991), p. 39.
11. Giddens, *Self-Identity*, pp. 182–3.
12. Giddens, *Self-Identity*, p. 185.
13. Grosskurth, *Melanie Klein*, p. 20.
14. See Hannah Segal, 'Silence is the Real Crime', *Int. Rev. Psycho-Anal*, 14 (1987), pp. 3–12.
15. Rae Sherwood, *The Psychodynamics of Race* (Sussex: The Harvester Press, 1980), p. 491.
16. Sherwood, *Psychodynamics*, pp. 492–3.
17. Sherwood, *Psychodynamics*, pp. 496–7.
18. Michael Rustin, *The Good Society and the Inner World: Psychoanalysis, Politics and Culture* (London: Verso, 1991), p. 20.
19. C. Fred Alford, *Melanie Klein and Critical Social Theory* (Yale University Press, 1989), p. 4.
20. Alford, *Melanie Klein*, p. 22; for his argument, see Ch. 5.
21. Alford, *Melanie Klein*, pp. 3–4.
22. Alford, *Melanie Klein*, pp. 19–20.
23. Cornelius Castoriadis, *The Imaginary Institution of Society* (Cambridge: Polity Press, 1987), p. 285.
24. Stephen Frosh, *Identity Crisis: Modernity, Psychoanalysis and the Self* (London: Macmillan – now Palgrave, 1991), p. 51.
25. Heinz Kohut, *The Restoration of the Self* (New York: International Universities Press, 1977), p. 86.
26. Jay R. Greenberg and Stephen A. Mitchell, *Object Relations in Psychoanalytic Theory* (Cambridge, Mass.: Harvard University Press, 1983), p. 363.

4   Poststructuralist Anxiety: Subjects of Desire

1. Elizabeth Roudinesco, *Jacques Lacan* (Cambridge: Polity Press, 1997), pp. 63–4.
2. Jacques Lacan, *Écrits: A Selection* (London: Tavistock Press, 1977), p. 2.
3. Jean Laplanche and Serge Leclaire, 'The Unconscious', *Yale French Studies*, 48 (1972), p. 154.
4. Jacques Lacan, 'Fonction et champ de la parole et du langage en psychanalyse', *Écrits* (Paris: Seuil, 1966), p. 319.
5. Cornelius Castoriadis, 'The State of the Subject Today', *Thesis Eleven*, 24 (1989), p. 7.

6. See Paul Ricoeur, *Freud and Philosophy: An Essay on Interpretation* (New Haven: Yale, 1970), pp. 395–406; Jean-François Lyotard, 'The Dream-work Does Not Think', in A. Benjamin (ed.), *The Lyotard Reader* (Oxford: Blackwell, 1990); Cornelius Castoriadis, 'Psychoanalysis: Project and Elucidation', in his *Crossroads in the Labyrinth*; and Jean Laplanche and Serge Leclaire, 'The Unconscious', *Yale French Studies*, 48 (1972).
7. Malcolm Bowie, *Lacan* (London: Fontana, 1991), p. 199.
8. Jacques Lacan, *Écrits: A Selection* (London: Tavistock Press, 1977), p. 152.
9. Louis Althusser, *Lenin and Philosophy and Other Essays* (London: New Left Books, 1971), p. 161.
10. Paul Hirst, 'Althusser and the Theory of Ideology', *Economy and Society*, 5(4) (1976), p. 406.
11. Christian Metz, *Psychoanalysis and Cinema* (London: Macmillan – now Palgrave, 1982), p. 45.
12. Slavoj Zizek, *The Sublime Object of Ideology* (London: Verso, 1988), p. 45.
13. Slavoj Zizek, *Looking Awry: An Introduction to Jacques Lacan through Popular Culture* (Cambridge, Mass.: MIT Press, 1991), p. 128.
14. Jean Laplanche, *New Foundations for Psychoanalysis* (Oxford: Blackwell, 1987), p. 128. All subsequent references to this work will be given parenthetically in the text.
15. 'Interview with Jean Laplanche: The Other within', *Radical Philosophy*, 102 (July/August 2000), p. 36.
16. See Rose in J. Fletcher and M. Stanton (eds), *Jean Laplanche: Seduction, Translation, Drives* (London: ICA, 1992), p. 61.

5 Psychoanalytic Feminism

1. Juliet Mitchell, *Psychoanalysis and Feminism* (London: Penguin, 1974), xv.
2. Mary Daly and Jane Caputi, *Websters' First New Intergalactic Wickedary of the English Language* (Boston: Beacon, 1987), p. 230.
3. Dorothy Dinnerstein, *The Mermaid and the Minotaur* (New York: Harper and Row, 1976), p. 186.
4. Nancy J. Chodorow, *The Reproduction of Mothering* (Berkeley: University of California Press, 1978).
5. Nancy J. Chodorow, *Feminism and Psychoanalytic Theory* (Cambridge: Polity, 1989), p. 71.
6. For example, see Issac D. Balbus, *Marxism and Domination* (Princeton: Princeton University Press, 1982), Ch. 9; and R. W. Connell, *Gender and Power* (Cambridge: Polity, 1987), Ch. 9.
7. Lynne Segal, *Is The Future Female?: Troubled Thoughts on Contemporary Feminism* (London: Virago, 1987), p. 140.
8. Jacqueline Rose, *Sexuality in the Field of Vision* (London: Verso, 1986), p. 60, no. 28.

9. J. Benjamin, 'Sameness and Difference', in A. Elliott and S. Frosh, *Psychoanalysis in Contexts: Paths between Theory and Modern Culture* (London: Routledge, 1995), p. 106.

10. Madelon Sprengnether, *The Spectral Mother: Freud, Feminism, and Psychoanalysis* (Ithaca: Cornell University Press, 1990), p. 246.

11. Jane Flax, *Thinking Fragments: Psychoanalysis, Feminism, and Postmodernism in the Contemporary West* (Berkeley: University of California Press, 1991).

12. Jacques Lacan, *Écrits: A Selection* (London: Tavistock Press, 1977), p. 287.

13. Jacques Lacan, *Encore: Le Séminaire XX* (Paris: Seuil, 1975).

14. Juliet Mitchell, *Women: The Longest Revolution* (London: Virago, 1984), p. 274.

15. Anthony Elliott, *Social Theory and Psychoanalysis in Transition: Self and Society from Freud to Kristeva* (Oxford: Blackwell, 1992), Ch. 6.

16. Rose, *Sexuality*, p. 7.

17. Rose, *Sexuality*, pp. 75–6.

18. Julia Kristeva, 'Women's Time', in T. Moi (ed.), *The Kristeva Reader* (Oxford: Blackwell, 1986), p. 206.

19. Andrea Nye, 'Woman Clothed with the Sun: Julia Kristeva and the Escape from/to Language', *Signs*, 12 (Summer 1987), pp. 664–86.

20. Drucilla Cornell and Adam Thurschwell, 'Feminism, Negativity, Intersubjectivity', in S. Benhabib and D. Cornell (eds), *Feminism as Critique* (Cambridge: Polity, 1987), pp. 149–51.

21. Luce Irigaray, *This Sex Which Is Not One* (Ithaca: Cornell University Press, 1985), p. 143.

22. Mitchell, *Women*, p. 291.

23. Judith Butler, *Gender Trouble* (London: Routledge, 1990), pp. 142–3.

24. Judith Butler, *The Psychic Life of Power* (Stanford University Press, 1997), p. 135.

25. *Radical Philosophy*, 67 (Summer 1994), p. 34.

6   The Dislocating World of Postmodernism

1. Zygmunt Bauman, *Modernity and Ambivalence* (Cambridge: Polity, 1990), p. 272.

2. Jean-François Lyotard, 'Defining the Postmodern', in Lisa Appignanesi (ed.), *Postmodernism: ICA Documents* (London: Free Association Books, 1989), p. 10.

3. Samuel Weber, *The Legend of Freud* (Minneapolis: University of Minnesota Press, 1982).

4. Gilles Deleuze and Félix Guattari, *Anti-Oedipus: Capitalism and Schizophrenia* (New York: Viking, 1977), p. 296. All subsequent references to this work will be given parenthetically in the text.

5. In an interview, Guattari comments: 'Lacanianism isn't just a re-reading of Freud; it's something far more despotic, both as a theory and an institution, and far more rigid in its semiotic subjection of those who accept it.' Félix Guattari, *Molecular Revolution: Psychiatry and Politics* (London: Penguin, 1984), p. 49.

6. Brian Massumi, *A User's Guide to Capitalism and Schizophrenia: Deviations from Deleuze and Guattari* (Cambridge, Mass.: MIT Press, 1992), p. 1.

7. 'In schizophrenia', Freud writes, 'after the process of repression the libido that has been withdrawn does not seek a new object, but retreats into the ego; that is to say, that here the object-cathexes are given up and primitive objectless condition of narcissism is re-established.' 'The Unconscious', in *The Standard Edition of the Complete Psychological Works of Sigmund Freud*, XIV, pp. 196–7. For a lucid discussion of the thought processes of psychotic states see Stephen Frosh, *Identity Crisis* (London: Macmillan – now Palgrave, 1991), Ch. 6.

8. Joel Kovel, 'Schizophrenic Being and Technocratic Society', in D. Levin (ed.), *Pathologies of the Modern Self* (New York: New York University Press, 1987), p. 336.

9. Massumi, *A User's Guide*; and also Ronald Bogue, *Deleuze and Guattari* (London: Routledge, 1989).

10. Jean-François Lyotard, *Economie Libidinale* (Paris, 1974), p. 133. All subsequent references to this work will be given parenthetically in the text.

11. Geoffrey Bennington, *Lyotard: Writing the Event* (Manchester: Manchester University Press, 1988), p. 39.

12. Peter Dews, *Logics of Disintegration* (London: Verso, 1987), p. 138.

13. Fredric Jameson, 'Postmodernism, or the Cultural Logic of Late Capitalism', *New Left Review*, 146 (1984), pp. 53–93. All subsequent references to this work will be given parenthetically in the text.

14. Jacqueline Rose, ' "The Man who Mistook his Wife for a Hat" or "A Wife is like an Umbrella": Fantasies of the Modern and Postmodern', *ICA Documents*, 6, p. 31.

15. Cornelius Castoriadis, *The Imaginary Institution of Society* (Cambridge: Polity, 1987), p. 3.

16. Cornelius Castoriadis, 'Logic, Imagination, Reflection', *American Imago*, 49(1), (spring 1992), p. 30.

17. Cornelius Castoriadis, 'The Retreat from Autonomy: Postmodernism as Generalized Conformism', *Thesis Eleven*, 31 (1992), p. 23.

Conclusion: Psychoanalysis as Critical Theory

1. Herbert Marcuse, *Five Lectures: Psychoanalysis, Politics and Utopia* (London: Allentane, 1973), p. 44.

2. Theodor Adorno, 'Sociology and Psychology', *New Left Review*, 46 (1967), p. 81.

3. Paul Ricoeur, *Freud and Philosophy: An Essay on Interpretation* (New Haven: Yale, 1970), p. 420.

Further Reading

For those wishing to explore further any or all of the various traditions in psychoanalytic theory the following books are recommended. The central works discussed throughout this book, plus other important texts, are listed as suggested reading in a set order.

Freudian psychoanalysis

Sigmund Freud, *The Standard Edition of the Complete Psychological Works of Sigmund Freud*, tr. J. Stachey (London: Hogarth Press, 1935–74)

Philip Rieff, *Freud: The Mind of the Moralist* (Chicago: University of Chicago Press, 1979)

Paul Ricoeur, *Freud and Philosophy: An Essay on Interpretation* (New Haven: Yale, 1970)

Peter Gay, *Freud: A Life for Our Time* (London: Dent, 1988)

J. Laplanche and J. B. Pontalis, *The Language of Psycho-Analysis* (London: Hogarth, 1980)

American ego-psychology

Anna Freud, *The Ego and the Mechanisms of Defence* (London: Hogarth, 1941)

Heinz Hartmann, *Essays on Ego Psychology* (New York: International Universities Press, 1964)

—— *Ego Psychology and the Problem of Adaptation* (London: Hogarth Press, 1959)

Erik H. Erikson, *Childhood and Society* (London: Penguin, 1965)

—— *Identity, Youth and Crisis* (New York: Norton, 1968)

—— *Gandhi's Truth* (New York: Norton, 1969)

Object relations theory

W. R. D. Fairbairn, *Psychoanalytic Studies of the Personality* (London: Routledge and Kegan Paul, 1952)

Harry Guntrip, *Schizoid Phenomena, Object Relations and the Self* (London: Hogarth, 1968)

Michael Balint, *Primary Love and Psycho-Analytic Technique* (New York: Liveright, 1965)

Jay R. Greenberg and Stephen A. Mitchell, *Object Relations in Psychoanalytic Theory* (Cambridge, Mass.: Harvard, 1983)

Stephen A. Mitchell, *Relational Concepts in Psychoanalysis* (Cambridge, Mass.: Harvard, 1988)

D. W. Winnicott, *The Maturational Process and the Facilitating Environment* (London: Hogarth, 1965)

—— *Playing and Reality* (Harmondsworth: Penguin, 1974)

Charles Spezzano, *Affect in Psychoanalysis: A Critical Synthesis* (Hillsdale: The Analytic Press, 1993)

Kleinian theory

Melanie Klein, *Love, Guilt and Reparation and Other Works 1921–1945* (London: Virago, 1988)

—— *Envy and Gratitude and Other Works 1946–1963* (London: Virago, 1988)

Hanna Segal, *Introduction to the Work of Melanie Klein* (London: Hogarth, 1986)

Juliet Mitchell (ed.), *The Selected Melanie Klein* (London: Penguin, 1986)

W. R. Bion, *Second Thoughts* (London: Heinemann, 1978)

—— *Seven Servants* (London: Maresfield, 1984)

Otto Kernberg, *Borderline Conditions and Pathological Narcissism* (New York: Jason Aronson, 1975)

Donald Meltzer, *The Kleinian Development* (Perthshire: Clunie, 1978)

Richard Wollheim, *The Thread of Life* (Cambridge: Cambridge University Press, 1986)

Michael Rustin, *The Good Society and the Inner World: Psychoanalysis, Politics and Culture* (London: Verso, 1991)

C. Fred Alford, *Melanie Klein and Critical Social Theory: An Account of Politics, Art, and Reason Based on Her Psychoanalytic Theory* (New Haven and London: Yale University Press, 1989)

—— *What Evil Means To Us* (Ithaca: Cornell University Press, 1996)

Thomas H. Ogden, *The Primitive Edge of Experience* (Northvale, New Jersey and London: Jason Aronson, 1989)

Self-psychology

Heinz Kohut, *The Analysis of the Self* (New York: International Universities Press, 1971)

—— *The Restoration of the Self* (New York: International Universities Press, 1977)

—— *Self Psychology and the Humanities* (New York: Norton, 1985)

R. Stolorow, B. Brandchaft and G. Atwood, *Psychoanalytic Treatment: An Intersubjective Approach* (Hillsdale, New Jersey. The Analytic Press, 1987)

Lacanian and post-Lacanian psychoanalysis

Jacques Lacan, *Ecrits: A Selection* (London: Tavistock Press, 1977)
—— *The Four Fundamental Concepts of Psychoanalysis* (London: Penguin, 1979)
—— *The Seminar of Jacques Lacan*, Vol. 1: *Freud's Papers on Technique 1953–54* (Cambridge: Cambridge University Press, 1988)
—— *The Seminar of Jacques Lacan*, Vol. 2: *The Ego in Freud's Theory and in the Technique of Psychoanalysis 1954–55* (Cambridge: Cambridge University Press, 1988)
—— *The Ethics of Psychoanalysis 1959–60: The Seminar of Jacques Lacan* (London: Routledge, 1992)
B. Benvenuto and R. Kennedy, *The Works of Jacques Lacan* (London: Free Association, 1986)
Malcolm Bowie, *Lacan* (London: Fontana, 1991)
Ellie-Ragland Sullivan, *Jacques Lacan and the Philosophy of Psychoanalysis* (Chicago: University of Illinois Press, 1986)
Ellie-Ragland Sullivan and Mark Bracher (eds), *Lacan and the Subject of Language* (New York: Routledge, 1991)
David Macey, *Lacan in Contexts* (London: Verso, 1988)
Louis Althusser, 'Ideology and Ideological State Apparatuses' and 'Freud and Lacan', in *Essays on Ideology* (London: Verso, 1984)
Christian Metz, *Psychoanalysis and Cinema* (London: Macmillan – now Palgrave, 1982)
Teresa De Lauretis and Stephen Heath (eds), *The Cinematic Apparatus* (London: Macmillan – now Palgrave, 1985)
Slavoj Zizek, *The Sublime Object of Ideology* (London: Verso, 1988)
—— *Looking Awry: An Introduction to Jacques Lacan through Popular Culture* (Cambridge, Mass.: MIT Press, 1991)
—— *Enjoy Your Symptom* (London: Routledge, 1993)
—— *The Ticklish Subject* (London: Verso, 1999)
Jean Laplanche, *New Foundations for Psychoanalysis* (Oxford: Blackwell, 1987)
—— *Essays on Otherness* (London: Routledge, 1999)
J. Fletcher and M. Stanton (eds), *Jean Laplanche: Seduction, Translation, Drives* (London: ICA, 1992)

Psychoanalytic feminism

Dorothy Dinnerstein, *The Mermaid and the Minotaur* (New York: Harper and Row, 1976)
Nancy J. Chodorow, *The Reproduction of Mothering* (Berkeley: University of California Press, 1978)
—— *Feminism and Psychoanalytic Theory* (Cambridge: Polity, 1989)
—— *Femininities, Masculinities, Sexualities: Freud and Beyond* (London: Free Association Books, 1994).

—— *The Power of Feelings: Personal Meaning in Psychoanalysis, Gender and Culture* (New Haven, Conn.: Yale University Press, 1999)

Jessica Benjamin, *The Bonds of Love* (New York: Pantheon, 1990)

—— *Like Subjects, Love Objects: Essays on Recognition and Sexual Difference* (New Haven: Yale University Press, 1995)

—— *Shadow of the Other: Intersubjectivity and Gender in Psychoanalysis* (New York: Routledge, 1998)

Madelon Sprengnether, *The Spectral Mother: Freud, Feminism, and Psychoanalysis* (Ithaca: Cornell University Press, 1990)

Jane Flax, *Thinking Fragments: Psychoanalysis, Feminism, and Postmodernism in the Contemporary West* (Berkeley: University of California Press, 1991)

—— *Disputed Subjects: Essays on Psychoanalysis, Politics and Philosophy* (New York: Routledge, 1993)

Juliet Mitchell, *Psychoanalysis and Feminism* (London: Penguin, 1974)

—— *Women: The Longest Revolution* (London: Virago, 1984)

Jacqueline Rose, *Sexuality in the Field of Vision* (London: Verso, 1986)

Julia Kristeva, *Revolution in Poetic Language* (New York: Columbia University Press, 1984)

—— *Tales of Love* (New York: Columbia University Press, 1987)

—— *In the Beginning was Love: Psychoanalysis and Faith* (New York: Columbia University Press, 1988)

J. Fletcher and A. Benjamin, *Abjection, Melancholia and Love: The Work of Julia Kristeva* (London: Routledge, 1990)

Luce Irigaray, *This Sex Which Is Not One* (Ithaca: Cornell University Press, 1985)

—— *An Ethics of Sexual Difference*, trans. Carolyn Birk and Gillian C. Gill (London: Athlone Press, 1993)

—— *To Be Two* (London: Athlone Press, 1999)

M. Whitford, *Luce Irigaray: Philosophy in the Feminine* (London: Routledge, 1991)

Teresa Brennan (ed.), *Between Psychoanalysis and Feminism* (London: Routledge, 1989)

H. Cixous and C. Clement, *The Newly Born Woman* (Minneapolis: University of Minnesota Press, 1986)

Drucilla Cornell, *Beyond Accommodation* (New York: Routledge, 1992)

Critical theory and psychoanalysis

Herbert Marcuse, *Eros and Civilization* (London: Ark, 1956)

—— *Five Lectures: Psychoanalysis, Politics and Utopia* (London: Allen Lane, 1973)

Theodor Adorno, 'Sociology and Psychology', *New Left Review*, 46 (1967)

David Held, *Introduction to Critical Theory* (London: Hutchinson, 1980)

Martin Jay, *The Dialectical Imagination* (Boston: Little Brown and Company, 1973)

Jürgen Habermas, *Knowledge and Human Interests* (London: Heinemann, 1972)

—— *Communication and the Evolution of Society* (London: Heinemann, 1979)

Psychoanalysis and post-colonialism

Homi Bhabha, *The Location of Culture* (London and New York: Routledge, 1994)
Frantz Fanon, *Black Skin, White Masks* (London: MacGibbon and Kee, 1968)
—— *Toward the African Revolution: Political Essays*, (New York: Monthly Review Press, 1967)
—— *The Wretched of the Earth* (London: Penguin, 1967)
Christopher Lane (ed.), *The Psychoanalysis of Race* (New York: Columbia University Press, 1998)
—— ' "Savage Ecstasy": Colonialism and the Death Drive', in Lane (ed.) *The Psychoanalysis of Race* (New York: Columbia University Press, 1998), pp. 282–304
Octave Mannoni, *Prospero and Caliban: The Psychology of Colonization*, trans. Pamela Powesland, 2nd edn (New York: Praeger, 1964)
Ashis Nandy, *The Intimate Enemy: Loss and Recovery of Self under Colonialism* (Delhi: Oxford University Press, 1983)

Postmodern psychoanalysis

Gilles Deleuze and Félix Guattari, *Anti-Oedipus: Capitalism and Schizophrenia* (New York: Viking, 1977)
—— *A Thousand Plateaus: Capitalism and Schizophrenia* (Minneapolis: University of Minnesota Press, 1987)
Félix Guattari, *Molecular Revolution: Psychiatry and Politics* (London: Penguin, 1984)
Brian Massumi, *A User's Guide to Capitalism and Schizophrenia: Deviations from Deleuze and Guattari* (Cambridge, Mass.: MIT Press, 1992)
Jean-François Lyotard, *Economie Libidinale* (Paris, 1974)
—— *The Differend: Phrases in Dispute* (Minneapolis: University of Minnesota Press, 1988)
A. Benjamin (ed.), *The Lyotard Reader* (Oxford: Blackwell, 1990)
Geoffrey Bennington, *Lyotard: Writing the Event* (Manchester: Manchester University Press, 1988)
Frederic Jameson, 'Postmodernism, or the Cultural Logic of Late Capitalism', *New Left Review*, 146 (1984), pp. 53–93
Jacqueline Rose, 'Fantasies of the Modern and Postmodern', *ICA Documents*, 6, pp. 30–4
Cornelius Castoriadis, 'The Retreat from Autonomy: Postmodernism as Generalized Conformism', *Thesis Eleven*, 31 (1992), pp. 14–23

Psychoanalysis and contemporary theory

Anthony Elliott, *Subject to Ourselves: Social Theory, Psychoanalysis and Postmodernity* (Cambridge: Polity Press, 1996)
—— *Freud 2000* (Cambridge: Polity Press, 1998; New York: Routledge, 1999)

——*Social Theory and Psychoanalysis in Transition: Self and Society from Freud to Kristeva*, 2nd edn (London: Free Association Books, 1999)

Anthony Elliott and Charles Spezzano (eds), *Psychoanalysis at Its Limits: Navigating the Postmodern Turn* (London: Free Association Books, 2000)

Peter Dews, *Logics of Disintegration* (London: Verso, 1987)

Stephen Frosh, *Identity Crisis* (London: Macmillan – now Palgrave, 1991)

Anthony Elliott and Stephen Frosh (eds), *Psychoanalysis in Contexts* (London: Routledge, 1994)

Cornelius Castoriadis, *The Imaginary Institution of Society* (Cambridge: Polity Press, 1987)

——*Crossroads in the Labyrinth* (Cambridge, Mass.: MIT Press, 1984)

Mikkel Borch-Jacobsen, *The Freudian Subject* (Stanford: Stanford University Press, 1982)

Jacques Derrida, *The Post Card* (Chicago: University of Chicago, 1987)

Journals on psychoanalysis and psychoanalytic studies

The following is a selection of academic journals which publish cutting-edge articles on psychoanalysis and psychoanalytic studies.

American Imago
Contemporary Psychoanalysis
Free Associations
International Journal in Psychoanalysis
International Review of Psychoanalysis
Journal for the Psychoanalysis of Society and Culture
Journal of the American Academy of Psychoanalysis
Journal of the Universities' Association for Psychoanalytic Studies
Lacanian Inc
Psychoanalysis and Contemporary Thought
Psychoanalytic Dialogues
Psychoanalytic Studies
The Psychoanalytic Quarterly

Index